Reflections in Place

Reflections in Place

CONNECTED LIVES OF NAVAJO WOMEN

DONNA DEYHLE

The University of Arizona Press | Tucson

The University of Arizona Press
© 2009 The Arizona Board of Regents
All rights reserved

www.uapress.arizona.edu

Library of Congress Cataloging-in-Publication Data
Deyhle, Donna.
  Reflections in place: connected lives of Navajo women / Donna Deyhle.
     p. em.
  Includes bibliographical references and index.
  ISBN 978-0-8165-2756-4 (hardcover : acid-free) — ISBN 978-0-8165-2757-1
(pbk. : acid-free)
  1. Begay, Jan. 2. Tsosie, Vangie. 3. Sam, Mary. 4. Navajo women—Biography.
5. Navajo women—Social conditions. 6. Navajo women—Ethnic identity. I. Title.
  E99.N3D425 2009
  305.4897'26—dc22

                              2009025778

Publication of this book is made possible in part by the proceeds of a permanent
endowment created with the assistance of a Challenge Grant from the
National Endowment for the Humanities, a federal agency.

14   13   12   11   10   09   6   5   4   3   2   1

Contents

III
Changing Woman at Taco Bell: Middle-Class Life in the City
Vangie Tsosie

IV
(Re)sculpturing Belonging: From Yeíbicheii to Hip-Hop
Mary Sam

Epilogue

Figures

Preface

This book focuses upon the rich complex lives of three Navajo women I have known for almost twenty-five years and their families.[1] As I write about their lives, I have found the concept of survivance, influenced by Gerald Vizenor and inscribed by Native voices at the National Museum of the American Indian in Washington, D.C., helpful in deepening my understandings. "Survivance . . . is more than survival. Survivance means redefining ourselves. It means raising our social and political consciousness. It means holding on to ancient principles while eagerly embracing change. It means doing what is necessary to keep our cultures alive."[2] Survivance is a positive, resistant standpoint embedded with actions meant to assert and claim one's Native identity and place in the world by rejecting the images of Indians created by whites.[3]

A hint of this presence and standpoint was played out for me one afternoon in 2001 with Jan Begay, her parents, husband, four children, a sister, and several nieces. Seeking jobs in construction and in oil pipeline fields, and seeking better educational opportunities for their children, they relocated from the Navajo Nation to Salt Lake City and were the only American Indians in a rent-subsidized apartment in a large, racially diverse housing complex. Just outside their door was a swimming pool. It was a hot afternoon, and I asked if they had been using the pool. "Sure, now that it's open, we go in, but only late at night," Jan said with a broad grin. "We go out late at night. Take the pool over! Look out, the Indians are coming!" She rolled, laughing into her mother on the couch. Elizabeth added: "Ernie says, 'Surrender your wagons! We Indians have you circled. We Indians have you surrounded.'" Everyone in the packed living room burst into laughter. They were Indians in the city, claiming place, and (re)claiming history, with their very presence.[4] Their standpoint strategically used and challenged the historic images of Indians victimizing innocent settlers, turning upside down this prevalent white discourse to proclaim their survivance and visibility in today's world—both in the city and on the Navajo Nation. In taking over the swimming pool at night, my friends may well have been avoiding a white gaze and creating a space of freedom. Many of the Navajo people I know lead lives where the intrusive power of a white gaze—informed by stories of white supremacy and the spreading of "civilization" across the continent (stories Vizenor calls "manifest manners")—creates obstacles which must be maneuvered around and circumvented. Adapting Foucault's[5] conception of surveillance to the racially polarized context within which the women in my study live helps reveal how dominant group members exert a gaze informed by the discourse of manifest manners that is used to predefine the identities of Navajo people, thus limiting the options available to them, and sometimes directing their activities. The surveillance exercised by white community members often assumed that Navajo people should act like white people, but really were not capable of doing so; consequently, the white gaze often judged Navajo people in terms of their ability to realize a substandard version of the white norm.

As I would come to understand, the Begays, like many Navajo people, endured racial and cultural struggles to remain connected to the Diné/Navajo landscape and place. I have seen survivance manifest itself by using what I call a "Native gaze." Navajo peoples in this community refuse to submit to the surveillance of their white neighbors. Jokes and moral lessons describe whites as rude, loud, disrespectful, immodest, selfish, uncaring, and shallow. The practices of playing against teachers with the use of silence or shout-downs, blocking teachers' interactions and effectiveness as instructors in classrooms, dismissing criticisms of themselves by employers in low-paying jobs, and circling an urban swimming pool all work to assert a Native gaze on a racially contested landscape.

In the fall of 1984 I moved to San Juan County in southeastern Utah, where I first meet Jan and her family. I was about to start an ethnographic study of the lives of young Navajo men and women, in and out of school, in a community bordering the Navajo Nation. District officials and Navajo parents were concerned with the high dropout rate of Navajo youth, and I was invited to conduct a study to find out why so many youth were not succeeding in schools. My research focus centered around two questions: "Why do Navajo youth leave school?" and "What factors help Navajo students succeed in school?"

During the next twenty-five years, I listened to Navajo youth talk about their lives and watched them grow up and have families of their own. I attended their high schools, joining them in over three hundred classes, and I interviewed 168 youth who had left school and another 100 who were either still in school or had successfully graduated. Individuals from a master list of almost 1,500 youth were tracked during the 1980s to examine graduation rates, employment, and post-secondary training. Teachers, administrators, political leaders, parents, and community members also answered my endless questions. With field notes of observations and casual conversations; audiotapes of meetings and events; formal and semi-formal ethnographic interviews; and ethnohistorical archival data, I documented their lives over these years. A critical ethnographic lens guided the analysis of my data, with a specific focus on dialectical power relationships surrounding race, culture, gender, and space. And, in accordance with the ethical stance of my profession, individual, community, and institutional consent was granted for this research.[6]

As an educational anthropologist, a college professor in a teacher education department and ethnic studies program, and a former high school social studies teacher, I was troubled by the absence of ethnographic research on American Indian adolescents' lives, especially since these youth had the highest dropout rate of any group in the United States. Murray Wax, Rosalie Wax, and Robert Dumont's 1964 book, *Formal Education in an American Indian Community,* examined school failure among Sioux youth; it was the only serious, in-depth research of its kind. No such study existed for similar experiences with Navajo youth.

What Wax et al. found were students who forcefully asserted they were "pushed out" or "kicked out" of school by institutional practices that discriminated against them, and by teachers who cared little about their lives. Youth argued that they wanted to stay in school, but that the costs were too high. School officials, on the other hand, spoke of traditional values and cultural differences that conflicted with those of the white mainstream, language difficulties, poverty, lack of motivation, little self-control, and a resistance to "white man's schools" as links to understanding why so many Indian youth fled schools before graduation. Sioux youth who left school were described, following a script of

manifest manners, as "blanket Indians"[7]—Indians who refused to move
to a higher level of civilization by leaving their reservation and "Indian-
ness" behind. Over the following two decades, this was a term I would
frequently hear used to describe Navajo and Ute youth who refused to
conform to white expectations of Indians. In 1933, Luther Standing
Bear (Oglala Sioux) spoke of this survivance.

> According to the white man, the Indian, choosing to return to
> his tribal manners and dress, 'goes back to the blanket.' True, but
> 'going back to the blanket' is the factor that has saved him from,
> or at least stayed, his final destruction. Had the Indian been as
> completely subdued in spirit as he was in body, he would have per-
> ished within the century of his subjection. But it is the unquench-
> able spirit that has saved him—his clinging to Indian ways, Indian
> thought and tradition, that has kept him and is keeping him
> today.[8]

What I came to discover in my own research were teachers who set
up norms of behavior based upon their conception of good (white) students and applied those norms to judge the academic and social activities of Navajo youth. As the youth I hung out with sought to navigate white surveillance, they adopted strategies of resistance against
school officials who demanded Indian youth judge themselves against
their white peers; to act differently, look different, or have different life
goals were signs of failure, of being a "blanket Indian." Choosing to
stay living at home on the Navajo Nation was described as being suffo-
cated by unprogressive families. Choosing basic-level education classes
to be among Navajo peers to avoid racial conflict with white peers was
described as a lack of academic motivation. Choosing to attend Navajo
ceremonies, as well as various Christian denominational services, was
described as clinging to the past. And, choosing to be with one's families over careers was described as a tragic flaw and laziness. Encapsu-
lated within what Vizenor calls a discourse of manifest manners were
practices emanating from the colonizing ideology of manifest destiny
that presumed white people's rightful ownership of land, of educational
opportunities, and of available jobs. Even the well-intended acts of
white educators towards Navajo and Ute students often served to deny
them recognition of who they were, what they valued, and what they
might become. White insistence upon interpreting Indians using the narratives of television westerns and local folk tales prevented them from

attaining awareness of the extraordinarily rich cultural practices of the Indian people surrounding them.

Unlike my previous research and writings on dropouts, parent involvement, and test taking,[9] which were guided by the aim of understanding the regularities of the social and cultural patterns that explained Navajo student school success, in this book I have tried to distance myself from broad essentializations concerning the values or opportunities of Navajo people and instead have sought to offer stories that do justice to my friends' commitments, insights, and senses of humor. I have adopted a post-structural perspective which focuses upon describing the many situations the women lived through, without attempting to reduce their complex characters to a single set of sociocultural or structural determinants.[10] My hope is to disrupt, at least momentarily, the visions and assumptions mobilized by the discourse of manifest manners.

My attempt at representing my friends with due respect led me to push beyond the earlier framework of my work, although I'm sure that this work continues to reflect the input of these modernist theories. This is particularly evident around the concept of "identity." Rather than being fixed in time and space, identity can be seen as flowing to and from a culturally constructed self and community, always changing, always developing, representing neither static nor rigidly lived identities. The narratives of these three Navajo women clearly illustrated both the agency and complexity of being and claiming place on the contemporary landscape. As contemporary postindian warriors, these women force us to contemplate how we can develop a more nuanced understanding of the interweaving of culture and identity, and school and economic performances.

At points in the book, I do, however, invoke the overarching concept of "culture," because Navajo and white people continually use this to talk about each other and parts of their own lives. Although not the same as their grandparents or parents, youth are consistently able to show me events that differed in beliefs and practices from their white peers. Clearly, cultures don't represent a seamless whole. And identities are situational, contradictory, and divergently shaped by social, political, and economic forces. Identity is "always mobile and processual, partly self-construction, partly categorization by others, partly a condition, a status, a label, a weapon, a shield, a fund of memories, et cetera."[11] It is more helpful to view Navajo-ness as a process, as a matter of survivance, not as an object or verse or practice that one expertly passes on to the next generation.

I have also sought to distance myself from the structural language of race war and cultural integrity, for—even though these women do indeed encounter a sharply polarized racial landscape—racial polarizations do not enter their stories in any uniform way, as structural metaphors seem to imply. Structural models, which overstate the power of economic or racialized institutions on individuals' lives, have the unfortunate result of reducing people to victimhood, and this undercuts their power and humanity. Rather, the women face the obstacles of race and pursue their own sense of Navajo-ness in complex and unpredictable ways.

My earlier suggestions that the most traditional Navajo students— not the most "assimilated" Navajo students—were most likely to succeed in high school had the unfortunate aspect of rearticulating the traditional/modern binary that is endemic to the discourse of manifest manners and that I have tried to resist.[12] Jan's, Mary's, and Vangie's Native presence represented a resilience that challenged white surveillance; these women actively chose where they wanted to go, and who they wanted to become.

In the present work, my attention has shifted towards showing that the traditional/modern binary is only an impediment to appreciating the lives led by the women in this book. Their lives do, however, share a matrilineal place on the Navajo landscape. My goal here is to create representations that are respectful of these women as they navigate difficult challenges; that capture the ways in which historically rooted racial warfare plays out in their daily lives in very different ways; that show the situational complexity of the women's lives; that show the vitality and spirituality of these women; and that demonstrate to us very different ways of being Navajo.

Interwoven here are ethnographic portraits of three Navajo women's lives—Vangie Tsosie, who moved to Salt Lake City for jobs and a family; Jan Begay, who moved between the Navajo Nation, nearby towns, and Salt Lake City working semi-skilled jobs with her family; and Mary Sam, who lived and worked part-time on or nearby the Navajo Nation. I met Jan, Mary, and Vangie in 1984 when they were in high school. In acts of coercion guided by white surveillance, their teachers pushed all three women into vocational education in preparation for appropriate "Navajo jobs" as career paths. Counselors and teachers repeatedly told me, "Navajos work well with their hands." This normalization of Navajo identity, which is a way that white educators expressed the expectations that Navajos were not able to meet white norms, operated to guide curricular decisions made on behalf of Navajo students. In Peter McDonald's 1971 Navajo Nation presidential inaugural address, this script of manifest manners had already been challenged. "Everytime someone says how good we Navajos are with our hands, I want to say, 'Why not give us a chance to show what we can do with our minds?'"[13]

Few of the vocational skills they learned have been helpful in the jobs they have had over the years; however, they all have been successful in working and providing for their families. All three women moved through high school by creating an environment where they could spend time with friends and family. Academic classes dominated by white students were avoided. Friendly teachers, regardless of the subject, were highly sought after. Jan and Vangie successfully completed school. Mary left school in disgust for the way she was treated when she became pregnant. Emerging from colonization, the assimilation practices of their teachers urged Mary, Vangie, and Jan to "move forward," leaving behind their families, and the Navajo language, culture, and homeland. This they refused to do.

Educational discourses about youth of color, including American Indian youth, position success as a progressive and upward move towards white values and middle-class life, often located away from youths' home communities. At the same time, white practices, historically grounded, made this path all but impossible. And, ironically, Navajo youth who moved along this path faced a historically contrived gaze that rendered them "progressive" as opposed to "traditional"— and therefore less Indian. This surveillance often was predicated upon Navajo youths' acts of resilience and survivance.

The judgments and acts of whites' surveillance often unfolded from the unquestioned script of manifest manners. Although without individual maliciousness or intent, teachers and administrators were often misguided in their beliefs, and this harmed Navajo youth's professional opportunities. Counselors and teachers, echoing the beliefs of their pioneer families, encouraged Navajo youth to leave homes on the Navajo Nation to find employment in the cities. The high school curriculum was often vocationally tracked for Navajo students, preparing them primarily for minimum-wage, dead-end service industry or manual labor. As Vangie's story illustrates, after fifteen years of consistent employment in Salt Lake City, Vangie's wages hit a ceiling of around $7 to $8 an hour. A twenty-five-cent raise was all that could be expected. She is an intelligent, hardworking woman, conscientious and thoughtful, with post-secondary training, and had no problems finding employers eager to hire her. None of her skills and education, however, led her to middle-class careers. In 2005, Vangie and Gordon gave up their expensive mortgage and house, moved into an apartment, and planned to move back to the Four Corners area to be near their family on the Navajo Nation. From Vangie's perspective, the urban landscape was somewhat barren, denying what her daughter Piper needed most, and provided little of the richness of family life back in her home on the reservation. Life in the city also held little permanence in the hearts of Jan and Mary. Life in the city could be interesting and challenging, but for Vangie, Mary, and Jan, it was not home, no matter how many years they lived away from the Navajo Nation.

Twenty-five years later, Jan, Mary, and Vangie are happy, productive, and vital women with lives enriched in different ways with husbands and children, parents and relatives, work and play. Secured by matrilineality, mothers and daughters have moved through these experiences together, and are now nurturing the next generation. They have faced family deaths, accidents, school success and failure, middle-class jobs and unemployment, job discrimination, poverty, limited resources and city resources, and racism, with visions of survivance-resilience, repeated attempts at obtaining school credentials, joining the middle-class, rock concerts in Albuquerque and shopping sprees in Park City, relentless searches for jobs, providing jobs for other Navajos, renewal with Navajo ceremonies, Native American and Evangelical Church meetings, and sharing of resources. A new child, a new home, a new job, a new friend, a new restaurant—all are greeted with pleasure. Most critically, their paths have not taken them far from their homes among the sacred landscape of Diné Bikeyah, Navajoland, and the Navajo Nation.

These three women's lives disrupt the traditional/modern binary that organizes much of the discourse of manifest manners. When Mary shows her pride in being Navajo, it is not a commitment to the stereotypical vision of a traditional Indian envisioned by school personnel, but rather a commitment to contemporary values about the life best lived. This does not mean, however, that Navajo worldviews, beliefs, and identities are best understood discursively as an "unscripted or open text." Unlike many cultural and ethnic groups in global contexts, Navajo people are not a diasporic group; they remained connected to physical place—what is today called the Navajo Nation. Sometimes this connection was spoken of ideologically, as in the "Glittering World,"[14] other times as a refuge from a hostile racial climate in towns and cities, and other times as an essentialized rhetoric of what was necessary to be Navajo. "Place" seemed a foundation for continuity for the Navajo families I have come to know. As Vangie, living in Salt Lake City, said, "I still have an umbilical cord to there. I'm connected."[15]

A community is made up of many different stories, sometimes speaking to each other, sometimes speaking past each other, sometimes invisible to each other, and sometimes ignored by each other. In this sense, a community is not a uniform group of people, but rather a location or place. A part of the story of this community is about the strained relationships between European Americans and Navajo and Ute peoples, all of whom claim a belonging to this place. This is the enduring struggle of the community. American Indian stories and experiences spoke of strategic and persistent battles for equality in a place that was once solely theirs.[16] On the other hand, European American stories spoke of a God-given right to claim the land they had plowed and tamed, which fed their livestock.[17] Local pioneer stories framed most Indians as undeserving, uncaring, and resistant to civilization. Their stories also spoke of wanting to be good neighbors by helping Native people "better" themselves. White surveillance was historically rooted in this community. This was not, however, unchallenged. Indians, as I will argue, turned the tables and enacted a Native gaze of survivance, which judged the practices of whites—unlike themselves—as undeserving, uncompassionate, uninformed, and wrong.

Historical relationships and structures between Indians and whites were carried into the present in local practices in employment, schooling, and social relationships. These historical structures infused, seeped into, and restrained, as well as enriched, local productions of identity and belonging. I borrow the concept of "history in person" from Holland and Lave, who suggest we cannot understand complex cultural contexts "unless our accounts encompass the working creativity of historically

produced agents and the interconnected differences among their interests, points of view, and ways of participating in the production of
ongoing struggles." Most specifically, inquiry must look "into historical structures of privilege, rooted in class, race, gender and other social
divisions, as these are brought to the present—that is, to local, situated
practice."[18]

The struggles against racism and colonization forces faced by the
Navajo people I write about are enduring and profound, and always
part of historical memories. Historical documents, interviews, poetry,
newspaper accounts, county fairs, and folklore recounting the Posey
War, the (non)use of land resources, Anasazi burials, and government
policies present counterstories of Indians and whites speaking past and
against each other. I try to peel back layers of time to show that first
encounters—specifically as viewed through place and belonging—are
enduring, continually brushing up against people's visions of their identities. Using a multitude of voices and experiences surrounding events, I
try to show this through Jan's, Vangie's, and Mary's lives and belonging
as Navajo women. My presence in their lives, historical and contemporary schooling issues, a lawsuit, and race relations are interwoven
throughout their stories. I placed theoretical arguments only lightly in
their stories. The reader is referred to these discussions in relevant footnotes. Jan, Vangie, and Mary have read their stories, each with smiles,
reflective nods, wrinkled foreheads, and suggestions for changes. I write
here about what I have come to know about their lives, always aware of
the opaqueness of my understandings.

Survivance and Surveillance: Tools of Resistance and Control

In much of the writings about American Indians, to "survive" is pictured as retaining something—such as a language or ceremony—of a
long-ago past, salvaging the remaining elements of a previously rich
culture, which easily ignores the contemporary dynamics that are occur-
ring around American Indian lives and ethnic revival. As Nagel counters,
"cultures are not created at some prehistoric point in time to 'survive'
or be 'handed down' unchanged through the generations."[19] To speak
of only "survival" is to ignore a Native presence. Survivance, however,
implies a life of bodily action, even if embedded within an oppressive
and racist landscape. As Vizenor explained: "Survivance, in my use of
the word, means a native sense of presence, the motion of sovereignty
and the will to resist dominance. Survivance is not just survival but also

resistance, not heroic or tragic, but the tease of tradition, and my sense of survivance outwits dominance and victimry. Survival is a response; survivance is a standpoint, a worldview, and a presence."[20]

Ironically, social scientists describe cultures on the one hand as dynamic and in an ongoing process of reinventing and reinvigorating; on the other hand, as having to be draped in their historical clothing and showing minimal change in order to be "authentic." This discourse does little to enhance an understanding of American Indians. Vizenor argues that we must move past the colonial invention of Indians—which is only a simulation of Native people. "The postindian is after the simulation, and the sense of a native presence is both resistance and survivance. So the presence of postindians teases the reader to see the absence, the simulation of the other, as a problem. . . . The postindian stands for an active, ironic resistance to dominance, and the good energy of native survivance."[21] This good energy of Native survivance can be seen in the break-dancers I saw performing competitively before their Navajo and white peers; in young Navajo writers and poets claiming a space for their voices; and in young elementary schoolchildren dancing the Yeíbicheii, in and out of school, while listening to hip-hop music with their older siblings. The silences I felt in response to racist, insulting encounters with teachers also shone with resistant energy, for in Vizenor's vision, "Performance and human silence are strategies of survivance."[22] Time after time, in classes I attended with Navajo youth, the air chilled with expressive silence.

White surveillance creates a strategically limited space for Indians that is frozen in an historical lifestyle; it is impossible for Navajo youth to (re)create the past in the present, unless it means artists recreating ancient Anasazi designs on Indian pottery or young women calmly walking alongside the sheep they are herding. This limited space is framed by non-professional jobs and the idea that there is little need for college. Indians are rarely allowed to move into the spaces maintained by whites, in effect keeping communities divided by retaining control over limited jobs. The practices of this surveillance can be seen through the legacy of manifest destiny with what Vizenor calls "manifest manners." Manifest destiny, an ideology which exerted an entitlement to lands and fortune based on white supremacy, resulted in the catastrophic deaths of millions of American Indians from massacres, diseases, and confinement to reservations. This history still saturates the social, political, economic, and physical landscape. Manifest manners is a way of bringing this distorted history into the present. In Vizenor's words, "manifest manners are the absence of the real in the ruins of tribal representations."[23]

An excellent example of what I believe is the discourse of manifest manners appeared in the March 9, 2005, *Salt Lake Tribune* in an article titled, "Bennett: Oil Rigs Won't Hurt Wildlife." After visiting the Arctic National Wildlife Refuge to examine what impact oil drilling would have in this refuge, Utah Senator Bob Bennett met with Alaskan Natives, saying most were in favor of oil development. In a critique of Alaskan Natives opposed to oil drilling, he said: "But when you ask how they live off the caribou, you find out they get on snowmobiles and go out and shoot them with rifles. Somehow, I don't think that's the culture of their great-grandparents that they talk of preserving." To have an authentic Native Alaskan voice, leave the snowmobiles and rifles at home, and pull out great-grandfather's harpoons and spears.

By constructing representations of Indian people that lock who they are into an imagined past and control future opportunities, whites create an imagined Indian with the ideology of manifest manners. This serves to maintain whites' powers in the larger social structure. As an art teacher explained to me: "Those students from Monument Valley, they are the real Navajo. Most of them still do chores around the house like herd the sheep. They are dignified. And quiet. And do what they are told in the classroom." Within this controlling discourse—manifest manners—Indian people are not Indian unless they look like the popular white constructions of Native peoples living serenely, without technology, close to animals and the land. Indians become a cultural category that must remain true to that historic portrait to be real. And, with a twist, this "authentic" Indian is best served by limited contact with "corrupting" Western values in economic, educational, and social institutions, increasing the likelihood of economic struggles during their lives. "The more traditional Navajos wake up to the sunrise with prayers every morning," a counselor told me the first year of my research. He had sighed and leaned back in his chair. "I often wonder if we are doing them a disservice. It is so beautiful down there. They have such a simple and pure life. We should have left them alone." This binary, using historical tools of surveillance—traditionality/modernity—can be viewed as one script of the discourse of manifest manners.

Vizenor argues that new stories need to be told as acts of resistance to white surveillance. Indians should not represent themselves in ways that bring satisfaction to whites' representations. "If a culture lives it changes, it always changes. If a people live, they imagine themselves always and in a new sense. And here we are in the city, and people are still trying to figure out what was in the past. Well, there isn't any past, we're it."[24] White narratives of manifest manners, however, still try to capture and frame "real Indians" as relics of the past. Here at the University of Utah, a story circulated around the Department of Anthropology in the 1990s. A professor had sent several white students to visit another professor who taught courses on American Indians. "We are looking for examples of pure Indians," said one. Another interjected, "We want to visit real Indians. We were told that the Utes are an example of a hunting and gathering Indian tribe." My colleague sighed and explained, "Yes, the Utes are hunters and gatherers. The Utes hunt at Safeway and gather at the 7-11." Frozen in time, "real" Indians cannot possibly be shopping alongside everyone else at the local store.

The very act of manifest manners assures that the presence of contemporary lives is muted in support of simulations of real Indians. In the communities I discuss, this is evident, for example, in the development of cultural units that use living Navajo people to talk about and (re)construct the traditions of the past. This capturing of the past to bring it into the future is both predicated on the concept of American Indian-ness as a vanishing way of life, and a vision of the "right" kind of Indian—both dialogues of manifest manners. Rather than seeing Navajo parents, teachers, students, sons, and daughters themselves as members of a vibrant community today, they are used as resources to teach about past traditions. This is manifest manners at work. And, in some ways, as I write about my involvement in the community over all these years, I, too, was part of the script of manifest manners.

In engaging in cultural descriptions of the Navajo people I write about as a white anthropologist, I face the dilemma of creating yet another set of representations of Indian people in another form of surveillance. The very quest of anthropology, in my case to document the lives led by Navajo women, has the continual potential to reinscribe the discourse of manifest manners. I struggle with this issue, for, in some ways, my own involvement has been framed by manifest manners, even when I thought what I was doing was worthwhile. I trained teachers on-site in the district with a multicultural curriculum that, for some teachers, reinforced romantic views of American Indians. For others, cultural values, such as avoiding a direct gaze out of respect, became a deficit stereotype: "Indians don't look you in the eye." And yet, for others, our discussion of power relations between Indians and whites was illuminating. As part of a court-ordered educational team, I helped reintroduce Navajo language and culture in schools based on the assumption that language and culture in schools helped Navajo students to secure their identity. Some Navajo parents, however, viewed this as yet another way to deny their children the same kind of education provided to white students.

Deborah House has recently argued that the claim by Navajo people about their "Navajo-ness" is a resistant counterhegemonic strategy that asserts a positive distance from the dominant white society.[25] Navajo traditions are used discursively to represent contemporary Navajo-ness as good and white-ness as bad. Vizenor might view the rhetorical use of cultural traditions, even if not practiced the way whites think they should be, as a power shift, "Natives, of course, use simulations too, but for reasons of liberation rather than dominance."[26] Owens describes the paradox of these conflicting representations. "European American holds a mirror and a mask up to the Native American. The tricky mirror is that Other presence that reflects the Euro-American consciousness back at itself, but the side of the mirror turned toward the Native is transparent, letting the Native to see not his or her own reflection but the face of the European beyond the mirror . . . leaving the Native behind the mask unseen, unrecognized for himself or herself." In seeking a voice and recognition, "the Native must step into that mask and be the Indian constructed by white America."[27] In some ways, Navajo people control the surveillant gaze of whites by reflecting back a mask of "Indian-ness" in order to protect and hide who they really are from the controlling eyes of whites. This is a Native gaze in action.

My challenge is not to use manifest manners to reaffirm again the traditional/modern binary that seems natural with a white surveillance lens. What might Navajo-ness look like if we recognize the extraordinary diversity of subject positions, social experiences, and cultural experiences that make up this constructed category? Norla Chee, a Navajo senior at San Juan High School, challenged us to see the possibility of this through her own eyes.

TONTO IS MY WHITE NAME
By Norla Chee

My reflection stares
Back at me
Staring
Back at neighbors staring
For a glimpse of dried bloody scalps.
I reflect in perfect English on the image
Of Mrs. Jones's wig arranged among my
Creeping charlies on the window sill,
As if it were an Oscar.
Neighbor boys with Taiwan arrows
And girls with pink feathers in their hair
War dance around my maple tree and shout
Hey-ye-ya hey-ye-ye-ya
Until I chase them off calling
Yei-iitsoh! Child-Eating-Monster God
I saw on a PBS special about traditions
In my blood. On Monday I'll stand
In line to collect unemployment, to buy
A $1.50 pint of Thunderbird, and to pass
Around traditions and the trouble with
Hollywood.[28]

Narrative Ethnography: Writing Lives

In a postmodern text, the ethnographer is no longer invisible, but rather he or she attempts to honestly intersect and mingle, visibly, in the text—forming a single multivocal text focused on human encounters. Barbara Tedlock, in *The Beautiful and the Dangerous,* calls this form of writing "narrative ethnography": "The world, in a narrative ethnography, is re-presented or perceived by a situated narrator, who is also present as a character in the story that reveals his or her personality."[29] In *The Heartland Chronicles,* Douglas Foley speaks of writing "reflective realist narratives" as a sharp break from writing scientific realism: "The key narrative move that creates linguistic reciprocity is the foregrounding of people, characters, and events over theoretical commentary."[30] No one master narrative voice is used; experience is privileged over theoretical jargon; cultural practices are foregrounded; and the narrative is mutually produced. This does not mean, however, that the texts are void of theoretical reflections or importance in either of these books. As Foley explains, "*Chronicles* is actually full of social scientific constructs, but my explanatory ideas rarely interrupt the narrative flow. They are either integrated into the stories being chronicled or are in the background and explicated succinctly." Within this kind of writing, a key issue is the disruption of the "Self," or the omniscient observer visible in scientific realist texts. In Foley's words, "*Chronicles* tries to disrupt various scientific and post-modern self-representations of the heroic author as the all-knowing scientist, philosopher, or poet."[31] Both Tedlock's and Foley's books are assertive moves away from modernist texts, which attempt to capture "authentic" peoples and cultures bound seamlessly together in self-contained static portraits.[32]

What follows is a similar attempt. Here, I, too, speak from a subject position that makes situated, partial knowledge claims. I do not attempt to hide my presence in the text. And I do not make grand claims about Navajo people. Rather, I try to respectfully and richly present the storied lives of three young women and their families. And in doing so, the history of the relationship between Indians and whites is critical.

Acknowledgments

I would like to give a deeply felt thanks to Jan, Vangie, Mary, and their families for their willingness to let me open up their lives to strangers, people who might know little about their lives as Navajo people. Their generosity, thoughtful critiques, deep insights, and humor have enriched this book, and my life. Nia Francisco, Joy Harjo, Nila Northsun, Luci Tapahonso, and Laura Tohe kindly gave me permission to use their poems. Their Native voices resound with the strengths and challenges faced by the Navajo people in this book. And, I'm delighted to thank Emmi Whitehorse for her exquisite painting to powerfully surround these women's stories. Although they must remain unnamed, I wish to also thank the hundreds of Navajo people and other community members throughout the Four Corners area who have patiently listened to my questions, tirelessly corrected my misconceptions, and honestly tried to teach me about their lives. Over the past twenty-five years, I have been privileged to learn so much, but also to see the unfinished path ahead. An elderly Navajo man told me, "To know about us, you have to grow old with us." This, I am doing.

I wish to thank numerous colleagues and friends who over the past twenty-five years have pushed me to think about my own assumptions and theoretical frameworks and, in the end, beautified this book with their suggestions: Margaret Brady, Susan Carter, Karen Gayton Comeau, Doug Foley, Norma González, Beth King, Margaret LeCompte, Teresa McCarty, Dan McLaughlin, Audrey Thompson, William Tierney, Sofia Villenas, and the faculty and students from the Education, Culture, and Society Colloquium. Bill Davis and Debbie Westfall graciously opened their homes to me during my stays in Bluff. Eric Swenson's dedication to social justice in San Juan County has been an inspiration for me; I applaud the good works he has done. I would like to specifically acknowledge the support and wisdom Wayne Holm gave me all of these years. The picture of us in folding chairs sitting on a bluff overlooking the San Juan River, turning each page of the first draft of this book and discussing the past one hundred years of this place, will always bring a smile and feelings of immense gratitude for his scholarly advice and friendship.

During the years of fieldwork, I received a Spencer Foundation Fellowship and several University of Utah faculty grants. I thank these institutions for their support. I have had an excellent research assistant, Greg Bourassa, who did the difficult task of preparing footnotes, organizing references, filling in scholarly holes, polishing the manuscript, and pushing the electronic "send" key to submit the final draft. Melissa Moreno assisted me with early historical research and Sharee Tso-Varela helped with my understanding of Navajo thought and language. My thanks to all of them.

Lastly, I would like to acknowledge Frank Margonis, my colleague, partner, and best friend for his always understated, brilliant, and sensitive insights. This book has been profoundly affected by our intellectual conversations. When I said I had been working on this book for ten years, he reminded me it had been fifteen. During all of these years, he believed in this project, and supported me in ways that are beyond words. Thank you, my love.

ETHNOGRAPHIC TIMELINE

	Legal/political context	Socio-economic context	Educational context	Navajo woman		
				Jan Begay	Vangie Tsosie	Mary Sam
2000s	*Sinajini v. Board of Education* consensus plan ongoing	2006: 42.9% of Navajo individuals and 40% of Navajo families live below the federal poverty level	2002: End of consensus team monitoring	2008: Moving between home and towns for jobs 2006: Moved to Denver 2004: Returned home at Navajo Nation 2002: Son born 2000: Daughter born	2008: Living on the Navajo Nation 2006: Returned to Navajo Nation 2004: Piper's Kinaaldá 2000: Bought new home	2008: Living and working in a city near the Navajo Nation 2007: Son born 2004: Moved to city
1990s	1995: *Meyers v. Board of Education* 1990s: Continuation of *Sinajini* and other cases 1991: Utah Navajo Trust Fund audit	1996: Electricity installed at the Begays on the reservation 1995: Navajos are a majority in San Juan County 1991–1992: Energy fuels, uranium processing plant closes 1990: First Navajo bishop, Episcopal Church, St. Christopher's Mission	1998: First Navajo woman principal 1997: *Sinajini v. Board of Education* consensus agreement & monitoring 1990: Vocational career center opened	1999: Moved to Salt Lake City for job 1992: Daughter born 1991: Daughter born	1993: Piper born 1992: Married 1990: Moved to Salt Lake City	1994: Moved to reservation 1992: Son born

	Col 1	Col 2	Col 3	Col 4	Col 5	Col 6
1980s	1986: First Navajo school board member 1986: First Navajo county commissioner 1984: U.S. Dept. of Justice directs redrawing of voting districts	1986: Cedar Mesa Pottery Factory opens 1985: Maryboy housing complex on the reservation	1983: Monument Valley High School opens	1988: Attended Southwest Indian Polytechnical Institute 1987: High school graduate 1981: Kinaaldá	1989–1990: Phoenix 1989: High school graduate 1980: Kinaaldá	1989: Three years living in Blanding 1989: GED & high school diploma 1987: Job Corps 1986: Son born 1986: Left high school 1985: Son born
1970s and earlier	1974: *Sinajini v. Board of Education* 1959: Utah Navajo Trust Fund established Early 1950s: Navajo removal north of San Juan River 1923: Posey War	1880s: LDS settlers arrive in southeastern Utah 1620: County's oldest Navajo hooghan	1978: Whitehorse High School opens 1978–79: San Juan campus of Eastern Utah College opens 1967: First non-foster-child Navajo graduates from SJHS	1969: Born	1971: Born	1969: Born

I

Place and Boundaries

Navajo Survivance and White Surveillance

September 1990

The First Utah Navajo County Fair

The sun had just burst over the rim of the red sandstone cliffs surrounding Bluff, the small river valley town on the border of the Navajo Nation, when people started arriving for the opening parade of the first Navajo fair in the county. The temperature was predicted to climb throughout the day into the 100s. Sun-protecting umbrellas lay scattered around the blankets. Families claimed front-row seats at the edge of the two-lane state highway with blankets spread on the dirt, coolers full of food, and aluminum folding chairs. Others helped put finishing touches on the floats, stuffing crepe paper into chicken wire, draping blankets over car hoods, straightening signs hanging on the sides of the vehicles, and organizing the groups that would ride the floats. Soon a full crowd of over four hundred men, women, and children, in anticipation of the start of the fair weekend, lined the highway that led through town. Blue-jeaned, tee-shirted, and Nike-shod Navajo youth mingled with their grandmothers dressed in bright velvet shirts embellished with silver buttons and full-pleated velvet skirts. Men wore blue jeans, cowboy shirts, athletic jackets, and boots. Only their hats were different: some wore cowboy hats with silver hatbands, and others wore baseball caps declaring "Mobil Oil," "Indian Run 1983," "Standard Oil," and "Coors." A toddler ran giggling to her grandmother, wearing a Ninja Turtles tee shirt and beaded moccasins. The young and the old, the tourist-brochure image of the traditional, the working-class, the middle-class professionals, the cowboy, and the heavy metaler laughed and smiled together as excitement grew. Over the next two days, ten thousand people would attend the fair's events, enjoying a rodeo, a pow-wow, traditional singing and dancing, a mud bog, a softball tournament, a 10k foot race, a carnival, and the Miss Navajo Utah beauty pageant, all accompanied by a barbecue, arts and crafts booths, and food vendors.

The line of over one hundred cars, trucks, and floats stretched through the back street of town, following the curves of the original 1880s main street, past large stone houses, mobile homes, log homes, an elementary school, a cafe, and a trading post, and spilling out onto the 1960s highway that now bypassed town. The parade route began at the old stone jail, built in 1896 and now a community library. The original sign above the door still proclaims the turn-of-the-century message, "Justice For All. Obedience To The Law Means Freedom." The county sheriff blocked the highway two miles outside of town, and six of his deputies on motorcycles, with sirens blasting and lights flashing, were at the head of the parade. Behind the police, Navajo war veterans proudly carried the American flag. The parade started moving slowly through town.

I stood alongside the highway with Jan Begay and her family. Indian clubs from the high schools, a local college, and a state university had brightly decorated floats carrying Navajo students dressed in the traditional velvet shirts and skirts of their grandparents. They were preceded by cars bearing their elected royalty—young women in white, pink, and red prom dresses sitting atop hoods draped with Indian blankets and shawls. Throwing candy, they waved at the crowd. A float with the Whitehorse High School jazz band received shouts of encouragement as enthusiastic trumpeters created rhythms of their own. Horn blasts, clapping, and children's shrieks of delight as they scrambled for candy greeted the students as they passed. Several of the elementary schools, the Head Start program, and the tribally run adult education program also entered floats. The floats burst with colors and cultures as blue jeans rubbed up against velvet and leather. The school district's Even Start Program was represented by its classroom on wheels—a large recreational vehicle that traveled to homes on the Navajo Nation to instruct preschool children and their parents who had not graduated from high school. At first glance the RV looked like a lost tourist, but soon the familiar face of the teacher and the banners draping the sides secured its place in the parade. People clapped as the teacher honked and waved to those lining the road.

Floats for political candidates dotted the parade. The Democratic Party's float—with red, white, and blue tissue paper–covered arches and banners proclaiming "Forward in Unity in the 90's"—was followed by eight Navajo candidates on horseback. With help from the state Democratic Party, these county elections were the first with a unified all-Navajo slate of candidates. The crowed roared with approval as they rode through town. Officials running for Navajo tribal elections also took the opportunity the parade offered to seek supporters.[1] Some walked through the crowd passing out pamphlets; others drove trucks pulling floats of relatives urging their kinsmen's election; and still another rode in the back seat of a red Mustang convertible accompanied by Miss Navajo Nation.

The surrounding communities and local businesses also had floats in the parade. Local Navajo chapter houses' floats showed women weaving, carding wool, and holding lambs. The float from a small sewing factory was full of Navajo seamstresses dressed in brightly colored velvet skirts and blouses and adorned with turquoise belts, necklaces, rings, bracelets, and earrings. Flattened on the front grille of the truck was the factory's proudest item—a spacesuit sewn for NASA. A cafe in town advertised its Navajo tacos in the center of a float full of Navajo and white children. Cedar Mesa, the local pottery factory, also advertised its wares. Young Navajo and Ute artists, including several high school students, sat holding the mold-produced pottery they had painted for the local tourist trade. They were casually dressed in Levis and multicolored blouses and shirts. A familiar, well-worn black pickup driven by a white lawyer who gave free legal aid brought warm applause. An exceptional crowd favorite was a local singing group. The pickup carried The Mesa Singers, six red-satin-shirted, traditional Navajo singers in cowboy hats, and pulled a flatbed with two sets of drums and twelve singers. The float hubcaps were carefully covered with construction paper and painted like Navajo wedding baskets. Powwow fancy dancers followed the float. Men leaned close to the ground, their brightly feathered bustles pointing to the sky, as they danced in sharp, strong circles. Women fancy dancers in beaded leather outfits carrying satin-fringed shawls glided through the air with light-footed grace.

And then there was the river-running company's float—a van hauling a large yellow raft. River guides, carefully protected with "Mae West" life jackets, hosed the crowd from the raft, shouting, "Cool down! Cool down!" The crowd screamed and laughed as grandmothers, parents, children, and other innocent bystanders scrambled to avoid the drenching. The final float of the parade was from the local bar. Amplified keyboards and guitars accompanied the country-and-western band as the lead female sang, "Don't Let Your Babies Grow Up to Be Cowboys." The parade ended as bewildered carloads of tourists and commercial semi-trailer trucks from the now-freed highway suddenly found themselves in the middle of the celebration. Truck drivers sounded their horns and tourists waved. The atmosphere was charged with excitement, enjoyment, and anticipation as people started to move to the fairgrounds on the edge of town.

Like their neighboring Utes to the north and east, the Navajo people in the county had lived in this homeland for many generations prior to the arrival of Mormon and other white settlers.[2] Although archaeological and ethnographic evidence suggests Navajo people could have been in what is now the U.S. Southwest as early as AD 1000, the earliest existing Navajo hooghan[3] in the county, tree-ring dated at AD 1620, was found in White Canyon west of Bear's Ears.[4] Several Spanish maps from the 1660s describe Navajo territory as extending far north of the San Juan River.[5] One map drawn by a traveler in 1839 showed Navajos living as far north as Monticello, Utah.[6] An old forked stick hooghan, one of the earliest forms of Navajo housing, lies in Butler Wash just north of Bluff and the San Juan River. This early home, constructed in the early 1880s, and other stone hooghans provide physical evidence that Navajo families lived in the canyon tributaries north of the San Juan River prior to any white settlers. Many accounts written by earlier explorers also clearly document Navajos, Utes, and Paiutes passing through and living north of the San Juan River.

Navajo family stories passed down from generation to generation tell of Navajos encountering the first white settlers near their homes; of fond memories of good homes with plentiful firewood, and adequate water and food for livestock; and of traditional herb-gathering areas and beautiful canyons. Their voices collectively speak of deep roots connecting the Navajo people to this area of San Juan County.

> My brother made me a small home in the canyon. It was a good home for my family, our goats and sheep. Everything we needed was close by. Our family and friends lived in the next canyon. We used to visit each other every day. In the old home, everything you needed was close by your home. It used to be a nice place to live. The firewood was right there; the herbs were right there. . . . In each direction was everything you needed. We had our own ceremonies. . . . That whole area is almost sacred to my family, a home. We survived many difficult times along Comb Ridge. In my

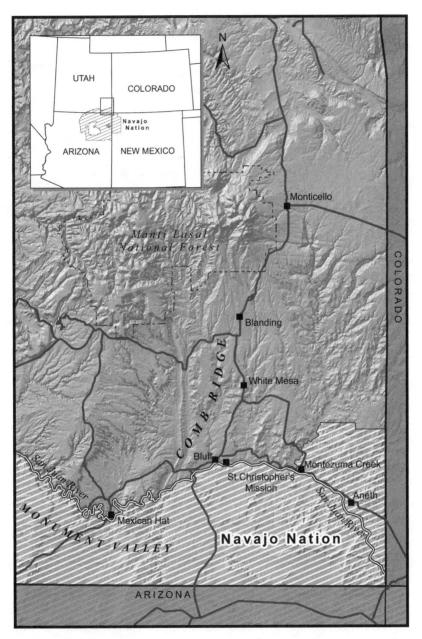

The Navajo Nation in Southeastern Utah

grandmother's time, the family lived along Butler Wash. The family encountered the Spanish in that area. My great-grandfather was taken hostage by the Spanish. During the hard time, they almost lived like the Anasazi. . . . It was a safe and productive place. A Navajo clan originated in that area.[7]

The existence of the Navajo County fair in 1990 was a direct result of the U.S. Department of Justice requiring redistricting of the county for the election of county commissioners. Prior to the late 1980s, no Navajo had ever held a political office in the county, despite the fact that they represented almost half of the county's population. With the redistricting by court order in 1984, the predominately Navajo population in the southern half of the county elected a Navajo representative, Mark Maryboy, to the county commission in 1986. His voice was the first in the political organization of the county to argue for public funds to be used to support a fair for the Navajo half of the county population. The white population in the northern half of the county had enjoyed publicly supported fairs for almost fifty years. Although the northern fair is open to all county residents, few Navajo families travel to the annual fairs.[8]

The Northern Navajo Fair chairman had told the crowd on this first day of the fair, "The color and excitement of the air will commemorate the establishment of a long friendship between the Indians and non-Indian from all over the Four Corners area, making it one of the highlights of the county events."[9] From among the more than sixty-five entries in the parade, Blue Mountain Diné won $100 and took first prize overall for the best theme float—"Forward in Unity in the 1990s." Bumper stickers proclaiming the pride of the moment, "NIHÁ-WHOL-ZHÍÍZII" (Our Turn Now), covered parade cars. The stickers' illustrations showed a dripping faucet asserting the need for running water in Navajo homes, a ballet box with a checked ballot urging community members to vote, a fistful of dollars as an asserted right to prosperity, a new public building for the neglected southern part of the county, and workers climbing off large trucks as a path out of poverty. This sticker, now faded, is still on the bumper of my truck.

As I walked toward the fairgrounds, the bright red sandstone bluff appeared as a large natural amphitheater surrounding a dirt-floor stage at the mouth of Cottonwood Wash. The summer heat undulated off the hundred-foot walls as wind carried thick red dust spiraling into the sky. Men were practicing for the rodeo calf-roping event. As their galloping horses cut sharply to the right and left, they appeared as phantoms emerging from dry red clouds. Practice halted and dust settled to the ground. The Ferris wheel of the carnival emerged against the deep blue sky. Its red metal gondolas gleamed in the sun as children's laughter brought others to join the ride. The smells of popcorn, cotton candy, and hot dogs mingled in the air with those of chili and fry bread. Behind the carnival, the finishing touches were completed on the leafed roofs of the traditional and powwow dance circles. And behind these large dance arenas, the water truck continued to deepen the mud in four-foot-deep trenches for the afternoon mud bog.[10] The fair's mosaic texture of a rodeo, a carnival, a truck mud bog, and traditional, country, and pow-wow dances provided a rich kaleidoscope of the complex and diverse Navajo narratives that emerge from this community.

A group of Navajo high school students sat drinking coffee with me at one of the Navajo food concessions. Red-checked plastic tablecloths covered two small wooden tables surrounded by metal folding chairs. A blue-striped awning on the old Airstream trailer provided temporary relief from the midday sun. The students had helped with the construction of the booths in the fairgrounds and talked about the racial composition of the crowd. "They say there will be ten thousand coming here this weekend. But not many whites. Because they are afraid." Another joined in, "No, it's not because they are afraid. It's because they think this is only for Navajo."

It was one month before the state and tribal elections, and the political booths in front of the food stands were active. "It's Our Turn," proclaimed the Democratic booth supporting an all-Navajo slate for county offices. The Republican booth urged voters to support the most competent candidates, a slate that was all white but "Works for the Navajo of Utah." Behind the Democratic booth, a white Vista volunteer stood next to a Navajo community worker passing out flyers and buttons for the Navajo candidates and brochures on water and land rights. Racial tensions rose higher as election day drew closer. It was 1990, and the local white postmaster had run off two Vista volunteers trying to register Navajo voters in the post office parking lot. "You outsiders need not come here. We can handle our own problems," he told them. "This is none of your business." Two community relations officials from the U.S. Department of Justice moved around the booths, listening to the advice and persuasion offered by those surrounding the booths. They would stay in the community until after the election. Of the 328 federal officials sent to nine states for the general election, 17 of these monitored voting places in San Juan County to ensure that proper information was provided to Navajo people.[11]

In 1868, a treaty was signed between the United States of America and the Navajo Tribe returning 3.5 million acres of land to the Navajo people. Navajo peoples, imprisoned at Hwé'éldi, or Fort Sumner, New Mexico, since the three-hundred-mile Long Walk in the winter of 1863–1864, were finally allowed to return to parts of their homelands. At the beginning of their incarceration, there were 8,354 Navajos living in the camp. It was a devastating four years in prison. Watched over by the U.S. Cavalry, Navajo people faced inadequate food from repeated crop failures; a lack of adequate clothing, homes, and firewood; raids by other tribes; and a smallpox epidemic that resulted in the death of over 2,300.[12] When Navajo people moved back into their homes in the northern part of the reservation, which extended into Utah, they were reunited with relatives who had escaped this devastating journey by "hiding" where they could, often with the help of their Ute and Paiute neighbors. Navajo people worked hard to reclaim their lives. Peach trees were replanted. Gardens of corn, squash, and melons reemerged near river's edges. Sheep and cattle again stepped on the red earth. Homes dotted the canyons and mesa tops. And, most importantly, children, grandchildren, and great-grandchildren were born.

One hundred years later, during the centennial celebration of this bitter event, a Navajo artist from New Mexico wrote these words:

MY PEOPLE (1968)
By J. R. DeGroat

we are many clearly of different clans
we are one by our same belief
we have beauty behind us
we have beauty before us

we are the child of whiteshell woman
to the east
we are the child of turquoise woman
to the south
we are the child of abalone woman
to the west
we are the child of jet woman
to the north

we are white corn; father and son
we are yellow corn; mother and daughter
we harvest corn, we feast
we offer pollen, when we feasted

we are shepherds, we clothe ourselves
we are horsemen, we travel around
we are craftsmen, we create
we are learners, we explore

we have industries, we progressed
we have schools, we achieved
we have hospitals, we are cured
we have churches, we are saved

we walked the Long Walk
but the Long Walk is not over[13]

A water truck drove slowly past me on the dirt road to the mud bog at the rear of the fairgrounds. Brightly painted and well pampered, large-tired trucks named Spikes, Cow Springs Special, Mud Eater, Blue Warrior, Ace High, Mud Goat, and Unlimited lined the mud-filled trench. Over fifty racers from as far away as Barstow, California, and Salt Lake City, had registered to compete in the Mud Bog Contest, which offered cash awards totaling $4,170. The president of the Southwest Mud Bog Racers Association, the only Indian-owned boggers association in the United States, explained that mud bogging had come to the Navajo Nation five years previously with a racing truck called Scorpion that offered to race any truck that was willing. That race sparked interest and excitement, and mud bogging grew by leaps and bounds. "Whatever is happening on the reservation, you have to have a mud bog to really draw a crowd," said the president. "And reservation mud bogs are drawing more and more big names; racers who are well known on the national scene."[14] A campaign for a fight against drug and alcohol use was one social purpose of the association. As the president asserted, "Participation in the bogs already has turned some people away from using alcohol." At the end of the event, the Top Pro Division winner was a white rider from California driving the three-hundred-yard distance in 8.65 seconds in a truck named Wasted Wages.

A truck called The Scalp Hunter perched proud, red, and high above its huge, sparkling-clean black tires. Inside sat Sam, Jan Begay's uncle, with long braids, a black cowboy hat, and mirrored sunglasses. He smiled broadly, revealing missing front teeth, as Jan and I approached. "Yá' á'tééh, it's good to see you here. This was my grandfather's truck. We used to haul water barrels from over the mission to the reservation. It was right after we used the wagon. It's a 1942 Ford. Now it is used for a different need. It is a warrior of sorts, a mean mud bogger."

He laughed as he talked about the supercharged truck. "My brother has been winning all sorts of contests around the reservation. It is a hot truck." As he stopped to rebraid his long hair, our conversation moved from mud bogging to Sam's return to the reservation. "I'm here to get some money for a while. I finished at the junior college in Alabama and now I am finishing at Washington State." The summer of 1991, Sam was accepted into veterinary school in Washington State. "I just have to finish some classes and get some money and then I'll go back." But then there was the pull of family and place. "My kids like it here. They are happy to be back here on the reservation. It's home." Sam never returned to veterinary school. He lives with his family near the Begays' home on the reservation.

As Sam squeezed his large frame out of the tiny cab, the Begays and other relatives stopped to welcome him back. Gentle handshakes were followed by teasing: "Hey, college Navajo. What are you doing back on this poor reservation? Now that you have gone to college, are you better than us poor, ignorant Navajo? Can you still say words in Navajo, or have you forgotten how to speak Navajo!" The soft laughter circled the small group as I stepped away from the conversation. Sam, a Roadman, or religious leader, in the Native American Church,[15] was being asked to run a meeting for Jan Begay and her sister.

Roars of supporters signaled the beginning of the mud bog as two trucks lined up on parallel trenches for the first race of the day. Sam walked over to watch his brother run the race. The red-painted Scalp Hunter teased the black Monster Masher as each driver gunned his engine and inched forward to the starting line. A flag signaled the start. Engines reached a high pitch as the trucks plunged into the mud-filled trenches. Mud flew into the air, dotting the spectators lining the trenches, as the two now-red-brown trucks emerged to cross the finish line. This time Sam's brother came in second. "It's okay. He'll try again. But it will take us a week to clean off all that mud and show the shine and power of Scalp Hunter again!" He laughed, gently shook my hand, and moved over to talk to his brother. As I watched him walk away, images of "war veteran," "college graduate," "Navajo father," "mud bogger," "Native American Church Roadman" and "veterinarian" moved through my mind.

The crowd had gotten much bigger during the afternoon. As I walked back to the carnival, I heard my name. "Hey, Donna, you need to buy one of these beautiful special handmade tee shirts. I know you have money!" I laughed as Jim, his sister Mary, and mother Carol came over with armloads of tee shirts. Carol, one of the few Navajo elementary school teachers in the district, explained: "Jim did the design and I bought the tee shirts for him. If we sell all sixty of them we can double our money and make $300." The shirts, in pale blue, pink, and white, displayed a black design of an eagle flying above traditional and pow-wow dancers. In one wing was a Navajo hooghan and in the other a bronco rider. Different-sized block letters above the design proclaimed, "First Annual Utah Navajo Fair." After I chose one and put it on over my shirt, Jim moved off to continue selling.

Carol was running a booth for the local elementary school, and Mary was helping. Stacks of school schedules, monthly activities, and parent permission forms filled the small metal table. Sitting in the booth, Carol talked about her and her children's schooling.

I went to the Phoenix Indian School. From the seventh to graduation. I liked it. It was before a school was here for Indians. The school was only for white kids. So I went away. I went to junior college. I liked it. Then I came back here and worked at the cafe. Then I didn't go to school for a long time. I worked and had kids. But I have finished college now. And I am back here again. At home. I didn't go to school here because Indians weren't welcome.

Treaty between the United States of America and the Navajo Tribe of Indians, 1868, Article IX

In order to insure the civilization of the Indians entering into this treaty, the necessity of education is admitted, especially of such of them as may be settled on said agricultural parts of this reservation, and they therefore pledge themselves to comply their children, male and female, between the ages of six and sixteen years, to attend school; and it is hereby made the duty of the agent for said Indians to see that this stipulation is strictly complied with; and the United States agrees that, for every thirty children between said ages who can be induced or compelled to attend school, a house shall be provided, and a teacher competent to teach the elementary branches of an English education shall be furnished, who will reside among said Indians, and faithfully discharge his or her duties as a teacher.[16]

The first district school in San Juan County started in November 1880 in Montezuma Creek. A month later, a log church and school was built as part of the Bluff City fort. Both schools were in one-room crude log cabins and "reflected the values of the predominantly Mormon community from which they took root."[17] By the early 1890s, sixty to eighty children were attending schools in the county. By 1914, both Monticello and Blanding enrolled students in high school programs. As more rural and isolated communities demanded local schools, more than two dozen single-room schools were opened from the 1920s to the 1940s. White children had access to private or public schools throughout a geographical area of almost eight thousand square miles. With the discovery of uranium and oil in the county, the student population increased 225 percent, from 800 students in 1948 to 1,800 in 1958. In *The First Forty Years: A History of San Juan High School 1914–1955*,[18] all the students were white. Their Navajo peers remained, for the most part, outside the districts schools' walls. Access to the local public schools for Indians did not systematically occur until the late 1950s, more than sixty years after their white peers enjoyed a public education near their homes.

Carol sighed.

They just hang around. They don't do anything. I can't stand it. The older ladies were saying that at least at the boarding school you learned to do things. You learned to clean real well. And now all the young kids do is to go over fast, and it is still dirty. At least they taught you responsibility because you took care of your home yourself. They don't learn any of this anymore. Not in the family or the school.

Even as Mary protested, "We're not all like that!" Carol expressed frustration with the Navajo youth in the community. "Kids around here just want a little money to buy this and that. They don't think to the future. They don't think that doing good in school will help. They want just enough money to buy something." Her comments narrowed to her oldest son. "I have been trying to get him to apply to the Institute of

American Indian Arts in Santa Fe. Jim is a good artist. His uncle went to that school. I got all the applications for him, but he is just sitting at home and doing nothing." She laughed as she told me why her brother was kicked out of the local high school. "They thought he was crazy. That he was a wild Indian. But he went up there and did real good. He showed them. Now he is working as a commercial artist."

Carol complained bitterly about the racial prejudice the Indian students experience at high school. "They treat Indian students like they are nothing. Not even human." When she moved Jim to Whitehorse High School, an almost all-Navajo high school in the district, his attendance improved, but his academic performance remained low. Her youngest son had just started high school. Concerned about racial tensions, she wanted to send him away to a private school. "I wanted to get him out of here." She explained: "The kids were saying that you were a nerd if you got As. And then they said to the Navajo kids that they were acting like *bilagáanas* [white people]. I could hardly believe it! In the seventh grade they were saying things like that." She blamed this on the influence of older Navajo students, "They make fun of getting good grades," and the influence of the white community in town, "They get into too much trouble in town. I don't know what they do in town. They hang around with bad white kids."

Mary and Jim were the first young Navajos to befriend me when I started my research in this community in 1984. I had rented a small house across from their trailer. They were involved in a break-dancing clique of Navajo youth, were uninterested in what school had to offer, and spoke of feeling unwanted and "marginal," surrounded by the white community. I remembered the last time I had seen them on a visit in 1988. I arrived in mid-afternoon. Carol was still teaching. Mary and Jim were home. Jim was stretched out on the couch watching a television soap opera. He rolled off onto the floor with a grin, "I guess I should go to school now, the professor's here!" We both laughed. School would be out in fifteen minutes. Mary was fixing sandwiches for herself and her two young babies. I helped her feed the youngest as she talked about school. "I should go back. But I just don't fit, and now I have kids. The teachers, you know, they look at you differently. They know you have had a baby, and they stay away from you. I didn't like the way they look at me. Maybe I will go back to the Job Corps. School just never worked for me." Pointing with her lips towards her brother, she continued, "Jim should do something. He just watches TV, listens to hard music, and smokes dope." Jim responded to his older sister's criticism. "At least the music is rad [radical]. School sucks! I don't like the way the teachers treat me. And the white kids are geeks." I remembered Jim as a defiant, assertive break-dancer who challenged the racism in his school and community with his performances who had told me, "It used to be cowboys and Indians. Now it is breakers and cowboys." I asked him if he and his friends were still into break dancing. "No, we don't do that anymore. We got tired. We listen to heavy metal now. And hard rock. It's tough music. We don't dance. We just listen."

Jim and his sister both eventually dropped out of high school—Jim with truancy, academic, and social problems; Mary when she became pregnant. Shortly before he left school for the last time, Jim told me, "It's a drag, man. It's boring." Jim had worked at the Cedar Mesa pottery factory during the past year, painting mold-produced "Indian" pottery to sell to tourists, but he was now unemployed and living at home. Mary tried to finish her high school diploma and complete a certificate for a heavy equipment operator at a Job Corps center in Montana, but dropped out when her boyfriend wanted her back home. She, too, was living at home with her two young boys and their father. She was looking for a job, but admitted, "It's not easy. I don't have a high school diploma, and I have two kids."

Images of Jim bragging about three hundred minutes of high school detention; refusing to arrive in agricultural science class with his textbook because its cover pictured a "dumb" cow; not wanting to visit his grandparents because he could not speak Navajo; wanting a job in order to "get away from this dumpy town that would never have a McDonalds"; and attempting to gain job skills through a mail-order art college passed though my mind as I thought back on that last day we had spent together. I thought of Mary as a young mother, a young wife, a loyal sister, a loving daughter, and a Navajo woman—all roles that overlapped and strengthened each other. I looked down at the flying eagle on the tee shirt Jim had designed for the fair and saw the pride of young Navajo youths as they moved through multiple cultural landscapes in a process of (re)creating who they were. And, they did this while asserting a Native presence.

The afternoon sun dipped below the bluffs, and I realized the rodeo was about to start. I had promised the Begay family, my closest Navajo friends, that I would meet them at my house to attend the rodeo, and I was late. Excusing myself, I hurried through the fairgrounds towards

my house. Pickup trucks were still arriving: some with horses standing in the truck-bed and others hauling custom-made horse trailers.
Young children, parents, and grandparents spilled from the trucks with
the excitement of new arrivals to the fair. Laughter burst from the children as they asked for cotton candy and carnival rides. Several tugged
on their grandmothers' arms to take them in the direction of the bright
lights and sounds of the carnival behind the rodeo grounds. Groups
of Navajo cowboys gathered to discuss their upcoming rides and the
condition of their horses. Women, many with small babies, visited with
arriving friends and relatives. Smiles added to the warmth of the twilight. I continued across the dirt parking lot, past a group of well-worn
trailers in the "Coral Mobil Home Park," over the bridge on the highway, and into the "white" section of this small town of several hundred permanent residents. Settlers from the Church of Jesus Christ of
Latter-day Saints (LDS) church founded the town in the late 1800s, and
the old stone settler houses still stand; they are still occupied by local
whites. I lived in one of these old homes.

In 1995, the Utah State Historical Society commissioned a history
book for the centennial celebration of San Juan County. The chapter
introducing the Ute, Paiute, and Navajo peoples to the reader is titled
"Setting the Foundation, AD 1100 to 1880." It is this "foundation"
or occupancy of the county that non-Indian settlers faced when they
arrived in this area. The history of the arrival of European Americans—
Mormon settlers—appears in a chapter titled, "Civilization Comes to
San Juan: Homesteading and City-Building, 1880–1940." From the
European American author's perspective until April 6, 1880, when seventy men, women, and children established Bluff City on the banks of
the San Juan River, "civilization" did not exist in this high desert country in southeastern Utah.[19] Archeological evidence, Navajo clan stories,
and chant ways suggest otherwise. The Great House which Bluff now
surrounds was occupied from approximately AD 700 (Pueblo I occupation) until around AD 1300 (Pueblo III). Archaeological and ethnographic evidence suggests that Navajos came to the Southwest as early
as AD 1000 and had relationships with prehistoric Anasazi.[20] Although
thousands of petroglyphs, cliff dwellings, and over thirty thousand
ancient Anasazi ruins are visible signs of a heavily populated region, the
Native peoples are carefully minimized and silenced in the discourse of
the descendents of the early Mormon settlers. Describing a somewhat
vacant landscape, one wrote, "Later came wandering Navajo and Ute

tribesmen who left little record more indelible than their horses' hoof prints."[21] Between six hundred to one thousand years of occupation by Utes, Paiutes, and Navajos are only a whisper on the pages of the county's official history.

The Begays, Ernie and Elizabeth, their daughters Jan and Val, and two grandchildren were sitting on the porch when I arrived home. We sat drinking coffee, talking and watching the blue sky fade towards a rich star-studded blackness. It was hot on the porch and the baby was fussing. Elizabeth picked up her grandson. His fat soft brown cheeks grew into balls as he laughed at her touch and closeness. Her granddaughter climbed into my lap. Elizabeth sighed, "I'm too young to be a grandmother," and with a smile told me her oldest daughter, Jan, was expecting her first baby. "Jan and Harry were in Albuquerque looking for a job after he was laid off from the uranium plant when they found out she was going to have a baby. So they came home." All her daughters were again home. Taking the baby for a diaper change, Jan said: "Mom was real lonely. Val was painting Indian pottery in town. And Della was in preschool. The others were in school. So she was all alone. She cried a lot. So I decided to move back. Mom needed us. Her daughters." Elizabeth said: "We thought about moving off the reservation so Ernie could get a better job, but then there was the sheep. I said we should get rid of the sheep. But I couldn't. They were my mom's. It is the wealth she gave me. It is part of my mom."

Elizabeth and I had spent many days together on the reservation over the past decade. As with Carol, more often than not the conversation turned to her own and her children's education. Elizabeth did not finish high school, but encouraged and takes great pride in her children's school successes. She paused from cooking one day and said: "I didn't start school until I was nine years old. I remember my parents telling me to just go take care of the sheep. I was four when I started herding the sheep. And then I went to school here for three years and then to boarding school." She shook her head as she continued: "I was real stupid. I had only six months to go. And I dropped out. I wish I didn't. I wanted to be a nurse, and I dropped out because Ernie wanted me to." She saw her boarding school experience as contributing to her poor academic performance at the local high school. "I wish I had never gone to boarding school. I was there for six years, grades four to nine. The reading level of the books was only about fifth or sixth level. And when I went to public school, I couldn't understand anything they were saying or read. They teach you better in public school. In the boarding school you are not taught as well as in public school. Because they know you are Indian."

Urging her daughters to "do better," she warned them if they drop out they would end up "sitting home doing nothing like I am." When she spoke about the future, she often had contemplated returning to school. "I want to go back and finish the general education degree. But I have all of this now to worry about." With a sweeping motion of her hands towards the trailer, sheep, and children, she said, "I have all of this to take care of now."

But when her daughter Val dropped out of school after the eighth grade, Elizabeth started to work on a GED. Val joined her in the adult education program the following year. Their persistence paid off. In 1992, Elizabeth and Val completed GEDs at an adult education center in Bluff.

A group of Ute and Navajo black-leathered, spiked-braceleted heavy metalers walking to the fair passed in front of the porch. Two elderly women in bright velvet shirts embellished with silver buttons, strands of turquoise, and full-pleated velvet skirts also walked past us on the way to the fair. Staring at the youth, Elizabeth broke the silence. "That is why I don't want to move into town. There is too much there for them to get involved in. You can't control them, and they go bad. The older ones do." The conversation turned to the struggle young Navajos face as they experience their lives and develop their identities. Ernie spoke:

> I think that the main problem is self-concept. They think that white people think they stink. Everyone stays away from them. Then they see a Navajo like Jan talking to white people, and they think she isn't Navajo. Their self-concept is hurt. They feel that they aren't worth anything and then they don't do anything. It's what white people expect anyway. They don't know a lot of Navajo, and not English either. The teachers don't understand how this can hurt them.

Elizabeth felt young Navajos were confused, "But the teenagers now. I don't know about them. They don't seem to want to learn anything." Both she and Ernie felt strong parent support was needed. Ernie had been the president of the local Parent Advisory Committee for the past two years and continually urged parents to become involved and supportive of their children's education. As he said one night at a parent meeting: "Some students are hesitant to go into school in the morning. You and I know how shameful it is to go into class with incomplete work. It hurts. That is what happened to us. Uneducated parents." Ernie's high school diplomas and college experience contradicted this modest comment. Elizabeth and Ernie were proud of their children's school accomplishments. "John got second prize for his poem at the elementary school," Elizabeth said, "and then he got a free pizza for reading a lot of books when he went over to the boarding school. Della is making straight As in her first year up at the junior high." "And my son Jack," said Ernie, "is a junior and he is on the football team. He is the only Indian kid on the team. They say he is doing good in school and could graduate early. But his standardized test scores are at about 15 percent. It is hard because he is a Navajo. They don't expect anything because they think he is an ignorant Indian."

Ernie's comments turned the conversation around to what it was like to return to the reservation and once again live surrounded by Navajo neighbors. Elizabeth handed the baby to Jan. She showed me two cassette tapes on traditional stories she had borrowed from a relative.

> I used to not believe, but then I came back and I saw things, and then I believed. The ceremonies and medicine men are important. I had to move away to go to school. I was in a foster home and then I lost much. I am trying to learn again. I don't know about the Four Corners much, the Navajo stories, but I want to learn again.

With the click of a recorder's button, Navajo stories have a path to come back into their daily lives. These new forms produced new stories that, in turn, (re)created what it meant to be "traditional."

In 1969, the Navajo Tribal Council passed a resolution for an official name change from "Navajo Tribe" to "Navajo Nation." This bold statement asserted a nationalist claim of political and cultural rights.

> The Diné—the Navajo People—existed as a distinct political, cultural, and ethnic group long before the establishment of the United States of Arizona, Colorado, New Mexico, and Utah, and
>
> The Government of the United States of America recognized this fact and entered into treaties with the sovereign Navajo Tribe, and down through the years both the Congress of the United States and the Supreme Court of the United States have recognized the inherent right of the Navajo People to govern themselves, and

When the geographical area occupied by the Navajo People was incorporated into the Union of states of the United States of America, no one asked the Navajo People if they wished to be so included, and

It is becoming increasingly difficult for the Navajo people to retain their identity and independence, and

It appears essential to the best interests of the Navajo People that a clear statement be made to remind Navajos and non-Navajos alike that both the Navajo People and Navajo lands are, in fact, separate and distinct."[22]

We decided to walk over to the rodeo. The young children grew excited as adult conversation shifted towards movement to the bright lights and smells of the carnival. As we passed the one cafe in town, Jan remarked that "Catfish" was closed today. I gave her a puzzled look. She carefully explained the descriptive categories Navajos used to name people. "We Navajo call him 'Catfish' because he has a long waxed mustache just like a catfish. And that guy that fixes cars, we call him 'Cigarette God Damn' because he always has a cigarette in his mouth and says 'God Damn.'" I remember back to the name "Crow" the Navajo students called the vice principal. I had no problem understanding why. Ernie laughed, "And they call us, the 'family that speaks English' or the 'Nissan Navajo.'" We squeezed into the grandstands at the rodeo. The first round of bull riding was finishing, and the next event was the bronco riding.

"Welcome ladies and gentlemen! We are very happy you have come to the rodeo today. We have cowboys from all over the country and even deep down on the reservation," declared the master of ceremonies. The crowd laughed as the announcer continued to name small community after small community on the reservation with the preface, "And as far away as the big town of . . . " Then the speaker switched to Navajo. He continued for several minutes. The crowed roared with laughter. Elizabeth leaned over to me: "He is telling funny jokes. They don't translate so well into English, but they are dirty. About cowboys sleeping with women and not being able to do anything because they are tired and bruised!" She smiled and continued giggling at the next joke.

The entry stalls started to fill with broncos. The crowd quieted as attention turned towards the cowboys as they climbed onto the wooden stalls for the first event. Several broncos bolted from the confining stalls, and deep-sounding thuds and crashes echoed up into the grandstands.

The announcer continued, "There are ten brave cowboys riding next, ladies and gentlemen. And our very own Navajo commissioner will be riding in this event." He continued, "Mark Maryboy is the youngest and first elected Navajo county commissioner in this state. It is because of him that we have this fair. Let's give him a hand of appreciation, folks." The Navajo crowd responded with warm applause. The first rider lasted only three seconds. The crowd clapped at the cowboy's efforts. Mark was the next rider.

I had met Mark when I started my research in this community. At that time he was director of tribal education for the Utah portion of the Navajo Nation. The school district had approved my research, and I had spent three months observing in the public schools before I discovered that there was also a local tribal division of Navajo education to approve my research. As I later learned, the divisions between Navajo and white organizations were sharp in this county. Both claimed the right to decide on the educational opportunities for Navajo youth and adults. Both were somewhat invisible to each other. And both complained the other was ineffective.

Mark was an ambitious young Navajo who fit in well among Navajo elders and youth. But as his political experience and public voice strengthened, the white community increasingly saw him as a "radical Indian." As Mark told me one day, "I'm not a token Indian. I have learned the white man's ways, and I will use them to fight for our rights as Navajos." During the first four years of his term as commissioner, he spoke in support of services for his Navajo constituents by challenging the white community's disproportionate use of the county's resources in a county that was 50 percent Navajo. Ranging from the rough quality of gravel used on reservation road to the lack of electricity and running water in these same Navajo communities, he continually argued for more resources and services. He used words like "discrimination" and "inequity" and made the local white population uncomfortable. And he turned to the world outside the county—the *Los Angeles Times,* the *New York Times,* the U.S. Department of Justice, and the state's television and newspapers—to voice publicly his concerns about over one hundred years of Indian subjugation by whites in this county. I remembered his face lighting up as he spoke of his biggest accomplishment for his people, a HUD complex of thirty-six houses on the reservation with electricity and running water. "They said I couldn't do it. I was too young. But I went to a workshop on community action[23] and they told us that it was amazing what can be done in a community if you work together. We did. And it worked." Reflecting back on his speech that day, he laughed, intertwining the fingers of both hands as he spoke: "The elderly don't trust me, yet. The old-timers talk about the four mountains and sacred songs. I didn't believe that, like the old guys. But I'm starting to weave a bit of that into my speeches. I just want to help the Navajo people."

Mark tried to mount his horse. The horse bucked, and he quickly pulled back. The bronco calmed and Mark was back on top. The stall burst open, and rider and horse plunged into the arena. The crowd roared. His black cowboy hat flew off in the first few seconds. Black-leathered chaps slapped against the horse as he sought a secure grip to balance with his raised arm. As the buzzer rang, he was still on his horse. He dismounted and landed walking. He came in second. A good ride. As he passed in front of the grandstand, several relatives called out, "Mr. Commissioner, you do as good in those meetings as you do on the bronco. Good job!" and "We thought you would fall off so you would show us how to act!" Mark smiled slightly as he reached down, picked up his cowboy hat, dusted it off, and walked back to the horse stalls.

The rodeo continued with barrel racing and calf roping and ended with a favorite event, bull roping. The red dust thickened to almost obscure the roping cowboy and his bull. In the stands, we sat with bandanas partially covering our faces. With tired and restless children in her arms, Elizabeth announced they were leaving. "We need to go over to the pump and get some water. And then go home and feed and water the sheep. We will be back later for the powwow. Us Navajo always like a dance! Just like you *bilagáanas*." They laughed as we left the rodeo grandstands. They returned home to the reservation, and I walked over to the dance arenas.

As the sun set, turning the red sandstone cliffs into silent flames, cars and trucks full of dancers started to arrive. Two separate dance circles, one for traditional Navajo round dances and the other for an all-tribes powwow, started to draw people from the bright lights of the carnival rides and concession stands. Families of grandparents, mothers, fathers, children, and babies in arms set up their chairs and draped brightly colored dance shawls and blankets across the chairs as they settled around the circled dance ground. A voice boomed from the announcer's booth. "Yá'á'tééhee! Welcome to the first Utah Navajo Fair! Get ready for Grand Entry. All you dancers out there get your regalia on and line up. Ladies and gentlemen, we have ten drums and over five hundred dancers. Our brothers and sisters come from as far away as Canada and Montana and from the cities of New York and Los Angeles." Dancers slowly moved into place as the line snaked around the enclosure. Purple-, red-, blue-, and green-feathered regalia, multi-colored yarn leg bands, beaded leather dresses, and shiny, colored satin dresses joined together as the dancers entered behind the head dancer bearing an American flag and the flag of the Navajo Nation.

The dance ground slowly filled and swelled as the announcer continued, "We have the best dancers in the country, all here to compete for prizes in men's and women's traditional and fancy dances." Fancy dancers spun and flashed brightly colored regalia and demonstrated quick, supple foot moves. The dust rose around the dancers to soften and dim their image as they continued to move clockwise around the filled grounds.

Jackie, a Ute, flashed a smile as she spun lightly and gracefully in front of me. Jackie went to high school with Jan, and was one of Mary's best friends. Competing in the woman's fancy dance division, she wore a turquoise- and brown-beaded white leather dress with matching knee-high moccasins and headband. As the dance ended, she came smiling over and gave me a hug. "Hi! I bet you didn't know I was a fancy dancer. I'm one of those modern Indians. I can do it all!" We both laughed as I reminded her of the break-dancing routine she had performed for the Indian talent show in high school three years before. "Yea, I wore a tight black leotard, and my sister wore all white. We lip-synched to a song by Salt and Pepper. It was a rad dance."

Two days after that dance, she sat with me on a wooden bench in the hallway between classes. "I like school, but I don't like my classes. They are boring. I don't go." Her truancy had resulted in a court-appointed placement in the Youth In Custody Program, and her file included a comment from a teacher whose class she had cut twenty-eight times the previous semester. "I wish she would come to class. She gets involved in all of the discussions. She is very bright. She would have all As if she were attending classes." Jackie dropped out of high school shortly after the assembly. Moving to Salt Lake City, she worked for several months as a hotel housekeeper before she returned to the reservation. She has worked odd jobs during the past three years, and was now enrolled in a local community college to finish her high school diploma.

As her sister joined us, Jackie concluded: "I don't break-dance anymore. Now I am into Indian dancing. I went on the powwow trail this past summer. We went to Montana, Canada, California, and Washington. It was lots of fun to meet Indians from all tribes even though I didn't win a contest, but maybe next year!" She bent down to help a younger dancer with her regalia. As she carefully arranged the beaded belt over the smooth satin dress, I was reminded of the time she gently coached and help write a social studies report for two younger Ute relatives and the time she left math class when her teacher tried to humorously pressure her with a play on her last name, "Cantsee." "When I came into class late, that teacher said, 'Oh, here is another Indian who can't see how to get to class.' I told him to go to hell and left class." The drums called for dancers to return for the next competition.

I spotted the Begays watching the traditional Navajo round dance at the other dance arena and joined them. Elizabeth greeted me: "Isn't this wonderful! There are so many dancers from all over the reservation. And it is so alive. These dances are important to our culture. This is like the squaw dances we took you to. It is all a part of being Navajo." We talked about the first time I was taken to a ceremony by the Begays. The Enemy Way ceremony[24] is a three- or five-day healing ceremony. The family of the individual who is ill arranges for a family from a different clan to "host" the prayer sticks, drum, ceremony, and dance. War veterans are highly respected among Navajos, and Ernie, who had served in Vietnam, was asked to do the honor of hosting a ceremony for another veteran from a different clan who had been having recurring nightmares.

The first evening of the ceremony occurred at Ernie and Elizabeth's. They were responsible for feeding all participants and accepting the drum and prayer sticks, which arrived, carried on horseback by the patient's kinsmen, at sunset. We spent the day preparing mutton stew, fry bread, and bowls of potato salad, shredded lettuce, carrots, and fruit Jell-O. Donations of sacks of flour and coffee arrived throughout the day. With the ceremony underway, the medicine man and the patient were in a nearby hooghan, and relatives and friends started to gather for the evening dance. The patient would remain isolated for the evening, and the Navajo crowd would eat and dance in support of the ongoing ceremony. As pickups and cars arrived, they formed a circle around the fire and dance area. When more people arrived, the circle deepened to become two, and by the end of the evening, the dance was surrounded by three concentric circles of pickup trucks and cars. Using a familiar image from my own cultural context, I saw a sort of "Navajo drive-in." And at center stage was the community, dancing in support of itself. The evening went well, with over five hundred participants. I was the only non-Navajo I could see, but as this was an area of the reservation in which I had spent much time, many of the Navajo people knew me and were accepting of my attendance. The janitor from the elementary school kindly said, "It's good to see you out here. Not many of you [whites] come out here to help us with our ceremonies."

The second night occurred at a halfway point between the two clan areas. We packed for the fifteen-mile journey, and the water drum was put into the back of my Honda station wagon. Half of the family piled into my car, and we took our place in the car caravan. Approaching the area, we stopped to let the riders on horseback overtake us. Ernie was leading the twenty riders. He smiled as they took their place in front of us. Streams of brightly colored yarn fluttered from the riders' saddles. Similar bundles of yarn, presents for the host's clan, streamed from car and truck antennas. Jack, a sophomore, inserted one of his tapes into my player. Mötley Crüe blasted out from the dashboard. We talked about music and Enemy Way ceremonies. "I listen to hard rock and heavy metal because they are cool," he told me. He shook his head from side to side and motioned with his outstretched hand moving back and forth as he continued: "I don't know much about the squaw dance.[25] But I like going to them. They are cool, and a lot of my friends go so we can be together, like, with Navajo people." We arrived at a reserved space in the circle surrounding the dancing area and central fire. As I helped unload blankets and food from my car, Elizabeth quickly removed the ceremonial drum, "You can't touch this, only the clan families can." I was grateful she had stopped me. Over two hundred people attended this second night.

The next morning, the caravan, with Ernie again leading on horseback, carrying the prayer sticks, moved into the home of the patient for the last day and night of the ceremony. Uncomfortable eyes greeted me as I once again helped to unload my car. I was at the home of the patient on a part of the reservation in which both the Begays and I were strangers. After several hours, I decided to leave. I was conscious of the discomfort my presence was causing the patient's family and wanted to avoid any embarrassment for my friends.

Several days later, I asked how the last night of the ceremony had gone. I was told several youth had tried to set fire to the hooghan in which the ceremony had taken place and how the police had to be called to remove two Navajos who were drunk. Elizabeth related: "It was bad. The fights and then the water drum broke, the one that was in your car. And then that man [relative of the patient] said the drum should not have been in your car. It was not traditional. I told him that was not true. You did not touch the drum so it was all right." Elizabeth seemed unconcerned, and the conversation moved to sheepshearing. A month later I found out, from their youngest daughter, that the situation was not "all right." Because of pressure from relatives, Ernie and Elizabeth had to have a medicine man perform a one-night ceremony to avoid "bad luck" because of the broken drum and to allay the suspicion that its cause was connected to my presence. They had paid a significant price for our friendship.

It was past midnight, and dancers were still arriving at the fair from around the Navajo Nation. The young children were asleep in Ernie's and Elizabeth's arms. Tonight's dancing would continue until almost three in the morning. I excused myself and left the dance. As I walked home, I passed through the carnival. Groups of teenagers mingled around the neon-light rides. Their dress was in sharp contrast to the youth dancing in the powwow. Beaded leather and feathers were layered with jeans, tee shirts, and black jackets. Laughter could be heard amid the clanking of the rides and loud enticements from the game booths. "Hey, all of you," called the man in the Pink Elephant booth to a group of girls. "Come here and win a soft toy for your sweetheart." The girls giggled as they moved to the House of Mirrors. As I turned to leave, I recognized several friends who had graduated a year before from Whitehorse High School. I had known Vangie since she was a tenth grader. I had heard Vangie had moved to Salt Lake City after graduation and was surprised to see her and her sister. While the majority of Navajo youth will stay in the community or local area, Vangie moved to the city. "Yeah, I moved up there. We are living in an apartment near the community college with our boyfriends. I might go to the college now that I lost my job." Unable to decide what she wanted to study in college, she instead decided to find work. With summer experience as a housekeeper in a local motel, she had no problem finding similar work. She explained why she was home that weekend. "I was working as a maid, but I got fired. You see, my boyfriend hurt his back, and so we had to come home for a ceremony. And my boss wouldn't let me have the time off. So I quit. He must not have wanted me to work for him, or he would have let me have the time to come home." She shrugged her shoulders and smiled, "I might go and study business or computers now. Something like that."

The sounds and lights faded as I walked away from the fairgrounds and into the dark and quiet night. Back at my house, I sat on the porch and thought about the day. The complexity of the Navajo people's cultural ways was usually opaque to outsiders. Within a discourse of manifest manners, the richness, humor, and wisdom of Navajo people were clouded over to produce a distorted picture of Navajo lives framed solely by poverty, alcoholism, and despair. Faced with racism in their schools and community, Navajo youth struggled and resisted—some passively, others forcefully—the attempts to erase the Navajo-ness of their identity. Cloaked in the strength and support of their families and friends, they faced an outside world that expected them to fail in schools. Some did. Most, like the youth I saw today, did not. The schools held out the promise that graduation would lead to good jobs and success. This part of the bargain often went unfulfilled. A meritocratic illusion is easily shattered by the experiences of many who sought jobs in either the cities or their local community. Even with degrees, Navajo youth faced a resistant white population. Many refused to withdraw from who they were, and moved and claimed their place amid the webs of Navajo cultural experiences on the physical landscape of the Navajo Nation. This was where they belonged: their place of power. White school officials despaired, interpreting this as a "return to the blanket," a rejection of the mainstream, and a course of ultimate failure. In short, they were not the right kind of Indian, according to the script of manifest manners.

Hardworking Men and Women in a Hard Land

Pioneers and County Fairs

The 1990 county fair in Monticello, the most northern town in the county, occurred a month before the first Navajo fair. The theme, "Partners in Paradise," was announced at the opening ceremony by the town's mayor, "We are all working together and we have our pioneer spirit to lead us forward." The crowd of several hundred clapped and warmly welcomed onto the stage the contestants for the Little Miss and Mr. Wild West Contest. A dozen blond-haired children, girls dressed in long cotton pioneer dresses and boys in jeans and cowboy hats, marched across the stage. Last year's junior royalty at the fair, Little Mr. Buckaroo and Little Miss Buckaroo, joined them. The three-day fair had started. As there would be at the Navajo fair, there were dance contests and a rodeo. But the complexions of the dancers and the sounds of the music were not the same. The "Dance-A-Fair" included the Canyon Country Cloggers, Mountain View Cloggers, Blue Mountain Cloggers, and the local drill team. Go Naked, a local rock group, played at the high school dance. Cultural entertainment reflected the diversity within the county—Mexican folk dancing, traditional American Indian dances, Polynesian music, and Western square dancing. The Lions Club sponsored a children's theater and a piano concert. The Boy Scouts served a Saturday country breakfast of pancakes, sausages, and biscuits and gravy. And each evening, a Western chuck wagon dinner was served to several hundred fair participants and visitors. Horseshoe contests started the fair in the mornings, and by the afternoons, judging for beard growing and a hairy leg contest had drawn a crowd who would stay for the rodeo dance featuring a country western band, The Silver Eagle Band.

The heart of the fair centered on livestock, food, and crafts contests. The overall Best of Show ended in a tie between a crocheted tablecloth and a gun cabinet. Best of Show awards were given for a decorated cake, 100 percent whole wheat bread, a Lone Star quilt, a women's three-piece pink pants suit, an etched-glass jewelry box, a cross-stitch picture, canned dill pickles, and apricot nectar and rhubarb pies. Steers, hogs, lambs, mini-lambs, and mini-hogs were judged for prizes in five categories: Grand Champion, First and Second Reserves, Rate of Gain, and Showmanship.

HOLD-OUT
By Edith McDowell Edson

Guess I do smell like a horse.
Been in the saddle all day.
Don't want feed lots, jeeps, and trucks
To lead cowpuncher astray.
It's my choice of what to do.
Herdin' cows is all I know.
Been wranglin' for thirty years
From Canada to Mexico.
Just ten dollars in my jeans,
But a cold beer in my hand;
Content with a cowpoke's life,
But people just don't understand
Why it is that we eat dust
And risk bruised and broken limbs
To see pinon, pine, and sage,
Bright sunset views from canyon rims.
Feed lots make life obsolete,
City living hems me in.
I'll be dusty, tired, and broke
But ride where folks have seldom been
Eighteen wheelers rollin' by
Replace cattle drives of yore.
We've traded blessed freedom
For the convenient modern store.
I'll head to San Juan County
Ranchers still run cattle there.
And I can raise my children
Where folks cherish fresh, clean air.[26]

Blanding was a quiet little Western town whose citizens prided themselves on surviving war, drought, "Indian uprisings"[27] and the Great Depression. The predominantly Mormon population viewed itself as a tribute to its settler heritage. Driving down the main street to the one stoplight in town, one passed the oldest surviving building, the Redd Mercantile, built in 1909. Its sandstone walls were chiseled by hand from a quarry fifty miles from town. Large red sandstone columns held up a porch that covered two sides of the building. Its early days were vivid to Gordon, the son of the owner, who had run the family business since 1939. "I remember we used to have cowboys sit out on the wooden porch years ago. They whittled away at the porch. In fact, they whittled so much my dad had to rebuild the porch. When he rebuilt, he put angle iron in it so the cowboys couldn't whittle it down so much."[28] With a resilient communal attitude, the population pulled together during times of economic stress. "Country people didn't suffer as much during the depression as city folks," said Gordon. "Country people raised what they needed to eat and used scrip or traded for other things they needed." In 1946, the store added a huge locker plant with five hundred rental freezers. "Locker plants were a real deal at the time," Gordon explained. "There were no home freezers. Every town had lockers. We kept frozen food and meat in the lockers for individuals. If someone needed a pig or beef cut up, we'd do it for them and then store the meat for them." In 1958, the locker plant was closed and the grocery department expanded. This became the only shopping center in a seventy-five-mile radius. Gordon talked about their stock: "I remember when our soap department consisted of Palmolive hand soap and Proctor and Gamble laundry soap. Most people made their own soap back then. There were only three kinds of cigarettes—Camels, Luckies, and Chesterfields. Bull Durham [tobacco] was five cents a bag or six for twenty-five cents."

Times changed, and change did not come easily to some of the town's older citizens. In 1990, ground was broken for a new location for the old grocery store. The new twenty-thousand-square-foot store included a deli, a bakery, twice as much grocery space, and a new parking lot—the biggest construction project the town had experienced in the past forty years. This took some getting used to among town folks. "We have had some old-timers complain, but most comments have been positive," said Gordon. "When we first talked about a new store, we said it was going to be south of town. That seemed a long way out." The new store is located six blocks from the center of town.

Early Encounters: God's Work

Early Mormon settlers obeyed the calling by President John Taylor of the Church of Jesus Christ of Latter-day Saints (LDS) in 1878 to move from their homes to "establish a colony that would cultivate better relations with the Indians, deprive a white outlaw element of a refuge from the law, and expand Mormon control into the area."[29] By securing the borderlands of Utah and preventing their occupation by non-Mormons, the settlement of the region was framed with nineteenth-century Mormon colonization.[30]

Early accounts of their settler lives were filled with struggles to survive in a land they viewed as desolate and hostile. "Our tents and cabins were clustered together in an open flat. It seemed to me that the glistening sun would burn my eyes out; I was half blinded from always seeing it; the barren cliffs seemed little less than prison walls," one settler recalled.[31] Another spoke of the harshness of the land. "With the spring, the sandstorms came, whistling winds from the southwest, loaded with blinding sand which beat its way into every crack and crevice of the old log huts; sun shone down on the white sand; it was blinding to go and look at it and it was dismal to look at the stern gray cliffs with their barren walls."[32] A typical description of Bluff contained little beauty: "a lot of rocks, a lot of sand, and more rocks, more sand and wind to blow it away."[33] Albert R. Lyman summed up many local feelings about the area with the phrase, "forlorn corner of the territory."[34] This was not, however, how Navajo people on this landscape described their homes.

MY FAVORITE PLACE
By Leland Chee (Navajo, thirteen years old)

My favorite place are the hills at my grandma's house. They look as big as the mountains to me. The trees reach clear up to the sky. The sand and pebbles seem to move me around.

The trail seems to stretch longer and longer. The rocks seem to be hard and slippery as bananas. The wind seems to be as smooth as a window.

Slow as your breath, the grass seem to be waving at you. It's like a pattern telling you to come. As you get to the top, you feel exhausted. You feel happy and excited to climb around on the steep rocks.[35]

In spite of the feelings of the harshness of the physical surroundings, early colonizers were comforted by the belief that any opposition to their efforts was countered by the protection of God. As Kumen Jones, one of the original settlers and the first superintendent of schools, wrote:

There are two powers that work among mortal men, a good and an evil power. Any movement for good and tending to move men upward is always met by evil forces which oppose and fight it. My purpose in this humble effort in writing about it, is to convince my children and descendants of the fact that this San Juan Mission was planned, and has been carried out thus far, by prophets of the Lord, and that the people engaged in it have been blessed and preserved by the power of the Lord according to their faith and obedience to the counsels of their leaders. No plainer case of the truth of this manifestation of the power of the Lord has ever been shown in ancient or in modern times.[36]

In a mid-1880s letter to the settlers, Apostle Erastus Snow, from the LDS headquarters in Salt Lake City, promised, "Inasmuch as the Latter Day Saints of the San Juan Mission would live their religion and obey counsel, the Indians who would not be friendly but would steal and persist in their hatred and meanness toward us, that the hand of the Lord would be manifest in their destruction."[37] In this context, white colonization, if ignored or challenged, generated extraordinary punishment.

This prophecy spoke to the power of God to protect devout members of the LDS church. As Kumen Jones wrote, "The story of Navajo Frank was one of the cases where the above promises or prophecy was fulfilled to the very letter. 'Aunt Mary' and myself and several neighbors counted, on one occasion, fourteen of the worst of the Utes and Piutes that had died off within a few years, all of them healthy looking men." In 1882, Navajo Frank, between the age of twenty-four and twenty-seven, was described by Jones as a Navajo who was "young, robust, friendly"; who spoke "Piute, Moki, and Mexican"; and who "was of a jolly, good nature, and what we would now call a 'mixer.'" One day, Jones caught Navajo Frank riding one of his missing horses and decided he was responsible for many missing horses over the past several years. Confronting him, Jones warned if he continued to "steal from the Mormons he would get sick and die." Several months passed, and Jones again encountered Navajo Frank. "He was thin and haggard. His full chest was all sunken in, and he made inquiry for Haskel [the Indian Agent], saying he wanted Haskel to write a letter to the Lord and tell the Lord that Frank would never steal from the Mormons again if his life was spared." According to Jones, Navajo Frank no longer stole local Mormon horses and soon regained his health. Albert R. Lyman also wrote about Navajo Frank, but in his account he did not regain his health.

> One of the most troublesome thieves among the Navajos was a great husky fellow called Frank. Very full-chested and robust, with the strength of a grizzly bear, he feared nobody and cared only for Frank. When Haskel warned him that if he continued to steal from the little settlement he would die, he laughed a big amused laugh, and said he was not afraid of the Mormon God. For a while he continued to steal, but not for long. One day he came slowly, looking for Haskel. His great chest seemed to have caved in, leaving him with barely enough breath to speak. To Haskel he said, 'You tell your God that if He'll let me live, I'll never steal any more of your horses.' 'I'll tell him,' said Haskel. 'I don't know what He'll do about it. You've made much trouble for us, and if you ever do it again that may be the end of you.' The old thief's conduct thereafter must have been acceptable, for he lived fifteen years or more, and was a hollow-chested invalid when I knew him in the nineties.[38]

Settlers faced a daunting task, surrounded by Indians who saw no reason to give them their land. In response, they turned to their religious beliefs and created representations of Indians that distanced Indians from deserving and civilized whites. Regardless of individual friendships between Indians and whites over the past one hundred years, Indian interests were not given equal treatment in the colonization of the region. A local historian, Charles Peterson, described the racialized practices of colonization: "For whites, the arrangement led to increasing control of the country and its resources; for Indians, it led to subjugation and poverty."[39] This part of white peoples' enduring struggle in colonizing the land still persists in derogatory talk about American Indians today.

> 'Although every student deserves an equal chance, I didn't think this is the way' (high school teacher).[40]

In 1993, Utah passed a law requiring school districts to waive fees for school supplies, such as textbooks, and activity fees for the children of families too poor to afford to pay. If a student qualified for SSI, Aid to Dependent Children, or free lunches, the youth qualified for the fee waiver. In a case filed by a family over fee waivers, a judge in Salt Lake City ruled broadly that everything considered to be a school program fee must be waived for students who qualified. Locally, this was interpreted to include a basketball tournament in Hawaii, art supplies, an out-of-state history fair, summer tennis camp, and rental band instruments. Ten percent of students in San Juan School District were granted fee waivers, for a cost to the district of $16,000 during the 1993 school year. This state law did not sit well with many of the local school administrators and teachers.

At San Juan High School (SJHS), the history fair fund was $900 in the red, the football athletic fund was down $500–600, the track fund lost more than $200, and the pottery classes lost $600 for supplies. All the teachers interviewed for a *San Juan Record* newspaper article spoke of the cost of resources for the other students. By law, a school could not limit the accessibility of programs to the children for the poor. In this district, "the poor" almost exclusively were Navajo and Ute students. These youth were depicted as a "drag" on the school system and as pulling other deserving youth down. In the article, the principal complained, "The school has so little money that now even its own office supply money has been depleted in order to pay for those students getting the fee waivers." An art teacher explained, "I think that the equal education opportunity is trying to bend over backwards to create a 'standard class' financial status. . . . Instead of the government bringing everybody up to one level, they have dropped the higher ones down. It's like cutting your own throat." The message was clear. Whites worked for what they had; Navajos and Utes didn't.

In the interview for the article, white high school students protested that Navajo and Ute students were getting something for nothing. The issue became framed as good white work ethic and bad Navajo and Ute behavior; poverty was pushed to the background. One young woman explained: "If a student works hard to earn the money to go on a trip, they should not be deprived of that opportunity. I think that the fee waiver law deprives students of the experience of earning their own money; it creates harmful work ethics." Or, as her English and drama teacher explained, "This law turns honest people to dishonest. It gives them [the student] something for nothing." White teachers' and students' beliefs spoke to the availability of money, if one just worked. The band teacher's comments embodied this belief. "I'm against the student fee waiver as it is now. I think that the students should earn the money needed by working around the school; there are plenty of maintenance jobs or other jobs that can be done. But I am also not against giving help to those who need help." Help goes to the "right" kind of Indian— hard workers doing manual and service jobs. The newspaper article ended, "Poverty is an increasing problem in the state, county, district, and school, but if the fee waiver continues, it would mean the end of many of the outside school activities SJHS students enjoy." This strategy of manifest manners assured the invisibility of Navajo youth in experiences rich in cultural capital in publicly supported schools. Opportunities for Indian and white youth were differentially framed by these racialized practices.

When I arrived at Whitehorse High School in the fall of 1988, I planned to spend the day in social studies classes taught by a Navajo teacher from the community. He greeted me as I walked into his class. "We don't have any textbooks this period. The previous teacher lent them to another school. I hope to get them back real soon. So the students are in the library, learning how to use the files, where things are. They need to learn how to use a library." Disappointed, I left and decided to observe a LDS seminary class.[41] I knew Vangie was in the class, but I had been avoiding attending religious classes in a public school context; I was uncomfortable with the thin lines and opposing views between LDS theology and Navajo religious beliefs.

Mike, the seminary teacher, greeted me warmly. I was teaching a University of Utah course on multicultural education for the district's teachers that semester, and he was one of my students. I saw Vangie and moved to sit next to her. Mike was talking about a story of the children of Israel surrounding the town of Jericho and knocking it down with their voices. The students were excited and engaged with the story. When Mike explained, "God told them to totally destroy the town, killing all, the old and the young," students protested. "But why should the babies be killed?" said one young man loudly. Vangie added, "They didn't sin! Why should they die?" Many students nodded in agreement. "I know this is a tough one," Mike said. "But it is like a cancer in the body. Like it says in your workbooks. You have to cut it out or it will spread. You have to stop it before it spreads." The students were quiet. Minutes later, the bell could be heard from the high school and the class was over. Several days later in a formal interview, Mike talked about his experiences as a seminary teacher in Montezuma Creek. "My wife and I love it here! The kids are really great. I told my dad it was like when he taught. The kids have respect. Maybe it's not respect. But they don't have disrespect. They're not as vocal as Anglo kids in disrespect." I had asked him for his thoughts on the difficulties Indians students had in their classes or in school. "I think probably the biggest problem would be the internal motivation that somehow is built into the Anglo culture and isn't necessarily as important for Indians. This type of learning in the Navajo culture would be the biggest problem." He paused, and continued. "I would go back in my opinion to self-esteem and motivation. Inner motivation. They seem to need a lot of external motivation. They don't get it from home."

I then asked him for his greatest difficulties as a seminary teacher. Cautiously, he talked about the main story in the Book of Mormon, which details the chronicles of families leaving Jerusalem, coming to the Americas, and choosing to follow different paths. "Nephites were the righteous ones, and the others followed the brothers Laman and Lemuel, who from day one are real antagonistic. They talk back to their dad. They beat on Nephi when he's a little boy. They're real rebellious, bad guys." Mike stopped and seemed uncomfortable before he continued.

> I really wondered how kids would take it when you start reading about, you know, Lamanites.[42] Almost every Indian knows the Mormons call them Lamanites. So I wondered when you first start reading in the book [Book of Mormon] and the Lamanites, it says, they are cursed with the darker skin. . . . The Lamanites in the front of the Book of Mormon are the real dirty dogs. . . . But the dark skin isn't the curse. It's the mark. They are marked with the darker skin than the Nephites. The curse was idleness and laziness. It was a curse they brought about on themselves when they broke away from Nephi. They went and lived in tents and in the wilderness. The Nephites built the cities of stone and were industrious.

Handing me a Book of Mormon, he explained that by the end of the book the divisions between Nephites and Lamanites no longer had the same racial profile. "So, now you've got brown and white Nephites, and some white who are not good. Brown and white Lamanites. So they start to intermix." He pointed to the first page of the book. "We believe that the Lamanites [American Indians] go right back to Jerusalem and are members of the House of Israel. And we believe that the Book of Mormon is about their forefathers. The very first mission of the church is to the Native Americans."

At the end of our conversation, I asked Mike about race relations in the community. He chose to focus on the lack of Navajo converts and Navajo students in seminary classes. He linked problems to historically established relationships. "I think maybe there were just some bad things that happened years ago in the history of San Juan County. There are some prejudices in our border towns, which are Mormon towns, which is sad. It doesn't come from the church. We believe there is a big difference between the doctrines of the church and how we all live our lives. We know none of us live up to snuff."

I thought back to the first time I had heard the term "Lamanite." I was in my second year as an assistant professor when a colleague, who is LDS, shared an LDS primary school alphabet book. The two-sheet spread showed young children dressed with Plains Indians headdresses, riding bikes, pounding on drums, dancing around a feathered figure tied to a stake in a burning fire, shooting arrows into the sky, and dancing with raised axes. The text read, "L is for INDIAN. Now, that isn't right! Good Mormon children can spell L———."[43] I was soon to learn who "Lamanites" were. I had only been in the district for three months when several Navajo parents complained that teachers referred to their sons and daughters in class as "Lamanites," rather than by name. In classes I observed, I never heard a teacher use this term; I did hear the label in teachers' lounges and after-school events. The label I most often heard in schools was "those Indians." Others also heard this label. Late in the fall of 1984, the principal of a high school sent a letter to all of his teachers. He started his letter, "I apologize if what I say offends," and ended with, "Sorry if I have offended—I believe that I have told the truth."[44] He wrote:

> I believe that we have a serious problem in the way we view Indian students. I have defended our faculty to a variety of parents, all of whom believe strongly that the faculty of San Juan High are openly prejudiced against Indian students. I have defended us even to the point of verbal shouting matches with at least two Navajo fathers and one Navajo mother. I still maintain that no one of us is openly and consciously biased. However, I really feel that we have a problem of generalization that is affecting our overall relationships with Indian students and their families. I have noticed, and am guilty of it also, that we talk about 'those Indian students.' Very seldom do we specify particular Indian students by name as problems; it is always just 'those Indian students.' Do we ever refer to problem Anglo students as 'those Anglo students'? Rather, we always refer to them as individual students, with names, who are problems. . . . I really believe that the single most important effort we can make with our Indian students is to genuinely get to know them and to convey to them that they have worth and are important in your

classes and in the school. Admittedly, we have jerks in the school, of all colors and sizes. Let's refer to them by name and attempt to be supportive of all students.

Treaty between the United States of American and the Navajo Tribe of Indians, 1868, Article IX

In consideration of the advantages and benefits conferred by this treaty, and the many pledges of friendship by the United States, the tribes who are parties to this agreement hereby stipulate that they will relinquish all right to occupy any territory outside their reservation, as herein defined, but retain the right to hunt on any unoccupied lands contiguous to their reservation, so long as the large game may range thereon in such numbers as to justify the chase.

Removing the (Un)deserving: Challenging Place on the Landscape

I am proud to say that Posey was my great-great-grandfather. He was an honorable and great warrior. He had a tremendous amount of power and influence and used that to defend his people and their lands. The white settlers could not understand why Posey refused to go to the reservation of Colorado, but he refused to relinquish his freedom of movement for the '$15 plus rations promised to the residents of the reservation.'[45] Through his persistence and determination, he won for his people their sacred homeland. The war was finally over![46]

Tonya Morris, a Ute senior at San Juan High School, wrote these words in 1988. Her story won an award as a Grand Champion essay in the Utah State History Fair, and would later be published in the county's literary magazine. I happened to be in town, so I attended the program to honor the year's academic awards and achievement. Although I didn't know her well, she was a close friend of Mary's and several of the Navajo break-dancers I had come to know. I remembered her as a proud and outspoken young woman, one whom several teachers had told me they especially enjoyed because she was "so talkative for an Indian." Tonya was a small and slight young woman, with words that challenged the traditional stories told by white settlers. She smiled broadly as she walked across the stage to receive the certificate from her English teacher. Tonya was the only American Indian on the stage.

As Tonya had written, for the Paiute, Ute, and Navajo peoples, Posey was a great leader who fought and gave his life to save the Ute homeland in Utah from encroaching whites. He was remembered as a trustworthy, brave, and loyal protector of the Ute peoples. His adopted son remembered him fondly. "Posey raised me. He was like a father to me. He taught me to be a good person," or, as one Ute woman stated, "He was like a Moses and a Savior of his people."[47]

Posey was born around 1863 at Navajo Mountain, Arizona, even today one of the most remote and isolated parts of the Navajo Nation. This was the area where many Navajo people successfully hid from Kit Carson's roundup of Navajos for the forced Long Walk of 1863–1864. The sacred mountain, with high alpine forests and deep desert canyons, provided protection for thousands of Navajo, Ute, and Paiute peoples throughout his childhood. This was to change with the coming of white settlers in the early 1880s. Although his bloodlines are considered Paiute, he married into a band of Witapunuche Utes, also called the Avikan Utes, who lived primarily in San Juan County. Over the next forty years, he gained the respect of the Avikan Utes: "His courage, loyalty, tenacity, together with his ability to win friends, were the traits that eventually notched him a place in the heart of this people."[48] Although white folklore described him as distrustful, he lived on the Utes' traditional homeland, side by side with the white settlers through the death of one wife, a new marriage, and the raising of two sons and one daughter. Approximately sixty years old, Posey was no stranger to the white community at the time of the "Posey War" of 1923; he was their neighbor.

For the Utes, Navajos, and Paiutes, maintaining a traditional lifestyle as hunters and gathers increasingly became an impossibility. As early as 1885, the lush grass was gone, the result of massive erosion of topsoil caused by the overgrazing from over one hundred thousand head of cattle in the county. With the loss of the grasses, herds of deer had disappeared. And with the expansion of white settlements, favored campsites and springs were no longer open for Indian use.

Conflicts over stolen cattle, flour, and food increased. Robert McPherson, in "Canyons, Cows and Conflicts" (1992), argued that although both sides committed wrongs, the main problem lay in the "values and ethnocentrism of the white man." In 1914, the citizens of Blanding wrote to the commissioner of Indian Affairs for outside help to remove local Indians. "The Indians are not making any decided advancement, and we feel that the strong arm of the government should manifest itself and have the Indians placed where they can be advanced along civilized lines and relieve the good people of the county of the burden of being preyed upon by a reckless bunch of Indians."[49] Stockmen who put pressure on the U.S. government for exclusive use of public land now shared land with Indians. Navajos and Utes were described as nomadic Indians wandering unpurposefully with their herds. "These savages are possessed of the most heathenish superstitions against abandoning those places where the remains of their ancestors lie . . . [and] they consider their reduction to reservations as a species of slavery."[50] McPherson wrote: "Some whites recognized that they were using Indian lands, but the majority viewed the Indians as a nuisance to be removed even if they were the first on the range. The law specified that Native Americans had as much right as whites to be on public land, but this was conveniently overlooked in favor of emphasizing that they had an area specifically set aside for their use, a reservation."[51]

Given hunger, their view that Indian lands had been illegally homesteaded, and the patronizing attitudes of the settlers, the Indians finally burst into frustrated violence in 1915 and 1921. Posey was a central figure in these conflicts. Before long, his name was synonymous with troublemaking and thievery among local Mormon settlers. About Posey, Albert R. Lyman said: "In spite of his unorthodox notions and habits, I did not regard him as a bad man. He was not bad at heart. Deep in his undisciplined soul were the intrinsic elements of manhood—courage, loyalty and love. He grew from infancy as free as a bird in flight. He loved the wild, free region, and he regarded the white people with their herds of cattle, sheep, and horses as an unjustifiable invasion of his own private domain."[52] This manifest manners discourse created an image of a free, unthinking Indian, who is only lightly connected to the landscape, and has little need for a place on the land. This image further paints Indians as undeserving "others." Suspicion and distrust came to a head in 1923 in what the press called the "Posey War"—the last war between Indians and whites in the United States. The *Salt Lake Tribune* headlines screamed, "Paiute Band Declares War on Whites at Blanding," and news reporters flocked to the region to get the story. The last "white uprising against Indians," as McPherson claimed, was a more accurate description of the event.[53]

Prior to 1923, Posey and other Ute leaders in Utah had been meeting with representatives of the U.S. government to appeal for the right to remain on their traditional land. An Indian agent, E. A. McKearn, had recommended approval of their request. The Utes were close to stopping their removal from Utah. Then came the conflict: two Ute boys were accused of robbing a sheep camp, killing a calf, and burning a bridge. They were arrested and tried. Posey attended the trial, concerned that any trouble might jeopardize the Utes' struggles to stay in Utah. He was there when the boys escaped, shooting the sheriff's horse in the neck. He ran west of town to alert his people of the trouble. As the town organized the posse, Posey sent his people southwest towards Comb Ridge, a rock escarpment about twenty miles from Blanding. Ordering his people not to kill the posse members, he stayed behind to give them time to escape over the ridge while he negotiated with the posse. This did not happen. As Tonya Morris, the young Ute historian, wrote, "Posey believed that he would be able to negotiate with the posse, but for the first time in his experience with them, the Mormons were actually shooting at him." [54] Posey was shot through his hip before he escaped and found his people, frightened, in the wash below Comb Ridge. In their shock and confusion, they wondered "why their Mormon friends had suddenly 'gone crazy' and were trying to kill them." [55] Posey told his people to surrender. He thought this strategy would help his people in the negotiations with the U.S. government to remain in Utah. To do otherwise might mean their death. He left on his horse and rode into hiding in the high desert country.

The town's citizenry quickly mobilized, and the sheriff deputized the men, saying, "Every man here is deputized to shoot. I want you to shoot everything that looks like an Indian." [56] The town's streets were sealed off, and any Indians who could be found were put in the school's basement for a week until a stockade could be built. Over forty Ute/Paiute men, women, and children near town were captured. The rest fled into the canyons in fear for their lives. Throughout the county, Indian people were rounded up. The daughter of a sheriff remembered the night a group of Indian people was captured and held near her house in Bluff.

> The Paiute women were sitting on the ground, and some of them were crying constantly. It broke my heart because the tears were streaming down their faces. They would take their dirty skirts and wipe their tears. It was a sad thing. These people had lost some of their loved ones. We walked out among the campfires. We thought maybe some of them would talk to us, but they didn't. They hung their heads in grief, and kept on crying. Their feet had been bleeding also. [57]

Within a week, eighty Indians surrendered or were captured and placed in the center of town inside a hundred-foot-square compound made of cattle fencing topped with barbed wire. The Ute and Paiute captives would spend a month, until Posey's death, in this stockade. "There they were provided with shelter, food, a hydrant, and necessary conveniences, and with armed guards around the outside. Into this pen, the roundup from the hills was brought like a herd of wild cattle in the spring. People came to look at them as they were accustomed to come and look at a corral-full of wild steers, or wild horses."[58] Some came to gloat over them; others came in sympathy. Albert L. Lyman quoted one man: "All that these people have been wanting for a long time was a damn good licking. Now that they've had it, we can live with them in peace as we have been wanting to do for forty-three years."[59]

Even in death, Posey could not escape the hatred of some of the local settlers.[60] A half-dozen men followed the U.S. marshal's tracks into the canyon country where he had buried Posey. His grave was found, his body dug up, and, much like the familiar photographs of hunters and their game, they were photographed with Posey's dead body. Several days later, the Indian agent again dug up Posey's grave to verify his death with photographs. Today, over seventy-five years later, "White children of a younger generation go in search of 'Old Posey's grave,' an activity inspired by fathers and grandfathers who remember him, while adults still hike the Posey Trail, talking about gunfights and the bravery of the posse."[61] Framed with the romance of the "Old West," the story of the Posey War embodied deserving whites' struggles to subordinate undeserving Indians. With a "licking," peace could be had.

In the late 1980s, local historian Stan Bronson sang a song of Posey to elementary students in the San Juan School District. It is a song of the long-time romance between Posey and his wife. It is a song of white revenge against a "plundering" "young buck" for which "blood and thieving was the only thing that could partly satisfy." And, it is a song layered with the superior claims of the white settlers in a discourse of manifest manners: "He stirred up trouble in a Mormon town. They were ready his game to play."[62]

Shortly after Posey's death, the Utes were granted permission to remain in Utah. They had won their battle; Posey's life and death were heroic. As Morris claimed, "He was feared by the white settlers in San Juan County because he aggressively tried to hold on to the land which he claimed for his people in order that they could continue to live there for future generations. The love he had for his people seemed to stand out over all other characteristics."[63]

"My mom was part Ute," Jan's mother, Elizabeth, told me as we crossed the San Juan River on our way into Bluff. "My mom grew up over there," she said, pointing north to Comb Wash. "My sister and her family still live there. Where the wash comes to the river. The land people [Bureau of Land Management] say they don't belong there, that they should move back across the river. But they won't leave." Startled, I connected dozens of stories I had heard about an angry and dangerous group of Navajos to Elizabeth's extended family. Just below their home is a well-known cliff dwelling and an outstanding petrograph panel; both sites are frequented by river-rafting tourists. "We don't stop there anymore," I had been told by the owner of a small river-rafting company. "There have been some shots fired from the Navajos living near there. I don't really blame them. Some rafters camped near the ruins and used their fence posts for firewood. Pissed them off." He had shrugged his shoulders, "They were just protecting their land." I shared this incident with Elizabeth. "Yea, I heard that, too. My sister and her family just want to be left alone."

The Navajo and Ute peoples' struggles to hang on to their homelands did not end with Posey's death. Almost thirty years after the Posey War, Navajo families in San Juan County awoke to a forced eviction from their ancestral homes by Bureau of Land Management (BLM) officials and white cattlemen.

We lived there for so many years; there are many memories. Many of our loved ones are buried there. We never bothered anyone. We lived well with the people of Bluff. Some of the people we were close to, they spoke our language. We were a part of their economy. We did business with them. Some didn't speak our language; they didn't want anything to do with us. After the establishment of Bluff [in 1880], the ranchers were very helpful. They would hold on to wandering livestock and feed the stock while it was under their care. We used to help one another that way.

The cowboys knew of our home. They used to come and visit before the relocation. It seemed like we had a certain co-existence with each other that wasn't troublesome; then all of the sudden it became bad. Usually the cowboys would be in the area, working with their animals. They even hired some of our young boys for day labor. They borrowed them to help gather up their cattle. The cowboys may have scouted the area beforehand, but they knew the area. We were so close together; we had worked around each other for so many years.[64]

As early as the 1880s, Platte D. Lyman wrote in his diary of contact with Navajo families in Cottonwood, Butler, and Comb washes, and of concern they were affecting his economic prosperity. "The Navajos have brought many of their sheep onto this side of the river, eating up a great deal of grass and scattering our cattle badly." In his diary in 1881, William T. Tew reported seeing "wandering bands" of sheep belonging to the Navajo north of the river, one of which he claimed numbered six thousand head.[65] Unlike the semi-arid landscape, in the higher mountains, shrubless meadow grass grew waist high and winter snows melted into an area characterized by deep sandstone canyons, soaring arches, springs, water seeps, and hanging gardens. Ute ranchers and Navajo sheepherders traditionally moved their livestock there for summer grazing. White cattlemen wanted this grazing land for themselves.

Increasingly, the white population of the county north of the San Juan River relied on livestock for their livelihood and on federal land on which to graze. White stockmen, many of whom were descendents of these early settlers, continued struggling to coexist with Navajo livestock in a limited ecosystem for the next fifty years. With the Paiute Strip and Aneth extensions, the northern border of the Navajo reservation was expanded in 1933. Each addition to the Navajo Nation required a redivision of the remaining federal grazing lands. White stockmen in San Juan Country viewed the removal of Navajos just north of the political borders of the Navajo reservation as the only way to protect their claim to the rangelands. These were acts done by white neighbors to Navajo neighbors.

The events that led to the removal started with a severe winter in 1950, which devastated the rangeland throughout the county. Some Navajos, who normally grazed their livestock south of the San Juan River near their homes, were forced to move them north for survival. The stockmen watched the range grasses for their own livestock dwindle. In the spring, when grazing improved, these Navajo families returned south to their homes with their livestock, leaving behind Navajo families who had lived and grazed their livestock for generations on this homeland north of the river. The stockmen decided these Navajos, too, would have to go. They had no place to go, however; they were already living on their homeland.

In 1952, the stockmen sought legal action to remove Navajo families from north of the river through the BLM and the Utah courts. The court ruled in favor of the white stockmen, declaring that the Navajos were "trespassing." Armed with a court order, a few of the local cowboys

and BLM employees posted notices on sagebrush and dead trees warning that if found in the area, Navajo livestock would be impounded.
Few Navajo people in the area spoke English, and even fewer could
read English. After several months, the forced relocation began. Livestock were confiscated and trucked away in some areas, and in others,
Navajo people and their livestock were driven across the San Juan River
by groups of men with guns and whips. Navajos were handcuffed and,
in some cases, beaten and arrested. Homes were torn apart for barriers
or burned to the ground. The Navajo people anthropologist Beth King
interviewed painfully spoke of the horror of the late-night attacks, the
fear they had for their lives, and the loss of everything they had.

> It was really cold when they were forced across the river just below
> Desecration Panel. I later met up with my father. He told me they
> were forced across the river. Some people were escorted across the
> river; other people just left. They had been threatened. The people
> were just told to leave. They didn't have time to pack up. Most of
> their belongings were still there. They had to sneak back to get their
> things. Bedrolls were still under the shadehouses; they had to steal
> their own stuff.[66]

> Two people on horseback caught up with us right at the river.
> The river was very high. We started to move our animals into the
> river. I was in my late teens. I remember the water being high. I was
> on my toes, and it came up at my mouth. We lost many of our ani-
> mals. I moved the horses across the river first. The cowboys started
> to harass my mother, so I went back to help her. They were whip-
> ping our animals to get them to move across the river.[67]

The families forced south of the river faced the shock of an upcoming winter without housing or food. Many had left behind productive
gardens and their stores of food for the winter. Some found shelter with
relatives, but many more had no families or grazing privileges in this
area. The pain of displacement, framed by bewilderment and sadness,
still hung on their words when they spoke to King almost fifty years
after these events.

> It was just the kids and I. I left my herd at the sand dune, so I
> lost most of my herd. It was almost like being a lost individual.
> I couldn't go anywhere. My home wasn't there anymore. I didn't
> know who I was, where I was going to sleep next, where our food
> would come from . . . it was like a dream. I started roaming around

with people in the Shiprock area. I had a small boy. I concentrated on him and left everything behind. . . . I felt so discouraged. Everyone kept it a secret; it was like a curse. No one wanted to talk about it, so we kept it a secret. At that time, all of my concerns and concentrations were focused on surviving—how to survive the winter, how to get along now, pick potatoes, and work, work, work.[68]

One time, my husband and I went back to the old homes. Everything was still standing. It was really sad because the hogans, shadehouses, and sheep corrals were still standing. Each individual was hoping they could move back over the years. Someday they would be able to live there again. But that never came about. People more or less waited and waited. There was never anyone to interpret for them.[69]

Although the forced relocation of these Navajo families from their homes remains invisible on the pages of the official history of San Juan County, it is documented in a lawsuit argued in the courts in Salt Lake City. In 1953, a small group of the relocatees, with the aid of a sympathetic white lawyer, brought legal proceedings against the BLM, and they were awarded $100,000 for their lost livestock.[70] Bureau of Land Management employees and their volunteers repeatedly expressed ignorance in court as to the ownership of the livestock they had impounded, although one BLM ranger aide admitted he knew the areas where they gathered the horses were cornfields belonging to Navajo people. It is reported that this appearance of ignorance angered the judge, who said, "It's nonsense, pure nonsense, and I don't want to hear any more about it."[71] In finding in favor of the Navajos, the judge stated the BLM agents had violated state statutes and BLM regulations, and ordered further investigations into the entire matter. There is no record of any further actions against the BLM or of restitution to the dislocated Navajo families. Elizabeth's extended family, however, still refuses to leave their land north of the San Juan River.

Grave Robbing and Pottery Factories: Trophies and Commodities

It was a warm late-summer weekend in 1984 when I moved to Blanding as an ethnographer. I was invited for a day's hike into the canyonlands to visit an Anasazi cliff dwelling by Ed, the principal of the elementary school, and Sandra, his wife. Over the years we had become friends;

he was one of my first doctoral students, and she was a librarian at the school where I started my research. I climbed into their Toyota four-wheel-drive truck, and we headed, with a picnic in our backpacks, to a canyon several hours west of town.

This was an activity I had done before—I had been hiking in this area since college—and a favorite weekend activity for many of the county's non-Indian population. However, this was my first time visiting a site like this. We walked several miles, down a dry wash framed by cottonwood trees full of shimmering green leaves, to a set of ancient steps carved into the red sandstone wall. I remembered thinking, "No way am I going to climb up there!" With effort, and much admiration for the people who had carved these steps to their homes, we made it to the dwellings at the end of the canyon high above the canyon's floor.

The sandstone block homes throughout the complex had been almost completely destroyed by pothunters. Pottery shards, painted black and white, and brown and cream, lay scattered around the floors of the ancient public spaces. The floors of the small clusters of rooms, built to contain as many as one hundred people in the forty-room complex, were each dug up to find any ancient pottery. Hopes for intact pots, worth thousands of dollars, to sell on the collectors' market paid off enough times to encourage the digging of each of these Anasazi sites throughout San Juan County. I was told there were over thirty thousand documented sites of dwellings throughout the canyon and mesa areas of the county, and less than 5 percent of the county had been inventoried. This site was typical of most in the area. The middens, the soft areas for garbage and burials around the houses, were dug up for burial pottery. The insides of the homes also showed signs of persistent trophy hunting. It was not a pretty sight.

As we sat down to lunch, we talked about the lives, homes, and canyon walls around us. Native peoples made these canyons, arroyos, and mesa tops their homes from around 11,500 BC to around AD 1250, when the populations moved south to more secure water sources in Arizona and New Mexico. With the homes now abandoned, only brief visits by tourists and pothunters disturb the silence of the landscape. "None of the Navajo people we know will go into these ruins," explained Sandra, "but the local whites feel they own this place and they come in here and dig." We all shook our heads, thinking of the federal laws established to protect these valuable sites of antiquities, and spoke of the pothunters critically. We saw ourselves as outsiders, but not thieves. "They just don't see anything wrong with it. This is public land, and they and their ancestors have lived here before any other Anglo people. They feel they have the right to dig in these old ruins," explained Ed. Sandra nodded and added: "It's the American way. If you try to stop them, you are going against the rights of the people here in the West. They don't want the federal government to tell them what to do. They believe it is their right as American citizens to dig these Indian graves."

On January 6, 1996, a hiker witnessed several people digging near Bluff at a site in Cottonwood Wash near the remains of a ceremonial kiva structure in an Anasazi ruin. A San Juan County sheriff's deputy received a call alerting him to the illegal hunting of Anasazi antiquities. A check with the landowner confirmed that permission to dig on the property had not been given. When arriving at the site, the deputy found a pickup truck with vanity license plates reading "ANASAZI." Three children nearby explained they were on a family outing. Their parents, James Redd, the only resident doctor in Blanding, and his wife Jeanne came running down a hill, asserting they had permission to dig on the property, and became annoyed when a local newspaper reporter arrived shortly behind the deputy. "They were real pissed off when I got there. They were red-handed digging a site. The Redds red-handed! There were bones everywhere," I was told. "They had dug a trench about fifteen feet long and five feet deep. They are avid collectors of American Indian artifacts." About thirteen to fifteen bones or bone fragments were unearthed and thrown to the side of the site as they dug for pots and the other material goods Anasazi family members placed in the graves of their beloved deceased.

After the local county attorney declined to take the case because of his close relation with the Redds, a neighboring county's attorney brought felony counts of abuse or desecration of a dead human body, under the state's 1898 "grave-robbing" law, against the Redds. At the preliminary hearing in March 1998, a district judge dismissed the felony charges of desecration after questioning whether pieces of bone actually constituted a "dead human body" under the law. The Office of the Utah Attorney General appealed the judge's ruling, arguing his interpretation was "so unworkable and so racist" that it was contrary to a basic human policy that all human remains should be treated with dignity and respect. The Utah Court of Appeals upheld the dismissal of felony charges on the grounds that the human bones unearthed were not in a recognized place of final repose, thus avoiding the issue of whether these bones were or were not "a dead human body," and shifting the discourse to whether or not they were intentionally buried.

This court decision disregarded a century of archaeological research showing that middens, refuge piles outside Anasazi dwellings, were places where the Anasazi buried their dead: they were not places where they simply "threw away" their dead. The State of Utah's case cited early work by Alfred Kidder, a renowned scholar in Southwest archaeology, as part of their petition. "These beds of rubbish were repositories for ashes, house sweeping, table leavings, broken pottery, and discarded implements; they served, as well, for the burial of the dead. The custom of interment in rubbish heaps is a very general one in the Southwest; it was caused, apparently, by no disrespect for the departed, but rather by the fact that the heaps offered as a rule the only soft earth for grave digging in a land of barren rocks and hard-packed clays."[72] Every archaeologist I knew in San Juan County identified middens as where the Anasazi buried their ancestors. And pothunters knew where to look for Anasazi burials and the pottery their families had so carefully included with the bodies of their loved ones. Pottery to collect and display on one's fireplace mantle, or possibly sell, came from middens.

This decision stunned those who had spent their careers working to understand, and respect, the Native peoples in Utah. As quoted in the *Salt Lake Tribune*, Duncan Metcalfe, archaeological curator of the Utah Museum of Natural History, said: "It's racist and shows Utah still has a pretty racist edge to it. If these were our ancestors, we would provide protections for interment. It's unbelievable." Added Kevin Jones, state archaeologist for the Utah Division of History, "It is a sad commentary on Utah when the courts rule that the very people for whom our state is named do not deserve the same respect and protections as the alleged pioneers."[73]

Local American Indian leaders also shot back with accusations of racism within the judicial system. "I am appalled the judges would rule this way," said Forrest S. Cuch, director of the Utah Division of Indian Affairs and a member of the Northern Ute tribe. "It is ethnocentric, Euro-centric, and confirms the perception that our state is very backward with its views of Americans. Our government and social system do not recognize or legitimize American Indian cultures or people as having a viable belief system, one that is viewed in the same light as the European belief system."[74]

Six years later, in 2002, charges of third-degree felony abuse or desecration of a corpse were dismissed against James Redd. Jeanne Redd

pleaded no contest to a reduced charge of "attempted" abuse or desecration of a body. The judge imposed no jail time or fine; she served six
months of unsupervised probation.

Navajo and Ute people faced the practices and discourses of manifest manners by their white neighbors which seeped below the ground
and back in history into the very bones of those who had lived there
before any white footprints touched the landscape. This white gaze
strategically dismissed the bodies of Indian ancestors as undeserving
of the respect accorded their own ancestors. Navajo ancestral ties then
became cut off or disconnected from the contemporary Dinétah landscape. What remained of importance to whites were not the people,
but the objects made centuries ago by their skillful hands. The objects,
divorced from their makers, became contemporary treasures to be protected. In some cases, this rewarded pothunters with added income; in
other cases, it yielded exquisite pottery for home decorations or gifts. I
was told by one trading post owner that by unearthing pots, gravedig-
gers were helping preserve the heritage of the ancient Anasazi.

Contemporary Indian artists also have a role in this "preservation."
The designs of Anasazi pottery regain life in a new way in the hands
of young Navajo and Ute pottery painters in American Indian pottery
factories today. At some point in their lives, almost all the Navajo families I have known in the area have had a relative who has earned a living painting pottery. Throughout the Southwest, Indian and non-Indian
craft stores and factories now flourish in many border reservation communities. The roles Indian artists play in painting "authentic" Indian
pottery for tourists boost the local non-reservation economy. This was
a safe way for whites to assert the worth of Indians.

I drove Jan's sister's husband, Kevin, up to his job at a pottery shop
in Blanding on my way back to Salt Lake City. It was near Christmas
in 1987, and the shop was busy shipping pottery to customers throughout the Southwest. Rodney, the white owner, greeted me warmly and
offered a tour. "We have about sixty or sixty-five on the payroll. I
employ mostly Indians, and all of the artists are Indians," he explained
as we walked into a large open room in a newly constructed metal
building. Each artist worked at an individual station; newly painted
mold-made pottery sat scattered around the working tables, and large
metal racks were full of white, unpainted greenware. "They work on a
contract; a loaded tray is assigned to them, and a price is figured out for

the completed tray. They can work whenever they want. It is primarily piecework. I start them on minimum wage, $3.65 per hour. But they can go much higher." He pointed to an artist, a young Navajo woman I recognized from Bluff. "Celia over there, she is the best and is making $15 an hour. They can really make as much as they want. Some stick with it, others never get much above about $6 an hour. The boys are slower than the girls are. But we have some excellent artists here."

Celia removed the earplugs to her radio when we moved over to her station. Her smile was confident and friendly. The shelves behind her were full of assorted pottery she had finished. On a background of tan, green, and dark-blue airbrushed zigzagged patterns, black and cobalt blue mountains circled small round pots with lids. Abstract, elongated black strokes of chevrons and sun-circles danced across the lid and belly of the pots. Tall, gently rounded vases were painted with scenes of galloping horses crossing brown and white landscapes. The lips and bottoms of each vase were carefully stenciled with brown diamonds and green chevrons. She was painting a tray of candlestick holders. Each, in multiple shades of black, pink, and dark purple, was painted in patterns traditionally used in Navajo rug weaving. "Celia makes more money than I do!" Rodney said, laughing. "She makes a little over $20,000 a year. And I give a Christmas bonus. And we are starting an inventory bonus of 5 percent. Last month Celia made an extra $100." With a grin and roll of her eyes, she put back her earplugs and started another candlestick holder.

Rodney had a good reputation in the community—both with whites and Navajos. He was described as caring about his workers and their families. My friends said it was a good place to work. Our conversation turned to jobs and Navajo youth in the community. "Many of them have been through all sorts of programs. Some didn't do well in high school. I have some high school students, like Julia over there," he said, pointing to a young woman with knee-length dark hair. I recognized her as one of the youth I had interviewed the previous year who had left school. "But they come back here and work in the factory. Take Nez over there. He is a graduate from Utah Tech in Provo. A welder. But he came here and is working here. It is a good place for them to have a job." At the same time, Rodney lamented the consequences for youth that returned to the reservation. "There is a good and a bad side to that. Over there they are getting strangled. It really strangles them over there. They can't make it on their own, and their families strangle them with responsibilities." In this discourse of manifest manners, the strong cohesiveness of the Navajo family was transformed from an asset to a liability.

After the tour, I was invited to visit with different artists. I went to Kevin's station to see his current design. He was working on a set of shallow, wide vases with delicate narrow openings. The dark-brown and rust background was spray-painted first, and then windows were painted around the vase, which took the viewer into a scene of an ancient Anasazi cliff dwelling on a sunny blue day. I asked him his thoughts about working there. "It's a good job. My cousin worked here; he helped me get the job. But I want to be an engineer. It's all right, but I don't want to be here forever." Henry, the artist next to him, laughed. "That's what I said years ago! And I'm still here. But it's good. And the tourists come in all the time to see real Indians making art. They want to know the significance of the designs we make." Kevin joined in, "Some guys were telling them all sorts of bull. Our boss laughed and said to all of us, 'Just don't lay it on too thick!'" We all laughed. It was then that I looked at the pot Henry was painting. The same Indian patterns circled the pot; the same vibrant colors glowed from the pot; the same land-scapes, with mesas and mountains, were scattered throughout the over-all design. On one side of the pot, arising between two canyon walls, were the unmistakable twin towers of the World Trade Center in New York City. He saw me staring at the pot, grinned, and explained. "Oh, I thought some tourist from New York might like this on an Indian pot. So I just put it in the design." I was speechless.

Contested Boundaries

Places in Place

Our grandfathers had no idea of living in any other country
except our own. . . . When the Navajos were first created,
four mountains and four rivers were pointed out to us,
inside of which we should live, that was to be our country,
and was given to us by the first woman of the Navajo tribe.
—*Barboncito, May 28, 1868*[75]

Requiring neither extended analysis nor rational justifica-
tion, sense of place rests its case on the unexamined premise
that being from somewhere is always preferable to being
from nowhere. All of us, it asserts, are generally better off
with a place to call our own. Places, it reminds us, are really
very good.

—*Keith Basso*[76]

The history of this place—San Juan County and the Utah portion of the
Navajo Nation—is a history founded on the contestations of space and
place. The sacred mountains, canyons, and mesas framing the boundaries of the Navajo homeland are part of the history, religion, and identities of Navajo peoples in this community. A sense of place within these
mountains provides the life-blood of kin, family, and community. Not
just a link to the past, the landscape provides a path and foundation for
the present and future. Navajo identity is intertwined with the piñon
trees of the high mesa tops, the silver green cottonwoods along washes
and rivers, and the red sandstone bluffs and buttes scattered throughout the landscape. Stories of battles and triumphs between gods and
monsters and the trickster Coyote intertwine with video games and talk
shows in Navajo homes on and off the reservation. Satellite dishes—
painted as Navajo baskets—point towards outside cities where friends
and families often live. Visits to health clinics in the cities and Navajo

healing ceremonies by medicine men and women at home assert the importance of mental and physical health, founded in traditional values. Navajo parents are (re)producing Navajo children who continually act both different from and the same as the previous generation. Navajo-ness exists in memories, in the talk of others, in what eyes see, and in identities asserted softly. And these connections rest on a landscape that has been the homeland of the Navajo community for at least six hundred years. This is the landscape that the Navajo women, Jan, Vangie, and Mary, and their families call home, even when they live in border towns and cities. This is the place they come from.

During the last century, white colonization swept across this landscape and boundaries were erected: fences around homes, fences around gardens, fences around fields. Fences became a symbol of ownership. Fences kept Indians out, while providing a safe space for white settlers. With practices guided by an ideology of manifest destiny, whites asserted their superior claims to the landscape. The descendants of these settlers are still struggling for control over this contested place and for economic prosperity. During the past 125 years, whites have consistently acted to remove Indians from the land and keep them invisible in community institutions. Indian grazing rights were challenged. Indians were refused entry into public schools. Indians were denied public offices. Indians ancestral gravesites and bones were desecrated. Local white employers and vocational educational programs limited employment opportunities. This history mirrors local practices experienced by the Navajo families I write about. As J. R. DeGroat, the Navajo poet, wrote, "We walked the Long Walk, but the Long Walk is not over."[77]

II

Traversing Landscapes

Negotiating Boundaries

Jan Begay

Graduation Day

Salt Lake City, June 2, 2003

I came home from the university and checked the messages on our answering machine. "Donna, it's Jan. Della is graduating! My little sister is graduating from high school. It's at the big expo place in Sandy. We want you to come with us." Several days later, I joined the Begays and over five thousand proud parents, family members, and friends watching the 651 graduates from Jordan High School. It was an important day. The last of Ernie and Elizabeth's children had graduated from high school. Elizabeth was pregnant with Della when I had first meet the Begays almost twenty years ago.

The crowd was casually dressed. Women wore long flowered dresses, slacks, and even shorts. Men sported polo shirts and khaki pants and shorts. Athletic shirts, baseball hats, and running shoes appeared on men and women, boys and girls throughout the exhibit hall. The Begays stood out in splendor, a dozen dark bronzed faces amid a crowd of light-skinned, blond-haired people. I saw no other Indian families. "There were only six Indian students at Della's school," Elizabeth had explained. It was still hard to believe. And, unlike the majority of the audience, they dressed to honor the occasion. Ernie wore light gray dress pants, a black tuxedo jacket, a formal white, long-sleeved shirt, a gray tie, and shiny black shoes. He had last dressed like this at Jan's second wedding. Elizabeth wore a long blue flowered dress with matching turquoise jacket and delicate needlepoint turquoise earrings. All of the sisters and brothers were dressed in pants suits and jackets. I smiled as I noticed both Jan and her mother were wearing beaded deerskin moccasins as a complement to their new outfits.

We spotted Della as she filed in with her graduating class. "She didn't think she would make it. We are so proud of her," Elizabeth exclaimed. Ernie nodded, "We had a hard time with her. She didn't fit in school. And she was so quiet." After Della's sophomore year at San

Juan High School, the family decided to have her join them in Salt Lake City. "Everyone else went to those schools down there. They were bad. Della stayed to take care of the house while we were working in the city. She had a hard time when she started here, because they didn't teach her anything down there," Elizabeth explained.[1] Jan leaned over to me and whispered: "The schools are much better in the city. That is why my kids are in school here. There are not many Indians, but they don't get treated so bad. When my girl started here in the second grade, she couldn't read! They didn't teach her there. But now she is getting special help with her reading here." Her sister Val joined our conversation. "I agree," she said. "I brought my daughter up here to go to school. She is doing real good in junior high, and she is going to go to Jordan High next. The schools are just better up here for our kids, my two boys, too." The move to the city for the Begays started with the need for jobs. Now, their decision was framed by providing a better school experience for their children and grandchildren. I agreed with the Begays: the school experience in San Juan County was not equal for white and Indian students.

FOR MISTY STARTING SCHOOL
By Luci Tapahonso

help her
my shiny-haired child
laboriously tying her shoes
she's a mere child of 4

she starts school today
smiling shyly
pink heart-shaped earrings
long black hair

> *we pause outside the house and pray*
> *a pinch of pollen for you starting school*
> *and you, the older sister*
> *and you, father of bright-eyed daughters.*
> *with this pollen, we pray*
> *you will learn easily*
> *in this new place*
> *you will laugh and share*
> *loving people other than us.*
> *guide her now.   guide us now.*

we tell her at school
        sprinkle cornmeal here
        by the door of your classroom.
    she takes some and looks at me
    then lets it fall to the threshold.
                to help my teacher, mommy?
                she asks
      yes, to help your teacher
        to help you
        to help us as we leave her now.
    oh, be gentle with her
    feelings, thoughts and trust.

i tell them again:
remember now, my clear-eyed daughters
        remember now, where this pollen
        where this cornmeal is from
remember now, you are no different
see how it sparkles
feel this silky power
it leaves a fine trail skyward
as it falls
blessing us
strengthening us.

remember now, you are no different
        blessing us
        leaving us.[2]

In May 1993, the newly appointed district director of bilingual education attended a parent meeting at an elementary school whose population was 100 percent Navajo. Over thirty Navajo parents and their children attended. I was asked to attend these meetings by Elizabeth and Ernie. The director, an experienced educator who did not speak Navajo, stood and spoke to the group. "We want to do what your kids need. So we are going to develop a bilingual program. So your kids can learn better in their classes. We think it will help." Parents expressed disbelief. "But you were supposed to be doing that when I was in school," one said, "and you still aren't. How do we know you will use Navajo to teach our kids?" Another agreed, "You were supposed to be doing that bilingual education because of the court case. But it still isn't going on." Visibly uncomfortable, the director nodded his head in agreement. "Yes. I know it wasn't done. But we are going to do it now. Trust us. We are now sincere." These Navajo parents had reason to question the sincerity of the district efforts at educating their children. They had heard the same refrain of "trust us" almost twenty years ago when they were students in this school.

In 1976, the San Juan School District came to an out-of-court agreement in the *Sinajini v. Board of Education* case[3] filed by Navajo parents. Although several other issues were included in the complaint (including the district's failure to provide a legally sufficient language program for Navajos), the most important issue in the case revolved around the long distances Navajo children had to travel to attend high school. In one instance, Navajo students were bussed up to 166 miles round-trip each day. In the other, Navajo students were bussed for as long as 112 miles round-trip each day. The 220 Navajo high school students who were bussed by the district rode on the bus an average of 86 miles each day of the school year. The average Navajo student traveled four times as far to school as did the average non-Indian student. Each year, on average, Navajo students traveled more than 15,000 miles, spending the equivalent of 120 school days physically sitting on a bus to attend school. For the students at the end of the longest bus routes, the figures rose to 30,000 miles each year and 240 school days on a bus. These trips for the most part were on rutted, eroded, unpaved dirt roads that frequently washed out during rains. The agreement required the district to build two high schools in the southern portion of the county within the Navajo Nation and to develop a bilingual and bicultural program for all grades. Within eight years, the high schools were built—one in 1978 and the other in 1983. The bilingual and bicultural curriculum sat unused, gathering dust in the district's material center for fifteen years. On paper, the language and cultural programs were excellent. In practice, they were nonexistent.

In 1991, the district was found to still be out of compliance with federal English-as-a-Second-Language (ESL) requirements by the U.S. Department of Education's Office for Civil Rights.[4] After three years of unacceptable bilingual plans from the district, Attorney General Janet Reno authorized the U.S. Department of Justice to intervene in the *Sinajini* case as a party-plaintiff. The Navajo Nation also joined the lawsuit. Based on a preliminary investigation, the Department of Justice decided that the school district had discriminated against American Indian students, violating federal law and the Fourteenth Amendment, by failing to adopt and implement an alternative language program for limited-English-proficiency students. The district was accused of denying American Indian students the same educational opportunities and services provided to Anglo students, such as equal access to certain academic programs, as well as denying qualified American Indian persons employment opportunities equal to those provided to Anglos. This suit represented only the second case regarding American Indians and education in which the Educational Opportunities Litigation Section in the U.S. Department of Justice had intervened during the previous twenty-five years. I would become a part of this case, as an expert witness and curriculum specialist, for the next decade. During this time, I witnessed some of the fears and critiques the Begays spoke of.

Learning Place
Home among the Sacred Mountains

In 2003, after Della's graduation, Jan, Val, and their families were happy living in the city. "I don't know if I could ever go back," Val told me, "because it is so quiet down there. I like the noise and different things to do. I think I would be lonely down there. The reservation is not for me now." Jan nodded in agreement. Elizabeth and Ernie, however, talked about returning home. "It's too noisy here. And gangs are all around. And we worry about our home on the reservation. Who is taking care of it? People can come right in, you know. We like our home down there. It is who we are."

In the summers, the Begay family moved next to their aluminum trailer to sleep, eat, visit, and relax under a three-sided cottonwood shade arbor. It was 1984, and I was visiting for the first time. Cinder blocks supported box springs and mattresses above the hard-packed, red-clay ground. A kerosene lamp and water jug hung from a twisted corner branch. Metal folding chairs surrounded a worn, lime green linoleum kitchen table. Tucked beneath each bed were boxes of clothes, toys, and books. A slight breeze stirred the cottonwood leaves above us, allowing us a moment to forget the 110-plus-degree heat.

Elizabeth picked up the binoculars from on top of a wooden orange crate and focused toward the east. A tiny cloud of dust was visible. "This way if we don't like who is coming we can hide," she told me. Several children chuckled. Peering through the lenses, Elizabeth deduced, "I think it's Old Bread Man." She handed the binoculars to her daughter, Jan. "Yeah, I can see his truck now, Mom." Across an unbroken horizon one hundred miles to the north, east, and south sat mountain ranges in Colorado, New Mexico, and Utah. No visitors arrived unseen. The bread man, a retired social worker, made weekly trips with gifts of day-old bread to Navajo families. He was welcome. Others were not. "It is mostly our family that comes to visit," said Ernie, Jan's father, "but some Mormon missionaries and those Seventh-day Adventist folks come." His youngest son blurted out, "Grandma used to have them cut wood for us!" The family laughed. Ernie explained, "There are lots of people who come to change Navajos. And we use them for what is good—cutting wood, food, and clothes. But we tell them we are Navajos. And we like this."

And here I was, another interloper. I said I meant no such harm. But of course, my presence was also more work for them. I had met Jan in my first week of school observations. Dark, tight curls and a quick smile framed her face. Relaxed and outgoing, she introduced herself after a reading class. "I lived around white people in Moab. So I can talk to you easy, like. You can ask questions of my parents, too. My dad is president of the parent group at the elementary school." I was invited to their home for a visit.

When I first arrived, Jan and her entire family had sat formally on the living room couch with a calendar trying to organize the months ahead to properly educate yet another anthropologist. I was painfully aware of a joke, started in the 1950s when anthropologists flooded the Southwest, frequently repeated throughout the Navajo Nation.[5] The U.S. census worker asked, "How many people are in a Navajo family?" To which a Navajo man replied, "A mother, a father, three children, and an anthropologist." Elizabeth pointed to the next weekend. "There is a squaw dance on Friday or Saturday. We can take you there." Ernie added: "My niece will be having her Kinaaldá sometime soon. My sister is real traditional and is having it for the second month, too." The calendar quickly filled with shopping trips to Farmington, Cortez, and Blanding, school visits, farming, laundry days, and chapter house meetings.

Della scurried across the dirt of the shade arbor to pick up her favorite stuffed teddy bear, as Jan moved over to pick up her baby sister. "I keep forgetting. Like you are not supposed to walk over the tracks of the baby before it has started to walk. It is bad luck. She may never walk. My parents are always correcting me when I do it wrong. They are telling me what is correct to do for Navajos." The baby was passed to me. "Here, play with the baby. And make her laugh," urged Jan.[6] Handing the baby to me, Elizabeth explained: "If you make the baby laugh for the first time you have to have a dinner and rock salt. The rock salt is for the baby to give to people so they will have a good life. It is part of our traditions." Jan urged, "Make her laugh; you have the money for a feast!" Everyone but the baby laughed. Elizabeth continued: "I used to not believe, but then I came back and I saw things and then I believed. The ceremonies and medicine men are important." Jan moved to sit next to her mother. "I had to move away to go to school," Elizabeth said softly. "I was in a foster home and then I lost much. I am trying to learn again. I don't know much, the Navajo stories, but I want to learn again. But the teenagers now. I don't know about them. They don't seem to want to learn anything." Jan disagreed. "I believe in it. It's like doing work. Like going to school. You are always learning. I like learning to be Navajo."

As the day cooled, cooking began for dinner. Ernie and his sons dug a cooking pit, gathered wood, and started the barbecue grill, an old refrigerator shelf perched on rocks. The younger children husked corn from the garden and washed the husks carefully in a tin bucket. Jan and her sister ground the kernels for the kneel-down bread with a cast-iron grinder clamped to the edge of the table. Elizabeth scooped the corn mush into her palms, quickly folded it into a fresh cornhusk, and stacked it neatly on the table. By dusk, several dozen stuffed cornhusks were ready. Elizabeth carefully lined the earthen pit with aluminum foil and filled it with the kneel-down bread. More aluminum foil sealed the bread from the fire built on top of the pit. The bread would cook for several hours; the family would eat some; most would be sold for seventy-five cents at tomorrow's Northern Navajo Fair. Elizabeth and Jan pulled a sack of Bluebird flour from under the table to finish preparing the meal with one of the family's favorite staples—fry bread. Dinner was eaten in the cool of the night. "You can't eat until you wash your hands," Elizabeth told the young children. They scurried to the bucket to wash their hands. We filled our cups with warm, sweet, cherry Kool-Aid. Fresh roasted corn and squash steamed on the plates next to barbecued sheep ribs and fry bread. The family ate quietly.

Notes for the Children
By Luci Tapahonso

4

Diné people far from home are always scheming and planning as to how to get some mutton and Bluebird or Red Rose flour. When we hear of someone going back to the rez, we offer them money and ask humbly that they bring flour or mutton back for us. If car space is a problem, we say 'Even just a bit of the backbone is okay.' Mutton has long been a staple of Diné life and is a literal reminder of the many meals at home, celebrations, and events of all types, fairs, and ceremonies. When we taste mutton, we are reminded of the mountains, the air, the laughter and humor surrounding a meal, but mostly we are reminded of loved ones. And everyone knows that only Bluebird or Red Rose flour will work for *náneeskaadí* and fry bread. Some elderly people say that mutton has healing powers and brings happiness because sheep have been a part of our history since the beginning of time.[7]

When I met Ernie and Elizabeth Begay in 1984, they lived in a trailer on the reservation with their four school-aged children. Over the next decade, their family expanded when two married daughters, Jan and Val, brought their husbands into their extended family household and added three grandsons and two granddaughters to their homes—much to the delight of Elizabeth and Ernie. By 2005, they would have the pleasure of being grandparents to fifteen grandchildren.

In the beginning, Ernie and Elizabeth had chosen to raise their children on the reservation surrounded by Navajo practices and beliefs, some of which they themselves were experiencing for the first time. Ernie's 1990 tax forms claimed twelve dependents supported on a $26,000 salary from a maintenance department job at a uranium plant. Their new pink double-wide three-bedroom trailer sat atop a cinder-block foundation, isolated amid a treeless landscape of red hills and mesas in the high desert. It would take twenty years of petitions for them to get a house, but in 2000, the Veterans Administration built them a small, three-bedroom cinder-block house. Elizabeth still lives in this home. Wooden sheep corals, livestock watering troughs, a cottonwood three-sided shade arbor, a basketball backboard and net, a red transmissionless Fiat, a '57 Chevy, an old and a new Nissan truck, and a Nissan Pathfinder surrounded the Begays' home. An old trailer, Elizabeth and Ernie's first home, sat next to the horse corral, storing feed and hay for the livestock. Their nearest neighbors, relatives, lived over two miles away. Standing next to the fire engine red outhouse, I could turn in a circle and see across soft rolling red hills to an unbroken horizon of mountains, buttes, and mesas.

White lace curtains framed an immaculate interior of wall-to-wall carpeting, patterned velour couches, and overstuffed chairs in the

Begays' trailer. Elizabeth's new black lacquered dining room table sat prominently in the airy kitchen. A large wood-burning stove warmed the family. Photographs of a family picnic, Ernie dressed in Army fatigues sitting on a tank in Vietnam, and the children in school filled the walls. Water for the family was hauled in fifty-five-gallon barrels from town sixteen miles away, and for the livestock from the river nine miles away. Peach ceramic end table lamps provided a warm glow in the living room as the family gathered nightly around the twenty-four-inch color television. Only the hum of the generator reminded a visitor that they were without electricity. When the generator failed, kerosene lamps provided night-lights, and the television wired to a car battery continued to provide the evening's entertainment. Jan laughed: "It works about eight hours if the battery is good, two or three if it's an old battery. My dad can never understand why the battery is down, but my sister watches TV all day!"

When I started my research, Jan and her family had just moved back to the reservation after living in Moab for eleven years. Scattered throughout these years were times of unemployment when the fluctuation of uranium prices in the world market forced plants and mines to lay off workers. Ernie had told me, "We decided to return to being Navajos again. We had Elizabeth's mother's flock of sheep, so we decided to learn to be sheepherders again!" He spoke contentedly about their life. "We don't have electricity. And we don't have electric bills. We haul water, and we don't have water bills. And out here we don't have to pay for a [trailer] space." Jan's aunt added:

> A medicine man warned us about what happens when you leave. He said, 'They educate us to be pawns. We are educated to do a thing, and then we become pawns.' So you see, we have our water, even though we haul it from sixteen miles away, we have our warm house, and our meat and food from the land. In town we have to pay for these things, and then we become dependent.

Over the years, family members supplemented Ernie's income with work in the uranium plant, on road construction crews, and as clerks, waitresses, cooks, motel maids, pottery painters, fruit pickers, and tribal temporary employees. Sons and daughters moved off the reservation in search of employment and back again when temporary employment ended. Whether on or off the reservation, everyone contributed to support for the entire family. All, who could, worked at jobs or at home. Pooled resources bought food, clothing, and necessities, and paid for several car payments and insurance bills.

At that time, 1984, the Begays were among the 50 percent of Navajos living on the reservation without water or electricity. Over the next decade, they struggled with the state of Utah, the county, the power company, and the Navajo Nation to bring electricity to about fifty scattered home sites in the community. On one of my visits in 1996, as I drove across the White Mesa Ute Reservation, I found myself blinking to adjust to the lights I was seeing sparkling across the horizon. My first thoughts were of fires, but I grinned as I saw in the twilight tall wooden telephone poles stretched across the mesa and bright-lit clusters of homes in all directions. Electricity had finally come to the community. Refrigerators, air conditioners, electronic toys, vacuum cleaners, microwave ovens, light bulbs, and computers soon filled these homes.

I remembered a conversation I had with Mr. Jones, Jan's high school counselor who had signed Jan's transfer back to a remedial class she had already taken. This was a racially polarized school, where whites were often the aggressors. In his view, economic progress and increased material wealth were tainting influences on Indian lives. Indians who chose to work towards having electricity and running water in their homes, for example, were turning their backs on their traditions. And this image—which did not represent Jan or any of her peers—in turn was twisted into evidence justifying lower academic expectations for the Navajo students who filled the district's schools. "Maybe our Anglo way is wrong; we should not be pushing them toward it. We have too much strain in our Anglo world; look how calm the Indians are." Shaking his head, he talked about the beauty of Monument Valley. "You should go up there on a nice day and see the sun set and rise. It's wonderful. I sometimes think that Navajos in this traditional environment might have been better off than now."

This romantic view of the "noble Indian traditionalist" was exemplified by a painting behind his desk. In it, a Plains Indian with a long feathered headdress is standing on a cliff with arms outstretched to greet the rising sun. "Our expectations for these Indian students are just too high. We judge them against the norms of the others [whites], and it is just too much for these students. It takes time to change." He explained that the Indians at Monument Valley High School were more traditional and had a better attitude than those at San Juan High School. "They are really involved down there, they are in the band, and sing; you should hear them put on a show. But not here. We have no participation in drama, choral, drill team." After a pause, he added, "Maybe the Indian students were still uncomfortable around the whites. White man still intimidates." Even within a thoughtful pause, a manifest manners script ends with the superiority of the white man.

The summer of 1986 was a scorcher; by noon, the treeless garden's air rippled with heat waves. When the river water started moving tentatively through the irrigated field nine miles from the family's home, Ernie and his sons moved to help Jan and her mother finish picking watermelons, squash, and cantaloupe. Later, Jan and I sat in the shade next to my car. Jan, who was a sophomore, talked about her personal journey since returning to the Navajo Nation. When her family moved back to the reservation, she experienced living among Navajo peers for the first time. Looking across the mesa, she sighed and spoke softly:

> At first they made fun of me, because I couldn't speak Navajo and I didn't know anything. I went to a dance and it looked so neat. I wanted to dance, but they said I couldn't because I didn't have any clothes or nothing. Then my uncle took me up to Red Mesa and he bought me everything. It's real nice. So I danced. It was hard, though; everyone out there knew how to dance and thought it was nothing. They, you know, had been brought up all their life with it. I had to learn it new.

With time she felt more acceptance. "They say I speak real good Navajo now. The only time we speak English is when we are talking about school or homework. And we are accepted now by people when they see us at ceremonies." Moving back to the reservation meant a shift from wandering around the town's stores after school to working at home. And with this shift came a reaffirmation of a life shared by many Navajo people. "We do different things. Like we herd sheep and study by kerosene lamp, and they make fun of us reservation kids. They call us 'sheepherder.' And they use this against us." And, as Jan would also come to learn, that frozen image of what it meant to be "traditional"—as described with a discourse of manifest manners by her high school counselor—did not represent the complexity of her life as she also moved in and out of heavy metal concerts, bars, and parties with friends and kin. The "authentic" label did little to describe Jan's Native presence.

Over the years, Jan learned more and more about belonging in the Navajo community. Part of this was experiencing the racial treatment of Navajos in the white-dominated town communities. "The way I see it, it seems like the whites don't want to get involved with the Indians," Jan told me one day. "The whites make fun of the Indians. How they act and stuff like that. The way we dress. I don't know. They think we're bad. We drink. Our family drinks. That is how they think of us. Dirty. Ugly. That is what they think of us." These feelings surrounded the treatment often experienced in Navajos' encounters with white-owned businesses.

Late one night, Jan's brother, swerving to avoid livestock on the road, drove the family pickup truck into a ditch. He was unhurt, but the truck was badly damaged. Their insurance agreed to pay for the accident. The car was taken to a mechanic in the local town. "He kept that truck for months. It never ran well again," said Ernie. When Elizabeth went in to pick up the truck, she discovered that the car had not been painted with care. "They didn't even sand off the red paint. They just painted over the top. I told them I would not pay for it. The guy yelled at me and said he would turn it over to his lawyer. I said fine. What did he think? I was a dumb Indian? I was not going to pay for a bad paint job. That's how they treat Indians here." Local whites refer to this as an "Indian job"—work that does not have to meet white customers' standards. The word "Indian" attached to an object or phrase refers to "lower," "cheap," or "undesirable." At the grocery store, Spam is called "Indian steak." At the state liquor store, Tokay wine is called "Indian wine." And when whites talk about the "Indian way," the message paints pictures of people living in squalor, filth, and poverty in log or mud hooghans on the reservation, attempting to practice long-gone and ineffective ceremonies. None of these images were beautiful. Within a discourse of manifest manners, white surveillance was often used to deny the vitality and beauty in the everyday lives of their Navajo neighbors or, as in the case of Jan's counselor, to create beauty in an image that was impossible for Navajo youth to reflect.

Being Navajo—in its various images in the Begays' life—became a growing comfort for Jan in a social landscape where just this identity was used to deny her opportunities open to her white peers and friends.

Resisting the discrimination experienced in bordertown communities, Jan turned inward to the support and strength of Navajo neighbors and life on the reservation. She seemed to have looked inside herself, sighed, and felt a sense of satisfaction. Sitting under a shade at her home on a hot, bone-dry day, she told me softly: "It's nice here. So calm and quiet. At first I didn't like it. I was mad and yelled at everyone. There was more to do in town. It was so hot and dry. But now I like it here. It means feeling isolated. We don't socialize with whites very well. Us Navajo like to be with other Navajo."

September 1984: Kinaaldá and Changing Woman

I was in the elementary school when I heard the news. Several second grade girls were talking in the corner of the room. "It started yesterday. Everyone's going!" With wide eyes and giggles, her friend replied, "I'm going to have one too, when I'm ready." Sally, Jan's cousin, was having her Kinaaldá.[8] Calling the girls back to their seatwork, their teacher explained, "They call it a healing ceremony, or something like that. I think of lot of them still do this kind of thing." I remembered the superintendent's comment: "I don't think that happens anymore. It's something that was done by traditional Navajos. In the past. They have lost many of their traditions, you know." The next afternoon, I joined the Begays at Sally's Kinaaldá.

In the story of First Woman and First Man in the Navajo creation stories, the position of Navajo women in their cosmology and social landscape contrasted sharply with the positions of women who were born into and reared in a patriarchal society. Navajo culture places women at the foundation of their society, as the guardians of strong family networks. Young Navajo girls (and boys) are born to their mother's matrilineal clan, and for their father's maternal clan. This positions a young woman with an identity that privileges a closer affiliation with her mother and her mother's clan than with her father's clan. Mothers and daughters share a place at the center of the fabric of Navajo survivance. As Ruth Roessel, a Navajo educator and author, explained:

> The Navajos have always said that as long as they have cornfields and Kinaaldá they have nothing to worry about. These two elements of Navajo life remain in the position of vital importance, and in both elements the women play the primary role. The cornfield, with its fertility and growth, and the Kinaaldá ceremony, with its

recognition of the coming of age of the Navajo girl to womanhood, combine to focus on the cycle of reproduction, without which there can be no food and no people.[9]

Cornfields dotted the landscape, and almost all of the young women in this community, including Jan, her sisters, and now her oldest daughter, Jamie, had Kinaaldá. "My mother was very traditional," explained Elizabeth. "She insisted that we all have it. All the relatives here have it for their daughters. They say it is because they can remember their parents this way. Because they want Navajo to go on." Kinaaldá illustrates the transition to adulthood in Navajo culture, a transition that ensures the continuity and expansion of matrilineal networks in the community. One young woman explained: "My mom won't let anybody go out without one. My mom says if you get one you are an okay lady. On my aunt's side, they didn't do any of those. They're just running around out there somewhere." Her sister laughed, "White people try to hide it. We celebrate it. It is womanhood. And everything."

Á tsé hastiin the First Man became a great hunter in the fourth world. So he was able to provide his wife Á tsé asdzáá the First Woman with plenty to eat. As a result, she grew very fat. Now, one day he brought home a fine, fleshy deer. His wife boiled some of it, and together they had themselves a hearty meal. When she had finished eating, Á tsé asdzáá the First Woman wiped her greasy hands on her sheath. She belched deeply. And she had this to say:

'Thank you shijóózh my vagina,' she said. 'Thank you for that delicious dinner.'

To which Á tsé hastiin the First Man replied this way: 'Why do you say that?' he replied. 'Why not thank me? Was it not I who killed the deer whose flesh you have just feasted on? Was it not I who carried it here for you to eat? Was it not I who skinned it? Who made it ready for you to boil? Is nijóózh your vagina the great hunter, that you should thank it and not me?'

To which Á tsé hastiin offered this answer: 'As a matter of fact, she is,' offered she. 'In a manner of speaking, it is jóósh the vagina who hunts. Were it not for jóósh you would not have killed that deer. Were it not for her you would not have carried it here. You would not have skinned it. You lazy men would do nothing around here were it not for jóósh. In truth, jóósh the vagina does all the work around here.'[10]

Jan talked about her own Kinaaldá in my first interview with her in 1984: "I was scared when I had my period. I was in Moab, and I had not been on the reservation. I told my mom, and she called my aunt, and they prepared it." Her fear, and excitement, centered on her new-ness to Navajo cultural practices and this landscape.

> I had my Kinaaldá. Everyone out here has had it. I was embarrassed because I didn't speak Navajo. I didn't know what to do. They had traditional clothes. I wasn't really involved with this stuff. I didn't really know much about it until after I had that ceremony. Now I know more what is going on down there. I got really interested in it, so I just went ahead. I didn't know how to do it, you know. Every-body used to say, 'Do this and do that. Don't you understand the language?' Even when my mom translated for me, I couldn't get it right, so they took my hand and made the cross over the cake right. I was so embarrassed. They were saying it to me in Navajo because only the old people know. They did it when they were kids. So they just showed me how to do it. So I went ahead and did it. But I didn't understand Navajo. They had a hard time with me. They would tell me not to talk the *bilagáana* [white person] way. They used to say that to me. Then they would try to teach me Navajo. It was kind of hard learning how to be Navajo.

Young women were lectured to and prayed on during Kinaaldá about appropriate values and behaviors that will enable them to take their place in the community successfully. Unless these lessons were affirmed, it was feared that the young woman will be isolated or "run-ning around out there somewhere." Undesirable traits such as laziness, stinginess, and meanness were discouraged. Cooperative traits such as being helpful and caring for others were encouraged. Positive physical attributes, such as good teeth, a straight back, a tall build, strong legs, and long hair, were discussed, as Navajos believe the girl's bones are soft, so they can be molded, and what she does during the ceremony will influence her health. Jan talked about her experience: "They made me bathe standing inside a Navajo basket and then they dressed me in Navajo clothes. Then they massaged my body with a stone to make me grow. And they tried to make me shorter. They thought I was too tall." Throughout this ceremony, the ideal of the sociable, healthy, coop-erative Navajo was explicitly communicated to these pubescent girls. I remembered watching Jan's aunt at Sally's Kinaaldá. Tapping Sally's mouth with a stone, her mother said, "Now you will not argue with your mother, or use bad words or talk too much." Sally had muffled a giggle as she looked up and smiled at her mother. Kinaaldá served to formalize young Navajo women's commitment and obligation to the family and community. It also marked a time when henceforth women were restricted from some parts of Navajo ceremonial life during menstruation.

As Jan continued her life in the community, she was rewarded with the support of other very much still practiced Blessing Way and Enemy Way ceremonies, other traditional healing ceremonies, discussions with elders for appropriate practices, and meetings of the Native American Church. Each time practices and ceremonies occurred, they were different from before: aluminum foil replaced corn husks, pickup trucks added to sheepherding, ceremonies moved to fewer days, and hip-hop replaced rock on the outer circles at Enemy Way ceremonials. Their roots, however, were still located in a sense of place and a Native presence.

School Days

Creating Safe Spaces in Contested Places

Shortly after a fight between a Navajo and a white boy, the journalism class called a "press conference" to discuss Navajo education and racial prejudice for an article in the school newspaper. The journalism teacher, who was also the faculty advisor for the school newspaper, suggested that the conflict between Navajo and white students was an important topic that should be covered by the newspaper. The students, fourteen whites and two Navajos, voted to invite Navajo parents, the high school principal, the Indian advisor, and myself to be interviewed. Ernie, who was president of the Parent Advisory Board, and Elizabeth also attended the after-school meeting. The press conference started with a short statement from the principal: "We don't accept discrimination here at San Juan High School. We want a safe place for students to learn. This is what we try to provide. Are there any questions?" A white student who was new to the district spoke first. "When I came, I didn't know about Indians. The kids here tried to scare me, told me about Indian witches and evil spirits. It made me afraid of Indians, that they were weird or gross, and they were out to scalp whites!" She argued that cultural information should be taught in their classes so, "Anglos will understand the rituals and ceremonies, so they won't think it's weird or gross."

There was a general discussion of how to counteract stereotypes and misunderstandings between groups. One white student suggested the solution was to help Indian students to become more "white" to get beyond discriminatory treatment. "What about, would it help if Indian students were on placement?[11] I had two Indians living with me. I didn't mind it. One graduated, and she is doing real well. Would that help?" A Navajo parent softly replied, "We do not want our children to have to leave their homes to get an education." The conversation moved to the burdens facing Navajo students who live so far from the school. Ernie explained: "Our kids are tired when they get home. They get up early and spend hours on the bus, and then they run around at school all day, and then they get home and it's dark. And sometimes they are tired and grumpy when they get home. And they have to do chores and then their homework. They are tired."

Towards the end of the press conference, the principal suggested that when students heard discriminatory comments they should correct them. One student replied: "What do we do when teachers say bad things about Indians? Like the AP [advanced placement] history teacher. We don't have any Indians in there, and he says really awful things about Indians." The vice principal told them to talk to the principal because "teachers don't do that when he is present. We need to know what is happening. You kids can tell us." The principal shook his head, "I'm sure most teachers don't do that. If they do you kids can tell us." He continued, "All students, Anglo and Navajo, are just the same. I don't see the difference. Kids are just kids."

A white student asked about the fight. The previous week a fight had broken out between a Navajo and a white student. Claiming his younger cousin had been verbally and physically assaulted, a Navajo junior struck a white student across the face in the school hallway during lunch. Navajo and white students had quickly gathered at the scene as the principal and the football coach pulled the boys apart. Police were called to the school; the white student was released to his parents, while the Navajo student was taken to jail. Sighing, the principal explained, "The fight between the Anglo and Navajo boy was an isolated incident. We have taken care of the problem." Ernie, who had been silent, stood to tell a story. "I hear that there was this Anglo kid who was caught stealing a little radio. But then the teacher found out the boy was from an important family here. So the teacher did nothing to the boy. So, you see, we still have this problem." The bell rang. The press conference was concluded. The students, concerned that discussions of racial prejudice would both demoralize Indian students and embarrass white students, decided not to print the story.

I remembered Elizabeth, angered after that school fight between her son-in-law and a white student, complaining bitterly about the racial treatment Indians faced in the school. "I should have told that vice principal that he knows what it is like." Elizabeth and the vice principal had been classmates twenty years ago. "You know what it's like for the high school kids. You used to do the same things the kids are doing now against Indians. You remember when you put the pins in my seat? All the things that you used to do to Indians, it is still going on here and now. You did it, and now your kids are doing it." Elizabeth's niece's words of racial fights came back to me with a stinging bite. "They always give us trouble. Like there is this one group of guys. I told one, 'Shut up you pale face, or you red neck!' When they are rude to me, I call them everything I know. They think Indians stink. I tell them, 'If you don't like Indians, why did you move here?'"

It was 5:00 A.M. on a cold winter day in 1985 when the alarm went off in the Begays' home. Elizabeth was already up preparing breakfast. The smell of coffee and warming fry bread filled the trailer and nudged the reluctant children out of their beds. A winter storm had blown in during the night, dusting the red mesas white. Rays of the rising sun broke through the clouds, turning snowfields into glistening, luminous pools surrounded by twisted blue gray sagebrush and brown tumbleweeds. At 5:30, Ernie left for the uranium mill. By 6:00, the children were ready for school.

Bundled up against the cold, Jan and her brothers and sisters walked the quarter of a mile down the dirt road to where they caught the bus. Jan's work with the tractor the previous day had leveled the deep mudded ruts, so this morning the walk was on a well-smoothed path. A warm burst of air greeted them as the bus driver, their uncle, opened the doors of the large yellow school bus. The younger children would arrive at their elementary school within an hour; it would take Jan an additional thirty minutes to reach her high school.

The school bus circled through the Navajo community, frequently stopping to pick up clusters of children standing along the two-lane dirt road. The bumpy ride sent books and notebooks flying for students who did not sit on them or hold them tightly. Above the driver's seat sat the empty metal frame of a failed experiment. Three years earlier the school district had installed televisions for educational programs to fill the long hours spent on the school bus. Students who watched complained of headaches. Most, however, simply ignored the monotone delivery of instructional information from white teachers in the distant community. The televisions were jarred into destruction within a few months. By the time the bus returned to the smooth, paved highway leading into town, fifty-five students filled its seats and they had traveled over thirty miles. The bus continued across the river and into the small border town of Bluff to the elementary school. Climbing off the bus, Jan's brothers and sisters waved goodbye as they ran into the one-story red brick building.

The bus left town and climbed up out of the river valley on to the top of the mesa for the twenty-six-mile ride to the high school. The bus traveled through the open cattle range of the White Mesa Ute Reservation and passed the uranium mill on its way to Blanding, a community of 3,500 residents sitting at the base of a pine-covered mountain. This is the place Navajos called "Amidst the Sagebrush," where Navajos had first worked for settler families at the turn of the century. Plowed alfalfa fields now lined the highway on the outskirts of town. Tourism was a major resource for the town. Billboards declared, "Welcome to the Gateway to Canyon Country," "Visit the Dinosaur Museum—Exhibits Change Every Two Years," "Home of the 1996 AA Football Champions," "Visit the Cedar Mesa Pottery Factory," "Stop at the Cultural Museum," "Best Food in the West at the Elkhorn Café," and "Stop at Gas-N-Go." The four motels were frequently filled during the summers. Two pottery factories offered tours of their facilities for tourists to see Indians painting mold-cast pottery. Over the years, all of the Begays' sons and daughters worked in these factories. The town's mayor had told me these were the best jobs in town . . . for Navajos. Trading posts selling Navajo jewelry, pottery, and rugs were scattered throughout the town. The school bus went through the only stoplight in town to pull in front of the two-story, red brick high school.

Jan was a tenth grader at San Juan High School, a racially mixed school in the predominately white community. Although Navajo and Ute students were almost 50 percent of the school's population, few families lived in town. The Ute students were bussed to school from their reservation, eleven miles away, and Navajo students were gathered from around the Utah portion of the Navajo Nation twenty-six miles to the south. They were bussed in and out each day. The arrivals of the buses were not always welcome; as a math teacher exclaimed, "When the Ute bus arrives, my day is ruined." By law the public school had to accept Indian students, but to many in the community, they were not welcome.

THE NAMES
By Laura Tohe

Lou Hon, Suzie, Cherry, Doughnut, Woody, Wabbit, Jackie,
Rena Mae, Zonnie, Sena, Verna, Grace, Seline, Carilene

"Virginia Spears," the algebra teacher calls roll
(Her name is Speans)
And Virgie winces and raises her hand.
"Here." Soft voice.
    She never corrects the teachers.

"Leonard T-sosie."
(His name is Tsosie.) Silent first letter as in ptomaine,
Ptolemy.
Silent as in never asking questions.
Another hand from the back goes up. No voice.

"Mary Lou Yazzy. Are you related to Thomas Yazzy?"
Yazzie is a common Navajo name, like Smith or Jones.
She rhymes it with jazzy and snazzy.
Mary Lou with puzzled expression. "No."
"Oh, I thought you might be. He's quiet too."

I start to tense up because I'm next
With my name that sticks out
Like her sensible black high heeled lace-ups,
Clap, clap, clap down the hall.
"Laura Toe."
And I start to sink,
To dread hearing it on the bus tossed around
    Like kids playing keep-away.

Suddenly we are immigrants,
    Waiting for the names that obliterate the past.
Tohe, from Tóhii means Toward Water.
Tsosie. Ts'ósí means Slender.
And Yazzie, from Yázhí, means Beloved Little One/Son.

The teacher closes the book and
We are little checkmarks besides our names.

Roanhorse, Fasthorse, Bluehorse, Yellowhorse, Begay, Deswod,
    Miilwod,
Chee, 'Átsidí, Tapahonso, Háábaah, Hastin Nééz.[12]

Few Navajos before Jan's parents' generation had been allowed to attend public school with their white peers. Local schools were not open to Indian children, and very few day schools for Navajo were established before 1920, leaving thousands of children without access to schools provided for their white peers unless they traveled away from home and lived in boarding schools. During the 1930s, Navajo children living on the northern part of the Navajo reservation had limited access to federal Bureau of Indian Affairs boarding schools in Shonto and Kayenta, Arizona; Navajo Mountain and Aneth, Utah; and Shiprock, New Mexico. These schools were small—the Aneth boarding school held a maximum of forty students—and left hundreds of Navajo children without schooling. Mission schools included St. Christopher's Mission in Bluff, the Navajo Faith Mission in Aneth, and the Seventh-day Adventist school in Monument Valley. Some families migrated to other parts of the country so their children could attend school. Other families chose to educate their children at home. The public school officials made no efforts to recruit these students into the local day schools.

It was 1986 and yet another blisteringly hot summer day in the Begays' cornfield and garden next to the river. The stillness was at once stifling and calming. Ernie and his sons were working on a pump, preparing to irrigate the field. "It's my father's field," Ernie said. "I came here as a child. For as long as I can remember, our family worked this field." The Episcopal church installed the pump for the four Navajo families who farmed this area. Across the dirt-brown river, nestled under red sandstone cliffs, stood St. Christopher's Mission. "I went there when I started school. It was for Indians," Ernie had told me. In the late 1940s, Ernie's six-year-old soft brown skin, round face, and apprehensive eyes were captured in a photograph at the mission.[13] The picture showed eight young Navajo boys and girls pressed tightly together in front of the mission's stone entrance. Ernie was dressed as the other boys in jeans, a shirt, a jacket, and a bill-capped hat. Mary's mother, Carol, was also standing in this picture. The girls wore long cotton skirts and velvet blouses with silver buttons. Several of the children were giggling and laughing. Most of the children stared timidly at the camera. The priest, in a long black robe, stood proudly behind his charges. The caption read, "A group from first school."

In the early 1940s, Father H. Baxter Liebler, a young Episcopalian minister from Greenwich, Connecticut, rode horseback into the southeast corner of Utah to bring Christianity to Navajo people. He opened a small church, St. Christopher's Mission, less than a mile outside of Bluff. A school was soon to follow. Local Indian labor was used to help with the building. Father Liebler explained: "I had been warned by the whites in Bluff not to pay a Navajo more than a dollar a day for any kind of work. Although I respected very highly their advice in matters in which I had had no experience, I couldn't help seeing in this 'warning' a rather desperate attempt to maintain a white supremacy and to leave unmolested a source of cheap labor."[14] In a 1994 preface to Liebler's 1969 book, *Boil My Heart for Me*, Paul Zolbrod provided a statistical context for the differences in living experiences between whites and Indians.

> According to the 1940 census, San Juan County overall had a population of 4,712, 1,443 of them Navajos. Countywide, there were 1,328 dwelling units. Of those, 460 were equipped with flush toilets, 595 with refrigerators, and 670 with radios—all north of the San Juan River, which marked the upper boundary of the Navajo Reservation. To the south, where the Navajos mostly lived, a mere 39 of 349 dwellings had private baths or running water. Three hundred twelve had no indoor toilets, and 297 had neither indoor or outdoor facilities. Only 37 of those homes had any electricity.[15]

These disparities framed a racially segregated educational system within the county's schools.

The Navajo families I talk about in this book started their schooling experience here at St. Christopher's Mission. Mary and Carol still attend weekly church services at the mission. Ernie, Elizabeth, and their children Jan, Val, John, and Matt attended special services when the children were in elementary school. Some of Vangie's brothers and sisters also attend the mission sporadically throughout the year. Fathers and mothers spoke with pride and ownership when they recounted their school days at the mission. The Episcopalian ministers, all white, spoke Navajo, listened to their stories, and tried to understand the daily practices of their Navajo parishioners. This was a safer place to be Navajo than in the county's schools.

St. Christopher's Mission School was closed in 1961 as educational administrators outside the county questioned the legitimacy of persistent and accepted racial segregation in the county's schools. Father Liebler explained:

This is not because we felt that the then suddenly available public school was sufficient, but because we wished to put no obstacle in the way of desegregation. The school in Bluff had definitely been for whites. There was no legislation, no ruling, no test case—it was simply accepted. We had an Indian school, and the county had a white school. For a time the county reckoned our school as part of its system, paying a teacher's salary and providing all supplies, from pencils to coal. But when the United States Supreme Court began to get excited about segregation, it began to look bad to have an Indian school and a white school in Bluff.[16]

Surrounded by a resistance to allow Indian students in classrooms, Indian youth started attending public schools in the late 1950s. White parents fought hard to maintain their sons' and daughters' exclusionary white setting, arguing that the Navajo children would bring the diseases of glaucoma and tuberculosis into their healthy schools. Hidden just below the surface were beliefs expressing the fear that Indian students would disrupt student discipline, dilute academic scholarship, and, in general, cause the decay of student morale. The president of the school board, George Hurst, explained: "It wasn't the kids [who didn't want the Indians in school]; the kids would go along. They used to say sheep and cattle can't get along together on the range. Sheep and cattle get along alright. It's the sheepmen and cowmen that can't get along."[17] Fear spread throughout Blanding about a "massive infusion of Navajo students."[18] Racist beliefs fueled stories that Indian parents only wanted to move to Blanding so that they would be closer to a new welfare office or to the alcohol sold in Monticello. "Others saw this migration as another step toward Navajo domination in the county, which would eventually lead to the decline of its white communities."[19]

Money was at the heart of the decision to admit Indian students into the public schools in the 1950s. Schools received dollar amounts for Navajo and Ute enrollments. Indian youth with parents living and working on federal land—the Ute and Navajo reservations—counted at twice the rate. For the first time, white school officials and community members saw Indian student enrollment as an economic asset, rather than as a liability. As a prominent businessman explained, "For a while, Indian funds were educating the white kids."[20] This did not stop local opposition to Indian students sitting side by side with white students. George Hurst reflected on this racialized context.

I remember when we put the first Indians in school. J. B. Harris was the principal and superintendent, and I was elected to the school board. We put the first Indians in our public school here in Blanding. One fellow said that they would impeach J. B. Harris and "that other son-of-a-bitch." . . . A very prominent man in the county said that. We have a lot of people right now [1971] that would kick them [the Indian students] all out of school if they could.[21]

A huge economic boom in oil and uranium helped increase funds for education. The assessed value of the district rose from $3 million to $153 million in the early 1950s. The school district moved from the poorest district per capita in the state of Utah to the wealthiest. Teachers' salaries were among the highest in the state. An impoverished school system could no longer be used as a rationale for the exclusion of almost half of the county's children. Even with the increase in revenues, Indian parents were not openly encouraged to enroll their children in San Juan County's schools. The persistence of one Navajo parent, Hugh Benally, started the dismantling of segregation when he demanded the rights as a taxpayer to have his children attend the local schools his taxes supported. After three denied requests, the district conceded to Benally's arguments, and in 1964, his son, Clyde Benally, became the first non-foster-child Indian to graduate from San Juan High School.[22]

Reading, September 1984

The bell rang and Jan went to her first period class, Reading. The class was in the old section of the high school; tall ceilings, gold shag carpet, and pea green–painted brick walls framed the classrooms. Pink, green, and dark blue plastic chairs with attached light tan desktops were clustered in groups of four throughout the classroom. On one blackboard, a series of six pictures of white students was displayed with advice for students about schoolwork: 1) Find a quiet room, 2) Take notes, 3) Review, 4) Don't panic, do your best, 5) Review, and 6) Budget your time. Jan had a difficult time following this advice. Jan's home had no separate "quiet room," and she could only review with herself. Panic, or dismay, was an emotion she sometimes felt when facing homework alone. And, her budgeted time outside of class was filled with tending sheep, fixing the family car, tending younger siblings, maintaining the road with the tractor, and helping with the family's evening meal. On the other side of the room were listed the classroom rules: no disruptive behavior, no gum or candy, no leaving class for bathroom or drinks, come prepared with paper, pen, and books. Jan had little problem fulfilling these rules. She enjoyed the time at school with her friends and tried not to offend her teachers. She was a comfortable and pleasant young woman; her teachers described her as a "good Indian student."

This was the first year of teaching for Mrs. Williams. There were twenty-one Navajo students with an average reading level of fifth grade. "I like to teach Indian students. They are more pliable. I can have more of an impact than on Anglo students because I can be more of a model," she said, handing a stack of reading books to a student aide. She smiled at the students as they moved to their seats. The students were relaxed, and so was she. Students were dressed in jeans and slacks, spiked wristbands and silver bracelets, baseball hats and headbands, sweaters and shirts, and cowboy boots and Nikes. There was a soft hum in the class as students caught up on gossip and shared news of their friends and families.

Every class began with ten minutes of phonics. "The head of ESL believes in this, so I have to do it. But I think it is boring. Baby stuff." She started with the topic, "something bright." As she read the roll, students got points for responding with something bright. A few students yelled out "snow," "sun," "diamond." Most refused to answer. Mrs. Williams appeared frustrated, glanced at me, and told the class a story about a Cambodian girl. "She came to this country with her family and didn't speak a word of English. She studied and worked hard and become the state's spelling bee champion. This is my lecture for today. Students that use the Indian language as the reason they can't read are copping out." Several students groaned; a few laughed. She continued: "You guys all speak two languages. Research shows that bilinguals are twice as smart. Language is not your problem. It's your attitude. You have given up because whites intimidate you." She lifted the book in front of her. "Look at this story. I don't have a second language. You guys should be smarter than me. But you waste time in class; it has to do with your attitude, not language problems. You need to work harder." Several of the boys grinned to each other, sharing pictures of the hot race cars and heavy metal bands pasted to their school folders. Facing the class, she exclaimed, "Don't you want to be a top student?" "No!" the class responded loudly. "We don't care." She shot back, "Why do you come to school?" The class replied, "Fool around. Goof off. Girl watch. Boy watch." Break dancing, undulating hand motions, and pencils pounding drum beats on notebooks rippled through the classroom.

She frowned, turned back to her desk, and said to a student in the front row, "You wasted a lot of time last week." Slumped in his desk, he muttered, "I don't care."

In a loud voice, Mrs. Williams spoke to the class, "Okay, we are going to do a team work exercise." Students groaned. She divided the class into three groups and directed one member from each group to go to the board. "I will say a word, and you are supposed to write the proper vowel on the blackboard." Chalks stood poised at the board as students looked at each other for the first move. "Train," said the teacher. A student wrote "t" and the other two quickly wrote "t." Team members screamed, "Don't copy. Don't cheat." Looking back at their teammates, students erased and wrote random letters until Mrs. Williams identified the correct vowel. They then dashed back to their seats as others ran to the board.

Jan was reluctant to take her turn and was pulled from her seat by one of her friends. "I can't spell," she protested laughingly. One of her teammates joined her at the board, wrote "heavy metal," and started to draw a spiked bracelet. The student atmosphere of the class was one of warm solidarity in opposition to the well-meaning teacher. They acted as if she was invisible. The bell rang, and Mrs. Williams threw up her arms and reminded students, "Make sure you work on your spelling list for the test tomorrow." Few of the students were listening as they gathered up their books and backpacks and left the room. She was embarrassed with my witnessing of this class, and explained that these students were "difficult." She named this resistance as another failure of Indian students. And, with a mix of sympathy and manifest manners, she shifted her gaze to look at Indian youths' families as the root of academic problems.

> I know why. They make it all the way to high school without being able to read. First, there is no support at home for academic work; in fact, some students were almost punished for doing academic work. And second, it is because of the local attitudes of the whites. They think, 'Dumb Indians,' and it has worn off on the Indians. And third, previous teachers just pass students through their classes; they don't care if students read or not. There is no accountability.

Three years later, in an exhausted manner, she said: "You are not going to like what I say about Indians now. I am a racist! I'm not kidding. Working with these Indian kids makes you a racist. They just sit there and do nothing." Even well-meaning teachers were no match for the collective resistance of the all-Indian classes. In this space, Navajo students were the dominant force as they turned a Native gaze towards controlling their teachers.

Biology, November 1984

Mr. Roberts had an established routine in his class. Students were to enter the class, pick up the daily assignment in the basket on the left side of his desk, and proceed quietly to their desks. In a class of twenty-six students, only four were Navajo. These students, including Jan, sat clustered in the back left of the room. Jan explained, "We don't feel wanted, so we sit together." Today he was discussing the cell. "Look on page thirty-two of your text. It explains the cell. Now answer the questions at the end of the chapter. The questions are on the sheet assignments you picked up." The class reluctantly settled down to the task. Mr. Roberts, with his head down, seemingly oblivious to the class, graded papers for the entire forty-five-minute period as students worked on their assignments. Two of the Navajo students were sharing a pencil. One would write for several minutes and then pass the pencil across the aisle. Two white students, seated next to Jan, started whispering and taunting a young Navajo, who was studying to be a medicine man, about his hair bun, lice, and the length of his hair. "Hey," said one, "how long did it take you to grow that?" The Navajo boy replied with a soft smile, "Ten minutes." Jan smiled broadly at me. Another added, "Does it itch like a woman?" They were ignored. The white students grumbled and continued their comments: "You are a bunch of dirty Indians," "Indians are so gross." Jan rolled her eyes at me as she struggled to answer the questions from a text that was written five grade levels beyond her reading ability. The class was quiet, and tense. After the class, Jan told me: "I hate this class, but I like the teacher. He tries, but I don't like the other kids in the class." Her cousin, however, did not view the teacher sympathetically.

> He is prejudiced; he talks about Navajos and welfare. 'You all listen, you aren't going to be on welfare like the other Navajos.' He shouldn't talk like that! And then the white students say things like that to us. Like all Navajos are on welfare. I'm not like that. We work for what we have. He shouldn't say things like that. It makes us feel bad.

When Jan went to biology class, she sat in the back and refused to utter a word. Jan had learned her silence from experiences with her teachers. "Some of them are all right, but they are prejudiced against the Indian students. Like they look at us when we ask questions like, 'Oh, I'm tired of trying to help you'; they care about the students that don't need help." She finished the first quarter with an F and moved back to Basic Science, which she had successfully taken the previous year, for the rest of the year. She was bored, but safe. Her counselor signed her transfer without questions.

World Studies, October 1984

Jan told me this was one of the most boring classes in her schedule. We sat in the back of the room as the teacher, Mr. Black, prepared to take roll. Shortly after the bell rang, a young Ute, Jackie, entered the class and moved to the back of the class to sit between two of her cousins. She wore a shiny, red athletic jacket with "The Ute Nation" printed on the back. The teacher was surprised to see her. "Jackie, what are you doing in here? You took this class last year. What class are you supposed to be in?" "None," she replied. "Come on, what class are you hiding from?" he persisted. She did not answer. "You are hiding from a class, but we get along so I guess it is okay," he said as he started taking the roll. Jackie was skipping physical education, but it was for a purpose. "When I call out your name, I will also call out your test score. If you don't want your grade called out loud, you should tell me." He had called several students' names and grades, when one Navajo boy shook his head, "No." He went to the front of the room to receive his grade privately. Several Navajo girls followed him. Mr. Black stopped briefly with the next Navajo student's name, and then called out the grade—a twenty-one out of a possible twenty-five. Students laughingly shouted, "He must have cheated!" "No," the teacher replied. "The others around him got only seven to nine, so he couldn't have cheated. And the highest was a twenty-two." Several students jumped from their desks, surrounded the student and exclaimed, "Now I know who to cheat from!" and "Maybe he got my paper by mistake!" and "Now, that's some smart Indian." From that point on, all of the rest of the students had their grades called out. The ones who got the lowest grades received the loudest clapping from the other students. Calling the roll had turned into a student support group.

Glancing at me, Mr. Black clapped his hands and loudly said: "Okay, let's settle down. I'm showing a film today. About the Donner party that got stuck crossing the Sierra Nevada. We are going to talk about mountain men and the problems of cannibalism for survival." A few students grimaced. The class became quiet. He sat on a stool in the front of the class and tried to create excitement over the act of cannibalism. "I know it's pretty gross. But they had to do it for survival. What do you think of that?" Easily two-thirds of the class ignored his question. Students constructed elaborate barriers by using their notebooks to block his vision of them, and theirs of him. Students were doing work for other classes, drawing in their notebooks, sleeping, and quietly reading books. Ignoring the inattention of a majority of the class, he started the video.

While all of this was going on, Jackie was writing reports for her two cousins. "My report is due next period. Make sure you write like I do." He handed her a sample of his writing. She leaned back in her seat and reached for the encyclopedias lining the back wall. His report was on Russia for an English class. The other report was on Hong Kong for a reading class. She worked quietly and swiftly on the two-page reports. She handed them their finished reports and helped them with reading and punctuation for an English class. As soon as she finished, she left the room. Mr. Black was still moving slowly through the video and did not notice her departure. When the bell rang, only two students were listening to their teacher. Jan had taken a nap.

A Place for Navajo Language
Challenging Goals

March 2000: Salt Lake City Visit with the Begays

"Our language is real important to us," said Elizabeth. "That is why we fought for that to be in the schools. In that lawsuit [*Sinajini v. Board of Education*]. Navajo language and culture is what we want in school. They say you do better in school with both languages. They said they would teach it, but they never did." She shook her head and frowned. "I had to learn English in boarding school, and so I never got to learn Navajo in school. But Ernie speaks it real good. And my kids, too. It was hard bringing them back because they didn't know Navajo very well." Jan joined in: "Gosh, I didn't know what was going on; I had lived in Moab since I could remember. I had to learn Navajo by the people in the community. I speak it real good now. But my kids don't speak Navajo. They were brought up in the city. And they don't teach it in the schools." I was visiting during my spring break when our conversation turned to the recent English-only bill passed by the Utah State Legislature. Jan was angry. "Look at those whites. They don't want anyone else to have their own language. Like, maybe they will outlaw us speaking Navajo!" Her sister added, "And it takes smarter people to speak more than just English." The family smiled and nodded in agreement. I was painfully reminded of my mono-language limitations.

October 1984: "Are You Friend or Foe?"

I had been living for several months in the district, starting an ethnographic study of Navajo youth and schooling, when, after interviewing the superintendent, I was told, "Go talk to the director of the Curriculum Materials Center. He can tell you about our bilingual program." Arriving at his office, I was invited in and asked, "Are you friend or foe?" He laughed at my stunned silence and continued: "I always ask, because it's not popular here. I am only one of two in the district that is supportive of the bilingual program. None of the principals are in support of bilingual education. One elementary school has a program, but it is just total immersion in English. Navajo will be used as a last resort, but it is not stressed or taught." He reached behind his desk and pulled a packet off the bookcase and handed it to me. "Here is a copy of the plan we developed after the court case. Look at it carefully. It says that we will provide cultural awareness for all students; that means the whites too. But that never happened. Their parents would never let it happen." He sighed and shook his head as he continued: "People here don't understand bilingual programs. They think, 'I can learn a foreign language. If the Navajos can't learn English, they must be dumb.' They don't understand that when we teach a foreign language in school, we provide instruction about the language in English, but they don't seem to make the transfer to the Navajo situation here." The director himself did not speak Navajo.

Copies of the court-approved bilingual plan were printed in his office and sent to all of the teachers. "There was money for bilingual then, but because we have a decentralized district, principals can do what they want, so the money was used for other purposes they felt were important. And when we had cutbacks, the Navajo aides were the first to go. We lost all but at the lower primary K–3." He took me for a tour of the curriculum center, specifically focusing on the Navajo materials he and his staff had developed. "We have nine films, like *Coyote and Rabbit*, *Coyote and Skunk*, and *Coyote Learns Subtraction*. The young kids love them. But the teachers don't use them much. And here is our section on guides, manuals, and textbooks. We developed fifteen on cultural awareness for our teachers. And over here, we have thirty-five Navajo-experience booklets with cassettes in English and Navajo. We have over fifty other filmstrips and instructional kits and packets in both Navajo and English. But our teachers don't use them." There was only one Navajo teacher in the district. When we returned to his office, he showed me a set of order forms. "Look. We have larger orders for our materials from New Mexico, Arizona, even Colorado. Schools with Navajo students love our materials. But our teachers here don't use them. They think it is not worth the effort. And that the kids need to be learning English. Isn't that ironic? This stuff is supposed to help them learn English." I left his office with a copy of the bilingual program. I was excited about the materials. I was angry they were not being used in the district.

Over the next several years, I asked the teachers in the district, who were overwhelmingly white, about the bilingual plan they were required to use. Responses ranged from surprise to disbelief. None of the teachers remembered seeing the district's bilingual plan. Over the next ten years of my fieldwork, I saw no uniform bilingual-bicultural program implemented in the district. On an individual basis, some teachers did attempt to integrate Navajo words and cultural information into their elementary classrooms. In some classes, an alphabet lining a classroom wall used Navajo words for letters. Navajo clan names were printed neatly on the side of a chalkboard in several classrooms. Occasionally, Navajo elders would visit classrooms. On a school level, yearly "cultural days" included Navajo songs and dances, Navajo food, and speeches from Navajo educators and politicians. In the high schools, the inclusion of Navajo culture and language was rare. Walking through the halls and classrooms at night gave one no clues that in the morning the schools would be filled with young Navajo men and women.

On the district level, little was done to implement the bilingual-bicultural program. In 1984, the superintendent explained that although he was concerned about equal educational opportunities for Navajo students, "there is no real bilingual program in place now. The use of a model that uses native language first is not enforced here in the district. There were not enough Navajo-speaking teachers, and later, cutbacks led to reducing Navajo teacher aides." And, he explained: "We have a decentralized district here. Principals have total control over their schools. And they don't support bilingual education." He explained that the lawsuit was the reason for the existence of even a formalized bilingual plan. "There is not interest in their involvement with Navajo language. We need to bring kids up to grade level to avoid any future court cases; then we will have done our job."

Interview: Mr. Sanders, Head Counselor, October 1987

During a break from his student meetings, I sat down to talk to Jan's old counselor. I asked him what the biggest academic problem for Indian students was. He answered without hesitation: "Bilingual education. The Navajo language. The bilingual education program has been a big reason for the academic problems because it hinders the students from learning English." I took a quick breath; a bilingual program did not exist in the district. He reached into his desk and pulled out a yellowed newspaper article from 1975. "I don't show this to everyone, but it does give support for the fact that students in bilingual programs don't learn English." He handed me the article. It focused on the mismanagement of a bilingual education program in southern Florida. The director was accused of using program money to purchase a Cadillac. The article did not talk about student success or failure in the bilingual education program. It did, however, show smiling children's faces in a classroom. As I handed back the article, he moved to talk about parent involvement. "It is badly needed, but the families don't know how to help. We have left out the parents totally. We leave them in the hooghan." He argued that caring parents were ones who visited their children's schools. "Like when I started here, in ancient history," he laughed, "there was a man who had seven children, and he still came to the school every Friday to check up on attendance and grades; he cared about his children." I heard this story from numerous counselors and teachers. None of them, however, could remember his name or his children. But everyone insisted he was real, and someone else knew someone who knew him. This surveillance set a parenting norm that was difficult for any parent—white or Navajo—to follow.

Mr. Sanders spoke of several years ago when Jan had been a student at San Juan High School. "At one time we had three levels: basic, college bound, and vocational. I thought it was working real well. The parents were happy and kids didn't complain. They had choices, and they were not really locked in until the twelfth grade. Our Indian students do better in the remedial classes, so that is where I put them." He smiled when he talked about the district maintaining a dual system for students. "The ACLU came and complained and shut us down. But we still have tracking now; that is what the district is back to, and it is best for Indian students." This was justified because of the different needs of individual students. "These kids need different kinds of things. We make the mistake of thinking that they are all college bound, and they are not. They are not all academic. And then we lose some of them because they don't care about the academics." He turned to an analysis of the homes of the students. "Many of these kids go home to a different culture. They are not academic kinds of kids. It's not that their home culture is no good. It's just different. And we try to teach them all the same." Pointing in the direction of the local college to the west of the high school, he said, "The best thing would be to run a top-notch vocational educational program. That is what our Indian students need. Only about 43 percent of our students are what I call 'post–high school' material. Many of these go to vocational institutions."

At the end of our conversation, I asked about the racial conflict I had seen in several classes. "Yes, we have a bit of a problem. But kids are just kids, and some don't like each other. The real problem is peer pressure." By this he meant Indian against Indian.

> We have some Indian kids that could compete with any of the Anglos. The ones that have yuppie parents. But some of them don't have the motivation to go on to college. And their relatives don't encourage them. Some get girlfriends pregnant, and then they have blown it. One came to me and told me his father had said that he had to 'get off the rez' in order to make something of himself. Now, that's progress when the parents will say that.

He explained: "The traditional Indians put the others down. It's the problem with their culture. If one does good, the others make fun of him, saying he or she is trying to be better." Two teachers entered the counselor's office and overhead his last comment. They both nodded their heads in agreement. One illustrated the point graphically with a story about lobsters.

> You know what they say about lobsters? You can put them in water this high [indicating a depth of a few inches], and they won't get out. As soon as one tries to climb out the others pull him back in. [laughter] That's what it is like with the Indians. As soon as one of their kind tries to better himself, the others pull him back in.

"Yeah," said the counselor, "the Navajo are real jealous people. It's hard for young Navajo students who do well in school."

Observations: Heritage Language Class, Fall 2002

District administrators, Navajo Nation's educational experts, and I formed the "consensus team" to oversee the curriculum and language programs put into place with the settlement of the lawsuit. Three years into our and the district's efforts, heritage (Navajo and Ute) language classes were finally available to all students, in all grades in all appropriate schools. Elementary schools require thirty minutes of literacy instruction in Navajo per day and fifteen minutes of a content area in Navajo per day. Secondary schools offer two levels of Navajo language classes. Navajo culture and government classes in Navajo were scheduled for EDNET broadcasting the following year. All English and

Navajo teachers became English-as-a-Second Language (ESL) endorsed and certified. Navajo and Ute language teachers were hired at each school site. We would monitor these efforts for five years.

During our spring visit to the district schools, we observed a combination third and fourth grade Navajo language lesson. The classroom was filled with Navajo and English literacy. The walls were covered with bright posters showing Miss Navajo Nation, Monument Valley, Manhattan, flowers, animals, and smiling children of all colors and nationalities. The Navajo fourth grade teacher was a recent graduate from the University of Utah, with a special certification in reading, but she was unsure of her Navajo language teaching skills, so she had joined with a more experienced Navajo teacher. Students were verbal, eager, active learners. Many Navajo language classes we had seen years ago in the beginning of the program "labeled"; that is, they named and described the objects with very little active verb-based interactions. Navajo language was present in the classrooms, but it was not used in conversations. I was reminded of a Navajo father who told me, "We need to use our language, not just put it in books."

This class was different. The two teachers passed out paper cups and half-filled the cups with juice. In pairs, the students took turns pouring the juice for each other and explaining the action in Navajo. A soft murmuring of Navajo rose from each of the pairs. Very little English, except in an emergency, could be heard. "Okay, I'll say this once in English for you," said a girl to her partner. "I am filling this in for you." And she repeated it in Navajo. With a nod of her head, her partner responded in Navajo. The Navajo language was being used, not just displayed. The class was intense, and exciting. Students were engaged learners, and students were learning. All of us, district and Navajo Nation committee members, were pleased with the day's observations. This was what we had hoped for. But not everybody in the community shared our pleasure.

Resistance to the use of school dollars for Navajo language and cultural instruction emerged in daily discourses. Local historian Robert McPherson clearly captured these feelings and what it meant for the consensus plan in his 2001 book, *Navajo Land, Navajo Culture: The Utah Experience in the Twentieth Century.* I quote at length, as he is an insider to these issues, having lived his life in the county and written dozens of scholarly studies on southern Utah.

While this plan was implemented in various stages in 1998, there are some people who still voice complaints. They argue that the system hinders the acquisition of English-language skills for those who need the help the most; that the whole plan is politically and legally motivated and does not consider the welfare of the children; that the Navajo tribe, which has a voice in the adoption of the curriculum, is foisting family responsibility for teaching language and heritage onto the schools, where it does not belong; and that there are not enough staff to implement a true bilingual model. After listening to these arguments, a Navajo man serving on the school board countered: 'I think we should withdraw every Navajo student from the San Juan School District. That's when you will be happy. Take care of it once and for all. Just sweep the floor and go home. You have no interest in educating Navajo students in San Juan School District.'[23]

A Native Presence

Shaped and Stolen Opportunities

When Jan started tenth grade at San Juan High School, she wanted to be with Navajo peers. She found them—in the lower-tracked classes taught in temporary trailers alongside the school. "I did okay before. I got As and Bs. But when I moved here, I didn't feel like I was smart. Because none of my friends were smart. Now I get Cs and Ds. And when I first went to my classes, I thought, what is happening here? I was looking forward to being with Indian students, and there were none in my classes. They were in the lower classes. So I changed." Navajo students saw survival strategies in the high school as enrolling in classes where fellow Navajo students would surround them, minimizing racial assaults in mainstream classes.

For three years, Jan moved between state-required core classes and vocational electives with little academic success. She took pre-algebra and biology as a tenth grader and failed both, but successfully completed them during the eleventh grade. After the first quarter of her senior year, she withdrew, failing, from Algebra I. She earned Cs and a few Bs in jewelry design, driver education, American history, agricultural science, welding, journalism, health, career education, drama, and physical education. She took, and failed to complete, accounting, Native American studies, chemistry, and advanced jewelry design. She struggled with failing grades in reading and English classes throughout high school. Her accumulative grade point average by the twelfth grade was 1.96. The tenth grade teacher's comments on her report cards acknowledged that she "contributes to class activities," but she was "capable of better and/ or more work." By the eleventh grade, her teachers' comments clustered around "excessive absences and/or tardiness" and "does not complete assigned work." None of the teachers marked the extremely negative categories; Jan was a "good Navajo student"—non-aggressive and polite, with a smile for friends and teachers.

In the beginning Jan enjoyed school. "School is okay. It gives you something to do," she said. She had a large group of friends and was well liked by her teachers. Her journalism teacher explained: "She is a good student, but she doesn't seem to have a direction. You look at her classes, and there is no career pattern. Auto mechanics, reading, computers." Like many of her friends, Jan enjoyed the social life in school, but expressed half-hearted commitment to academic work. And, like her friends, she challenged the belief that school success was a path to social or economic success in the community.[24] "I have lots of friends; we take classes together, like basic reading. It's fun. But it doesn't mean anything for my real life." Jan avoided classes where she would be among only a few Navajo peers. "Those white kids don't like us. . . . I think that most of them think Navajos are disgusting. That is what I think." Her English teacher agreed with her assessment. "The good Navajo students are being pushed out of the academic classes because of white peer pressure or because teachers don't want them in their class. I even tried a seating chart that forced integration, Indian/white, Indian/white. But I gave it up. The white kids just talked over the Navajo kids like they weren't even there."

Wandering in and out of school during her senior year, Jan exclaimed, "I'm just sick of school!" She was suspended for truancy and caught drinking during school, but she did not drop out. Preparing to graduate, she said, "I've always told myself I was going to finish school. So I could get on with my life." Her friend responded strongly, "Get through high school. High school is important in all this. Just to get through. Then after that you can worry about what you want. You can do what you want after high school." School was rarely seen as critical to individual life situations in the community. "It's okay. I like it. I just want to get over it. School is good just to know what's going on in the world," said Jan's friend.

Family Webs: From Native American
Church Meetings to College

I met Elizabeth and Jan at the Laundromat in the small river town of Bluff. Situated in an attached room to the lodge, it was chocolate brown inside as well as outside. The dark space seemed claustrophobic on some days, while on others the brown walls were somewhat encapsulating and comfortable. As it was Saturday, this blistering hot day was full of Navajo grandmothers, mothers, daughters, and grandchildren doing their weekly wash. "We are going to have a Peyote meeting for the girls. For Jan's birthday, too. To help pray for them to finish school. If you could come, it would help to have an educated person like yourself, a professor," gestured Elizabeth. Jan had been suspended from school for truancy. The family was struggling to provide her the support she needed to stay in school. Ernie had taken a day off work, and he and Elizabeth had met with the principal, who had told them: "Maybe Jan just needs to drop out for a while. See what it's like just sitting at home and doing nothing. She just isn't trying. Maybe then she would want to be in school. She would learn about the importance of school." The Juvenile Court counselor had told them: "If she doesn't go to school, we will find a foster home for her in town. She has to be in school. That's what the law says." Elizabeth and Ernie saw the problem and solution differently. "Jan is having problems. The medicine man said it was because she had seen her grandmother's dead body, and maybe that we parents were not paying enough attention to her. Being too busy with other things. Maybe she was not believing in God a bit, not as a Christian. Maybe she said a prayer that was not answered. So we are going to have a ceremony for her." The next weekend I joined the family and friends for the all-night ceremony.

The white cloth–covered tipi was visible several miles from the Begays' home. Ernie and his brother had spent the day erecting the tipi, the traditional Plains Indian structure used for most Native American Church meetings, and gathering the wood for the ceremony. This same tipi would be used for Jan's wedding ten years later. As the sun set, family and friends moved into the tipi. We would leave when the meeting was over at 6:30 the next morning. Sam, Jan's uncle, was a Roadman of the church and conducted the meeting. Of the twenty-eight participants, I was the only non-Navajo. Sam started the meeting with an explanation of my presence. "We are glad to welcome a teacher here to support our efforts with Jan and Val. To help these young people with school." Then, as he would do throughout the night, he turned to me as he began my instruction. "You are born over here," he said pointing to the left side of the altar, "and you go around this way, clockwise, always around like that. Indians believe in the circle, so everything must go around in that way." He leaned over and whispered to me, "If you need to leave, let me know. I will help you do what is the right way." I am still thankful for his guidance.

As we sat around the half-moon-shaped altar representing the path of life—from birth to death—songs and prayers started with the passing of the prayer sticks and a drum and continued over the next four hours until holy water was brought into the tipi at midnight. I spoke and offered prayers during the meeting when I was invited to do so by the Fire Chief, who spoke to Jan and her sister first in Navajo, and then for my benefit in English. "You are young still. You do not know what will happen to you in ten years. It is important that you take this path, and finish school. Your parents love you very much. You must get your education. I pray for you; it is so important." He spoke passionately for twenty minutes. Tears were rolling down his face as he pleaded with his kin relations to succeed in school. As the singing resumed, more participants spoke of their own problems and offered prayers for the host's daughters. Ernie's brother spoke:

> I want you to have the good in life. It is hard. It is like a job. You are in school and you must work hard, like a job. We want you to get a good education, and then someday, you might have a job like a secretary or something like that, in an office. I can see that. Your parents try hard, but it is up to you. To get an education. We know it is hard, but it is important.

A half dozen of Jan and Val's high school friends were at the meeting. Some sang as the drum was passed around. Others spent the reflective time examining the contents of each other's wallets, thinking of lives beyond the tipi walls and softly whispering to their neighbors. None volunteered prayers or testimonies; the adults did these activities. At the first break at 11:00 P.M., they shot out of the tipi and scrambled into family cars. As I looked up, I saw a hand slip under the tipi and pass a Pepsi through to Jan. She smiled. Within minutes, her friends reappeared and moved to their places inside the tipi. All of their jacket pockets bulged with Pepsis. The adults would not drink until holy water was brought in around midnight. Sam explained: "When I brought in the water I poured a little: it was to bless the people who are no longer with us. To remember them. When she [his wife, who also brought in holy water] did, it was the woman who is blessing those who are to be born, the new life which is coming on the earth."

The meeting ended at dawn, with a second pail of holy water and ceremonial food. A dinner of roasted sheep ribs, mutton stew, salad, fry bread, punch, cantaloupe, and jars of Thousand Island salad dressing were passed clockwise around the circle. Afterwards, the men remained in the tipi, stretched out comfortably as they smoked and told stories. They spoke in English. There were jokes, often sexual in nature. Sam turned to me and asked if I had heard any jokes about Navajos. Blushing, I acknowledged I had, and they were often not flattering. He laughed, "We have jokes like that about white people too," and told a joke about a Navajo elder who shared a ride behind a hippie on a motorcycle to an off-reservation town.

> That Navajo elder was dressed up real well to go to the town. He wore new polyester pants and shirt and carried his things and money in a paper bag. He went to the highway and started hitch-hiking. Pretty soon a big Harley Davidson with a hippie came to a screeching halt, and the hippie said, 'Hey, brother, get on and I'll take you to town.' The old man was hesitant. But he decided, 'A ride is a ride.' He climbed on. The hippie roared off, and the Navajo almost fell off as he grabbed the seat in front of him. Faster and faster they went down the highway. Pretty soon the old man tried to spit out his chewing tobacco, but couldn't because the hippie was going so fast. All he could do was hang on as the hippie went faster and faster. Pretty soon, the spit started to go out of the sides of his mouth. His hair, which was in a bun at his neck, broke apart and now was standing straight up. The spit from his chewing tobacco went in his hair and glued it straight out. The hippie goes faster. The slick polyester pant legs flap in the wind as they slowly creep up his legs. His polyester shirt shakes in the wind as each button exploded, exposing his hairless chest. They finally arrive at the border town. As the old Navajo man climbs shakily off the bike, a group of hippies surround him and the hippie. Staring at the Navajo elder, they say to the hippie, 'Hey, man. What a cool chick you have here! What a beauty! Where did you find her?'[25]

Everyone roared with laughter at the ignorance and bad taste of white men. It was a biting picture. I remember feeling very uncomfortable after my laughter. Sam turned to talk directly to me. This time he spoke seriously about the general concerns Navajo parents have for their children, schooling, and the changing Navajo culture. His voice echoed Native survivance.

> I went to many different churches, but I felt I was a stranger: they left me empty. But this church, the Native American Church, is ours. I found the way here. It is Indian. It speaks to me. The things our grandparents knew, we do not know now, and our children

will never know. There is a new life, forward, to live in this here dominant culture. This is what I think. Our children need to go out and get the best they can. Go to school and college and get everything they want. And then come back here, to their homes. Here between the four sacred mountains. In the past, Navajo parents told their children to go out and get an education. Go to college. And they did, and they stayed in Albuquerque, in the towns, and then the parents were sad because they said they never saw their children again. It was like a spiral going up. But Navajo parents now have to tell their children to go out and get their education. To college. And graduate school. And then to come back home. Where they belong. Here on this land. This is where they belong. They need to bring their education back here to the reservation, their home. Then we can be a whole people. This is what I think.

Sam tried to explain that although there was some fear, and even resentment towards white people, there was at the same time a general feeling of pride towards what Indian people had contributed to America. The paradox of what had been gained and lost was clear in his words as he pointed to a tiny flag sewn on his baseball cap.

I am proud to be a veteran. Many of our people have served in the war. We are proud of this. I used to think that the flag was for whites; us Indians had the eagle feather. But then I thought that for every star on that flag, that Betsy Ross made, it represented Indian blood spilt. As each state was added to the nation, it was because they had removed the Indians. Indian blood was shed for that star. So I see the flag as being for Indians. It is our history here. It is because of us that this country is great.

Just as Sam finished speaking, a group of women entered the tipi carrying a large chocolate cake and placed it in front of Jan's sister, Val, who was grinning from ear to ear. Elizabeth and Ernie started the singing. "Happy Birthday to You" filled the warm enclosure. Young children tumbled into the tipi, singing, as they moved close to Val to ensure getting a piece of the still-warm cake. The new day was greeted with the chocolate-covered faces of the next generation.

After the ceremony Jan felt better. Several months later she told me: "I can't believe it. I got that red car and I have a date to the prom. And my parents are happy now. Things are now okay. It made me feel real good. I liked it. I believe it was good for me." For now, Jan felt in balance with her circumstances. The meeting had been a success. She would have several more meetings before she successfully graduated from high school.

May 20, 1988: The Accident

When I got home from San Juan High School, there was a small bag of brown herbs wedged between the screen door and the front door. Beneath the bag was a note. "I came by to see you. I wonder if you can come over to the house. Jan got hurt. She got in accident. Elizabeth. This is Navajo tea." I quickly changed and went to the Begays' home. Jan's youngest brother, John, answered the door, "You have to be quiet. 'Cause of the sickness and ceremony." Elizabeth, John, and Ernie stepped outside. "Jan said that she fell out of the car," said Elizabeth, "but a door just doesn't open up. She was pushed or she jumped!" John interjected, "She wouldn't do that; she isn't stupid." Elizabeth shook her head, "We are going to investigate. We aren't going to let it drop. We want to find out what happened. I think it was her cousin. They were drinking. We heard that Jan has been drinking and partying a lot up at the college."

As we entered the mobile home, I faced a medicine woman grinding roots and herbs in a metate, a grinding stone used by Navajo and other Native people for centuries. Her large turquoise cluster bracelets filled both wrists, and she wore a blue crushed-velvet skirt and blouse. A large turquoise circular cluster pin held her blouse tightly at her neck. She sat cross-legged on a bed of blankets next to the couch, grinding and sprinkling the herbs into a pot to soak. I quietly asked Ernie if my presence at this difficult time was acceptable to the medicine woman. He replied: "Yeah, it is just that she said we should be speaking Navajo. We are called a family that speaks English. We need to be quiet and speak Navajo." Listening to Ernie, she nodded, and with a pointing of her chin directed me to sit. The entire family quietly sat around a burning bed of coals in a short and small metal barrel placed in the center of the living room. Jan was groaning and sitting on the couch. Both arms were bandaged from wrist to armpit. Drainage and blood had seeped through parts of the white bandage. As she struggled to sit up, I could see her back was also bandaged and seeping. Everyone bowed his or her heads as the medicine woman prayed before giving Jan the first drink of tea. Jan was helped to her feet by her mother and led clockwise around the ceremonial coals. Each of us followed her path around the fire. Jan cried out with pain as she sunk back down on the couch. Her younger brothers and sisters were crying softly when Jan fell into a troubled sleep.

Elizabeth prepared a dinner of hamburger, canned corn, potato and tomato stew, fry bread, and Navajo tea. We ate in silence. In the kitchen cleaning up, Elizabeth said softly, "She was supposed to go to the doctor today, but Jan said she didn't want to go. And we didn't have a car." She pointed with her lips to the medicine woman in the living room. "So I brought my own kind of medicine. She is real good. She used to be famous for women who had a hard time with a baby. She would turn the baby around so it would be all right and could be delivered." The services of the medicine woman would cost $50 and last until noon the next day. All night, the family surrounded Jan and prayed for her recovery. I left around midnight. As I walked to my car, I heard an owl hooting in the distance. I remembered Jan's teachings as I tried to learn about Navajo beliefs: "They say when you hear the owl around that someone will die. Or will be hurt. It is a bad sign." I felt deeply depressed.

Several days later Jan was feeling better. She talked to me about her ordeal.

I had a fight. My sister and I. Up there at a friend's apartment near the college. She was drunk. And she says things when she gets drunk. I was too. I drank a case of tall ones. I just left. My friends and I went driving. They were singing and having a good time. I don't remember a thing. I passed out. And the next thing I remember was hitting the road and rolling about three times. It was dark and I couldn't see a thing. I stood up and knew I was all right. And I thought, 'What happened? Dang! I must have fallen out of the truck.' Then I found myself in front of the bar. I thought, 'What am I doing here?' I was getting sober. It was about two in the morning. I told my friends I had to get home. Blood was spurting all over me. I was really hurting. And then they went and decided I had to go to the clinic. They went and got the ambulance, and they took me out on a stretcher. They x-rayed me everywhere. 'Cause I hurt everywhere. And then they scrubbed me to get the dirt out. It really hurt. I went to a friend's home and slept all the next day. Then my dad came by to give me a job application for summer work at the plant. And he caught me. I didn't want my parents to find out. He cried when he saw me. Mom and Dad came back up for me. And Mom wanted to take me back to the reservation. And then that medicine woman came to work on me. I have had medicine men before, for ceremonies, but not a woman. It was real neat. I could ask questions, and she would explain things to me. The guys, you don't want to ask questions to. They get mad if you don't know. She said that wine was made by the white man and used by the white man. But us Indians didn't have it. It wasn't made for us. So we abuse it. We just drink to get drunk. The white people can use it socially, but us Indians abuse it. I try to not drink. But when I start I can't stop. I just drink until I get drunk and pass out. The medicine she gave me was very good. It works on you. Like you are crushed on one side and the vessels with the blood are flattened. And the medicine works to open up those vessels and get the blood going again to those places. I have learned my lesson. I'm not going to drink again. I need to get it together.

The Coyote, who is a sly person, has started The People to become drunk and stuporous. Now, we have a sickness called 'alcoholism' which has spread widely among The People both young and old. This horrible sickness can destroy you, your physical being, your dignity, and make you an unwanted person and dangerous. I hope you contemplate on this very carefully; someday you may remember what I told you and say, 'Grandfather told us about this' . . . it will make me very happy that you have listened; then again your children will say my parents taught me this and you too will be proud and happy. I know because I had this experience myself. My parents taught and lectured this to me; how else can I be telling you these. Our children are very precious to us, and we want the best for them. I have this kind of feeling to all young people, no matter who they are. I do not want them to destroy themselves. Life is too short and precious to take for granted. Especially while you are young, you have much to live for.[26]

On the Path to Work: Passing through College

In August 1987, Jan received notification that she had been accepted for the fall semester at the Southwest Indian Polytechnical Institute (SIPI), a vocational post-high school for Indian youth in Albuquerque, New Mexico. "Look! I got in! And now I can go into electronics. Like I had wanted to," she exclaimed. Ernie took time off work from the uranium mill, and the entire family drove Jan the 350 miles to school. Sitting on the bluffs overlooking the Rio Grande River, with the Sandia Mountains in the distance, the school seemed somewhat isolated from the surrounding urban population. Unpacking the car, Jan smiled and sighed. "This is my first time living in a real city. I'm so excited and at least I can see some mountains here like at home." After she had moved into her dorm room, we went to Wendy's for dinner. Saying goodbye to their oldest child was difficult. Elizabeth spoke to her daughter about having opportunities different from her own. "I wanted to go to school, to be a nurse or teacher. But I stayed and married Ernie. It is your choice now to get an education. And you can do whatever you want. Any kind of job you want, I pray for you that you will be happy." Her eyes swelled with tears as she gave her daughter a hug goodbye.

Jan enrolled in Basic Reading and math as prerequisites for the electronics program she wanted to enter. Within two months, she was able to increase her reading from a 6.5 to a 8.1 grade level. She would have to score at the tenth-grade level to qualify for the electronics program. She was proud of her accomplishments: "I learned a lot. When I started I was a six and now I am an eight. And I showed it to my principal and he wanted to know why I did so much better in the test and flunked my reading and math in high school?" She laughed. "It is because I sit in class and listen. And we are all Indian." She was also frustrated, "It just doesn't go into my head," and described her difficulties as starting when she was a child.

> I missed a lot of school when I was young. I went to boarding school when I was about fourth grade. My dad was drinking, and so my mom felt it was better for my sister and I. We only stayed about one-half year. Then I got sick. A busted appendix. And my sister broke her arm. So we left. And stayed with our grandmother. I didn't go back to school that year. I just stayed home. I wish I could start over again in the beginning, and I would learn much more. My younger brother and sister are lucky. They are going to school and doing real well. They are smart and go to school all the time.

Jan was homesick. During the first three months at SIPI, she returned to her home on the Navajo Nation four times. Sometimes she hitchhiked; other times she caught rides with Navajo friends to nearby towns where her parents picked her up. It was always a happy gathering when she returned to the folds of her family. Although Elizabeth and Ernie often said to her, "We don't want you to fall behind in your

work," they were thrilled to have her home. It was sometimes hard to
return to SIPI. Elizabeth explained: "The last time she didn't want to go
back! She is having problems there. Socially. Not academically, she says
that is fine. The Indians there are not friendly because she is not like
those Indians. And she thought all Indians were like her. She didn't say
anything when we took her back. Just sat there. She didn't say she was
happy or anything like that."

I was on my way home to Salt Lake City after Christmas in Albuquerque with my parents, and Jan caught a ride back to her home with
me. After one semester she was leaving SIPI. I helped her move out of
the dorm. As we drove, she talked about her experiences at SIPI. "I'm
glad I went. It was cool. I learned a lot. But all the other students were
much older than me. My friends at SIPI were surprised that I was in
school so soon after high school. I think that if I had known now about
it I would have taken time off. Not gone to school so soon." But Jan
relished the social life at the school. "We have lots of fun. My friends
are on tribal money, so they have money to spend. They eat out a lot.
So I get to have hamburgers and pizza a lot. Some of my friends have
apartments in town, and once a week or so they invited me over for dinner." She developed a friendship with an older Eskimo[27] male student.
"He took me and my brother to the new Holiday Inn for dinner. It was
real beautiful. But the guys are so much older than me they scare me!
So I just go around with my girlfriends." One of her girlfriends took
her to mountain beer parties. "Sometimes we would have keggers up
at the stone house. There is one guy who is always buying kegs of beer
and inviting us up there. We do cookouts, too. It's real beautiful in the
mountains and lots of fun." The dorms were also exciting social locations. "There were a lot of parties at SIPI. We are not supposed to drink
in our rooms, but last night a bunch of us girls had champagne in our
room. Andre for $2 a bottle. In another room they had Jack Daniels,
champagne, and two cases of beer. Everyone was going to their room to
party. But they didn't get caught."

Jan, however, had been caught. She had been evicted from the dorm
and put on probation from SIPI. She could not afford to live off campus, and decided to leave school. She told her parents her dorm had
been closed for the rest of the year, and she, therefore, could not continue her schooling. Her mother, however, did not believe her story. "She
told me that her roommate was kicked out because she had a boy in
her room. And drinking. But I think it was Jan was the one to get suspended. I told her, 'Is it because you got kicked out?' She just looked

at me. I told her, 'Don't you think I can think with my mind of what is happening? Because I am a parent.'" Jan was embarrassed, but happy to be returning home. On the freeway, we passed a large yellow billboard advertising forty-nine-cent hot dogs and Western cowboy and Indian souvenirs at Stuckey's. The fifteen-foot sign showed a Navajo woman, dressed in a traditional red velvet shirt and skirt, sitting cross-legged in front of a loom weaving a rug. Jan spoke: "It makes me proud. You know, that we still have our culture and everything. Our language. It makes me feel good that we are still Navajo." Jan settled comfortably back into her home. The following semester she enrolled in the local community college in Blanding. This two-year community college that Jan attended is where most Navajo people in San Juan County finish their time in higher education.

As in high school, Navajo youth at the community college were encouraged to seek terminal degrees in vocational areas. The academic dean explained: "We have looked into the economic development of the next decade, and it is in the service industry. Our students want to stay in this community, and these are where the jobs will be." I argued for encouraging more students to go towards four-year professional degrees, reminding him that the better jobs in the county required a college degree. He argued: "Most of the jobs here are in the service industry. We are happy if we can keep a Navajo student for a one-year program. That is success."

The college had a large vocational program. During the 1992 winter quarter, out of the almost one hundred courses offered, two-thirds were in vocational or technical areas. Certificates of completion, requiring one year of study, were offered in accounting, auto mechanics, general clerical, secretarial occupations, office systems, practical nursing (LPN), stenography, and welding. In addition to these specialties available to all its students, the college offered special vocational programs for Navajo students that were co-sponsored by the Navajo Nation. Designed to fill immediate job needs, these certificates were offered in marina hospitality training, needle trades (sewing), building trades, sales personnel training for supermarket employment, security officers, building maintenance training, pottery trades, modern office occupations, restaurant management, and truck driving. These "Navajo only" certificates were designed to prepare Navajos for local employment. An instructor explained: "These programs are designed to prepare the student for good jobs that are out there. They are extensive, lasting for three quarters. One quarter they are prepared with communication skills. And then how to get along with their bosses. It is the general social skills, work skills, and the particular skills for the job." These programs were not without criticism. Another instructor explained:

> We trained forty or fifty people at a time to run cash registers. That's good. But how many stores around here are going to hire all those people? They're training for limited jobs. Why send everybody to carpenters' school? In this small area we have tons of carpenters. Why teach them all welding? You can do it at home, but how many welders are there in this area? Probably every other person is a welder.

During the 1980s at the community college, Navajo youth and adults earned 95 percent of the vocational certificates.

At the community college, Jan again enrolled in basic-level classes. Back at home she was happier. "I like my classes. And I like walking around town with my books, you know, being a college student." But she still struggled with her classes. "I have problems with math. It just doesn't go into my head. They told me at SIPI my math scores were holding me back. I couldn't go into electronics. And that is what I wanted to do. I have been working on it here. But it is so hard." Homework was a major obstacle. "I don't do any homework. Like it is so hard because I have questions all the time. And so when I study I can't because I don't know the answers. Or how to do it. To do it I have to have someone right next to me. And my teacher is getting tired of my questions. So I don't do homework." At the end of the year she decided to quit the college. "I wanted to take a break and get a job. I took Biology 200, and English 80, and History 300, and weight lifting. It was hard. But I enjoyed biology. I want to find a job."

Most Navajo women wanted jobs in the community. Women who had higher degrees landed the few professional jobs available. In this racially polarized community, whites maintained established networks to most of the jobs, and constructed a job ceiling that drastically limited Navajo women's access to managerial- and professional-level work. Even though whites and Navajos had equal population numbers in the community, whites held over 90 percent of the professional and managerial jobs. Whites held over 85 percent of the teaching positions. Only one school principal, a man, was Navajo. Other than secretaries, there were no Navajo women in the school administration. This would change in 1998 when a Navajo woman became principal of an elementary school. Given this racially defined job ceiling, coupled with vocationalized training in high school and matrilineal networks that pulled at women to stay in the community, most women were unemployed much of the time or were headed into low-paid, service-level jobs.

The unemployment rate of Navajo people was 41 percent, over four times the unemployment rate for whites. I followed 537 young women over a ten-year period and found an unemployment rate of 67 percent. Even of the women who were employed, only 27 percent were employed full time. The most optimistic analysis placed one out of every four women in a full-time job.[28] Under these conditions, extended families, with multiple wage earners, were critical to economic survival; young women pursued any kind of job available and worked hard to contribute to the family. Mothers sought to keep their daughters, who had the potential to bring additional wage earners into the family, close to home. Mothers also tried to hold on to their sons who, if married, would leave home. Matrilineal networks were an important factor in the economic survival of families. Mothers and daughters were positioned to support each other.

I still smile when I remember my own wedding in the late summer of 1991. We had sent the Begays an invitation, but had not heard if they were coming. I should not have doubted their generosity and support. The entire family, including Jan's three-week-old daughter, joined us for our celebration in the mountains above Salt Lake City. During the ceremony, alongside a creek next to a lodge, we welcomed our families and friends to speak. After many had spoken, Ernie rose and introduced himself. "We are Navajos from the Navajo reservation. We see Donna here as our daughter. She had become a good sheepherder." I heard chuckles from my friends and colleagues. "But then she wasn't coming around anymore. So we decided we had to come all the way up here to Salt Lake City to see what had happened to her." He looked at me and grinned. Soft giggling arose from Jan and her siblings. "And we found her here getting married to a man we didn't know. But we came to support her on this new life." Later, Elizabeth would remind me of what this meant. "We look forward to having our new son-in-law come chop wood for us," Elizabeth had said, laughing. Always with a broad grin, for the past fifteen years, she has teased me with the request, "When is my son-in-law going to come work for me?" Using cultural traditions for economic gains from whites is the strategy of a Native gaze. I'm afraid I have not been a dutiful daughter.

The employment of Navajo women is focused on wholesale and retail trade, services, and government, where they outnumbered Navajo men by two to three times. Navajo women, using local family networks, managed to secure frequent, although minimum-wage, jobs in local motels, cafes, stores, and offices. Nearly 70 percent of extended families with mothers and children also received some kind of federal assistance, such as Aid to Families with Dependent Children and surplus commodities. Jan's aunt explained:

> Now it is opposite as in the past. It is the women who go out and get a job. The Navajo men don't. The ladies get jobs. After all, the kids are to be fed. But the men want to be superior. They want to tell the women what to do. But we are strong. And women are concerned about the family. You have to take care of your children.

Most of these women were in low-paying pink-collar jobs: they were licensed practical nurses, office workers, seamstresses, pottery painters, motel maids, cooks, waitresses, and clerks. These jobs provided no benefits and most were seasonal. Even with a high school diploma, if they remained in their home community, as most, including Jan, did, daughters could look forward to a future of semi-skilled jobs mirroring those of their mothers. One young woman expressed the situation clearly: "I would like to go to college to get a good job. But I'll probably get secretarial jobs. I would like to live close to my family down here. My aunt left and it was very hard on them. They had to come back every month or so. It's very hard. I would like to live somewhere close around here. Not far. I'll find a job here." Jan most clearly spoke of the local employment possibilities. "My cousin, she is washing dishes at the cafe and is only getting $2 an hour! When my sister and I worked at the motel as maids, we got more than that. But there aren't many jobs, so you take what you can get."

In Jan's words, the Begays were a family who were "just the kind of family that moves to the job. We go where the jobs are. We have to, together, to make it." Jan and her sister Val and their families moved to Salt Lake City in 1999 in search of jobs. Ernie and Elizabeth followed them shortly, leaving their home on the reservation tended by their youngest son and his wife. Over the years, both sons and wives would join them in the city. At first, Elizabeth would spend the days in a rental apartment in a large complex tending to her five grandchildren. Three were in diapers; two had just started attending a local elementary school. By Della's graduation day in 2003, Elizabeth proudly announced, "I got all my kids to finish school. Now I have fourteen grandchildren to go!"

After they moved to Salt Lake City, Ernie, Jan, her brother, and her husband first worked in an oil field outside of Green River, Wyoming. Every morning, they climbed into Ernie's Dodge pickup and drove the 130 miles to work. Ernie was a foreman of a team of twelve who checked pipelines and other installations throughout the oil field. The hours were long, and the pay slightly above minimum wage. But they were together. When that pipeline was built, they sought jobs in town. A new Wal-Mart needed day laborers. A water line break required Ernie's skills. Temporary job assignments required relocating to Nevada for three months. There, the family lived in a pop-up trailer pulled behind their Dodge King Cab pickup. Back in the city within the year, they hunted for new work. To enhance their opportunities, Ernie joined the Teamsters Union, and his children joined the Laborers' Union. Ernie explained: "I thought the union would be good to join, and to help us secure jobs. But it hasn't helped. I'm waiting for a new job, but I am number 85 on that list!" Jan interjected: "We just go to the job site now. Wait each day. We are driving daily to Price [a two-hour drive] to get on another pipeline. It's day to day. You never know if you will have a job the next day. You can just show up and they say 'Go home.'"

Life in the city produced mixed experiences. In 2003, Ernie and Elizabeth decided to move back to their home on the Navajo Nation after Della's graduation. They were content with their decision. Elizabeth had softly said, "It's nice to be back here. This is where we belong." Jan's sister Val found her skills as a pottery artist helpful in the city and chose to stay. For three years she worked painting "Indian style" designs on pottery night-lights for a company in Salt Lake City, while she also painted her own pottery to sell to tourists in areas around the Navajo Nation. Val now works making dentures. "It's a wonderful job. Clean. The people are nice. And the pay is good." One brother and his family have remained in Salt Lake City where he is employed as a welder. Another brother also moved back to the Navajo Nation with his wife and daughter. Jan's last job in the city was working at Wendy's with her younger sister as they hunted for better jobs. During the summer of 2004, I gave recommendations for inquiring employers at a computer chip factory, an office supply warehouse, and a sign-painting factory. "She is so discouraged," Elizabeth told me. "She can't find anything. She might move back here to the reservation soon if she can't find real work." By the fall, Jan and her husband had gathered their children and belongings and returned to Ernie's family land to live with Elizabeth—just in time to enroll them into Bluff Elementary school.

Bluff, Utah, March 11, 2005: Interview with Jan Begay

Jan and I settled comfortably into the overstuffed chairs in my motel room to talk about this book. "Mom and I started reading it like at 9:00 last night. I read it out loud to her. And we couldn't put it down! We read until 2:30 in the morning!" Jan exclaimed. She laughed. "Dang, I was so stupid sometimes, and some of the stuff I didn't remember until I read your book. How did you remember so many things?" I reminded her of the yellow pads of paper I always carried around, often stuffed into a large leather purse. She nodded as she looked at the yellow pad sitting on the table between us. We both laughed. I asked for her reflections on what she had read.

She spoke first about the difficulty of moving back to the reservation for her high school years. Her struggles were framed by seeking a place in the community, as well as in the school. "Our relatives thought us kids were really stupid. They would say, 'They speak white.' You know, the language. They don't say English. They say white. It's like they are stupid, they don't know nothing." She shook her head. "But inside we knew things they didn't know. Like I knew what was going on out there in society. And would tell them." And in school, she felt very little acceptance. "I learned the hard way. I feel like I was pressured a lot at school. All I did was try to compete with them. But I couldn't. With the white students." Jan's troubles were seen as a means towards gaining personal belonging.

> I kept getting slipped off. Out of the circle. When we were trying to be in the circle. But it wasn't working. And then, I felt like part of my life I gave in. I gave up. I'm just going to do the bad things. That is what I did in Albuquerque. I did the drinking and things. Until my accident. When I was reading about that I went, oh yeah, that was what had happened. And then that medicine woman came.

And you came. And that was when things started changing for me. I started to think highly of my traditions. . . . And then I realized the things my mom and dad were trying to teach us. And then they were having a hard time too, because they were away from their society too. I was trying to avoid it, but I was getting ready to have kids. It's hard to explain, but it felt so good!

Throughout our talk, her central thoughts were of her children. "The only reason me and my husband stayed up there [Salt Lake City] was because of our kids going to school. To get a good education. It didn't matter if I worked minimum wages or what, as long as they were going to school." I had heard this from most of the Navajo women I had come to know. With the loss of Ernie, extended economic networks were strained. And, Elizabeth was alone. Jan spread her arms with a smile: "And now we are back down here. We would spend most of our paychecks coming down here every two weeks, anyway. To check on my mom." Jan shrugged her shoulders: "And, we were barely making it on five bucks an hour. And my mom would cry. She was so lonely." Ernie died unexpectedly of a heart attack in 2002, seven months after his youngest daughter, Della, graduated from high school. Elizabeth buried Ernie at home next to the graves of his parents, wearing a new tuxedo suit identical to the one he had worn at Della's graduation. After a pause, she continued: "And I'd end up coming down and visiting. And then she would be okay. And then two weeks would come and I'd get paid. And it would be time to come down again. I was worried about my mom. And I didn't want her to end up missing us."

I asked Jan to think about the future and imagine the lives of her children. "I don't want to pressure them. But they are pressuring me!" She rolled forward with a laugh. "What do I want for my kids? I want to stay here with my mom. I teach them what I know. And what I was raised with. And then my mom helps out. She has more stories, and it's like we never had time to do that when we were growing up." Jan spoke of days filled with long bus rides, home chores, and school chores. Valuable time was "when we had meetings or ceremonies. And then they would teach about it. When we were growing up." She expressed her hopes for her children's school experiences. "And I want my kids to go to school. And to learn their culture. And Navajo. And to get a better education. I really want that for them . . . and then they can spend time with their grandma. We are more stronger, then." I think Jan saw the confusion on my face, and explained:

And so we come together as a family. And we watch each other. One gets ill, and we do something right away. Like a ceremony. Or something's wrong, we talk about it. Being an aunt, and a mom, I would try and help them as much as I can. My brother and sister ask me, 'Hey, Jan, what do we do?' So my kids see that. So they understand it and they learn it better.

Jan glowed as she focused on her children. "They learn quicker than the way I used to. And it seems like it's so easy for them. And they are more spoken out . . . my daughters, they compete with the whites. They didn't take shit. I think my oldest daughter misses the competition with the whites. I think she gets a thrill out of beating the whites!"

I thought back to a conversation I had with Jan's daughter Tosha's sixth grade teacher. "She didn't know nothing. Not a word of Navajo when she came here. Now she is in my culture and language class, and she is real sharp. And she is learning real quickly." She rummaged around on her desk, looking for a stack of student papers. "Here it is," she said, handing me Tosha's paper. "This is the best paper in the class. It shows real understanding and imagination. And she has just moved here! She has only been in school in the city where they didn't have Navajo language classes or cultural classes." The top half of the page was filled with a rounded house, a dark-red smokestack sticking out of the top, a doorway framed with forked stick entry poles, and a warm-red sandstone color rubbed onto the sheet. The title of her paper was "The Hogan."

THE HOGAN
By Tosha Begay, age thirteen

H is for having special ceremonies inside one.
O is for the opening in the east where we walk in and out
G is for groups of men and women who come together to talk
A is for the altar in center where sand comes together to make
*   something beautiful*
N is for North Star which every night we see in the night lights.

Jan saw in her children's future, lives connected to old and new ways of being Navajo. "Just like that story my daughter wrote. That poem. See how beautiful it was. It's how fast they think. And that they have that thought." This was not dependent on Navajo language fluency. I asked Jan if her children spoke more in Navajo or English. "English.

They speak more English," she quickly replied, paused, and thoughtfully continued.

> But they express their feelings and their thoughts in the Native way. They have the mind and the thoughts in the Native way. And their traditions. They see it! The traditions. They see it! But they translate it in English. It's quicker and easier for them. They have better ways of saying it. In English. But their minds think in Navajo.

III

Changing Woman at Taco Bell

Middle-Class Life in the City

Vangie Tsosie

My clan is Bitter Water. I am Bitter Water. That's my identity. My connection to the land, to creation, to religion is directly connected with the beginning: Bitter Water Clan created by the Holy People through Changing Woman.[1]

Luci Tapahonso

A Navajo Blessing Ceremony

A New Home in the City

Notes for the Children
By Luci Tapahonso

1

Long ago the Holy Ones built the first hooghan for First Man and First Woman with much planning and deliberation; then they started in the east doorway, blessing the house for the protection and use of Navajo people. They moved clockwise from the east and offered prayers and songs in each direction. They taught us in hope that when we moved into a new apartment or home, we would do the same. They taught us this so that any unhealthy memories the house contained would leave; this was taught us so that the house would embrace us and recognize our gratitude. The Holy Ones knew that homes need prayers and songs, just as we do. To acknowledge a new home in this way ensures that the family will be nourished and protected. You can ask a medicine or clergy person to do this. And the Holy Ones appreciate it if you must perform this yourself. They understand English too.[2]

The sun was just peeking over the mountains on a warm spring morning in 2000 as I drove into the new housing development west of Salt Lake City, hunting for Vangie and Gordon's new home. In line with the local housing boom, three hundred homes were planned for this area. Mudded fields were dotted with homes in various stages of completion. Banners draped the entrance to the development, "Starting in the low 100,000's," "Beautiful one and two story custom homes ready now," "Why rent when you can have your own home." Brightly colored balloons flew high over model homes on each side of the street. As I drove down the street, people were starting to leave for work. Children were bundled into sport utility vehicles. Front driveways were being cleaned.

Open garage doors showed new, uncluttered spaces. One got the feel of overnight transformations as each home on the block was quickly occupied with new life. Buildings becoming homes. At the end of the block, surrounded by one-story houses, I found Vangie and Gordon's new home. I took a quick breath. The two-story home was beautiful. Sandstone-colored stucco walls framed the large arched windows of the cathedral-ceiling rooms. The mountains to the east filled the views from the living room's windows, and the mountains to the west filled the views from the windows in the kitchen and family room. On a spacious corner lot, the 2,500-square-foot house was their dream home. As I pulled alongside the house, I saw Vangie and Gordon inside the open garage. They smiled broadly at my expression of amazement. Today was moving day, and I had come for a Navajo house blessing, a Blessing Way ceremony.

We sat around in the empty room on the beige carpet in the formal dinning room. Gordon's father, John, a Roadman in the Native American Church, and his mother, Dora, came from their home on the Navajo Nation to perform the ceremony.[3] While John was outside preparing the coals, Dora carefully laid out the medicine bundle on a pillow and placed an eagle feather next to the bundle. "We have to prepare it just right for the ceremony," she told me. Out of several small plastic bowls she pulled Ziploc baggies full of cornmeal and laid them next to a Navajo basket. In the center of the room, she placed a folded towel and moved back to lean against the wall. She looked around the room, grinned broadly, and shook her head. "We couldn't believe it when we drove up. We were looking at the little houses on each side and then we saw this big house. We didn't believe it was the right house. I thought, Navajos don't live in houses like this. Only rich white people live like this." I agreed it was a spectacular house. Gordon's sister and her three young children stretched out in the sunlight next to the window. Vangie's niece Max and her two-month-old baby joined us quietly. Vangie, with seven-year-old Piper in her lap, sat next to her mother-in-law. We all admired the room in silence.

John and Gordon came into the room with the hot coals in a bread pan and carefully placed the pan on the towel. Opening the medicine bundle, John graciously turned to me and spoke in English. "This is the medicine bundle of my grandfather. He passed it down to me." He showed me four large leather bundles. "Each of these is for the sacred mountains. The North. The West. The South. The East. Each has special things, like dirt and pollen from these mountains." He carefully arranged them side by side as he stretched out a large animal skin. "I try to do what is right for my children. So I come here to do this Beauty Way ceremony. The songs and prayers speak to sky and earth and are necessary to happiness in the new home. I am just learning it myself. I try to do what is right for them. I just wanted to explain this to you." Dora handed him the Navajo basket, being careful to point the spirit-line—an opening in the circular design—to the East. "Yellow corn is for the man. And white corn is for the lady," John explained, as he poured the cornmeal into the basket. "And then you mix it. So things will work out good, together." He then started singing a Talking God hooghan song. We were surrounded by the rhythmical echoing of his voice.

John passed a small leather pouch to Vangie. He explained: "This is special pollen. We take some out on our finger and touch it to our lips. Then on our head. It is to bless you." The pouch moved clockwise and ended up in my hands. I followed John's instructions and handed him the bag. "Thank you for helping us here in this blessing," he said softly. John handed the basket to Gordon to bless the house with corn pollen. He instructed his son on the clockwise direction to walk around the coal pit and how to rub the pollen around the window frames and door openings, to the south, west, north, and east directions. As John continued singing, Gordon walked clockwise around the coals, and with broad careful strokes, he rubbed corn pollen on the frame of the large living room windows. The snow-capped Wasatch Mountains glistened through the window. As he passed, he sprinkled corn pollen around our heads. Framed by his father's singing, Gordon moved from room to room, up and down staircases, as the blessed corn pollen protected and warmed their new home. Only when the basket was empty did he return to sit next to Vangie and Piper.

"We must now bless ourselves with the cedar smoke," John said, as he sprinkled cedar needles into the coals. The coals briefly came to life. Again, moving clockwise, each of us drew the smoke to our bodies with our hands as we bowed our heads and washed ourselves in the purifying smoke of the cedar. Vangie and I smiled broadly at each other; we had shared parts of each other's lives over the past sixteen years. Looking at the center of the room, I noticed that the smoke from the coals vanished on the journey to the ceiling.

Twelve of us tried to squeeze into the large, red-vinyl corner booth at Dee's Family Restaurant. We needed to expand to a nearby table. Our spirits were high, the smell of cedar still surrounding us. Gordon grinned. "I like the lumberjack breakfast. It's got everything." His mother and father nodded. "But Piper and I like the pancakes," Vangie inserted. I voiced interest in the breakfast burrito. Gordon's sister and her family decided on bacon and eggs. The family had gathered for the blessing and would soon return to the reservation. "We need to go back home soon, to see my family," explained Vangie, as she helped Piper pour the maple syrup on the pancakes. "Gordon is going to have a ceremony. His back is kinda hurt. So we need to go home. Probably next weekend." This lead to teasing comments about being "city Navajos." "Yeah," said Vangie, "we go back and forth a lot. We put a lot of miles on the truck. It's moving Navajos!" The booth was filled with laughter.

Our talk turned to the house and their future plans. They would put in a sprinkler system the following summer and hoped to put up a fence this summer. A new elementary school was being built directly behind their back yard. "Piper will go to that school next year. She'll be a first grader," said Vangie as she smiled down at her daughter. Piper grinned broadly as she shook her head in agreement. I remember frequent conversations over the years about moving and staying in the city for access to better schools for Piper. "I'm going to be in the grade one!" she exclaimed. "We know this guy who is a painter," said Vangie. "We are going to have him paint a mural on Piper's wall. You know, like with characters from stories. I think it will be about $200 to do each one."

A year later I stood in Piper's room, turning in a circle to see brilliant dancing paintings of Snow White and the Seven Dwarfs, the Little Mermaid, Tarzan, and Winnie the Pooh and friends. Piper was surrounded by the comic book characters of middle America. At the same time, Japanese comic books filled the upper deck of her bunk bed. Five years later, when they left the house, Vangie told me, "Piper cried when she had to leave her room. She didn't want to leave. So she took pictures of them. I don't know if the new owners will love them so much!" She giggled. "Maybe we should have cut the sheetrock off and took them with us!"

REMEMBER
By Joy Harjo

Remember the sky that you were born under,
know each of the star's stories.
Remember the moon, know who she is. I met her
in a bar once in Iowa City.

Remember the sun's birth at dawn, that is the
strongest point of time. Remember sundown
and the giving away to night.
Remember your birth, how your mother struggled
to give you form and breath. You are evidence of
her life, and her mother's, and hers.
Remember your father. He is your life, also.
Remember the earth whose skin you are:
red earth, black earth, yellow earth, white earth
brown earth, we are earth.
Remember the plants, trees, animal life who all have their
tribes, their families, their histories, too. Talk to them,
listen to them. They are alive poems.
Remember the wind. Remember her voice. She knows the
origin of this universe. I heard her singing Kiowa war
dance songs at the corner of Fourth and Central once.
Remember that you are all people and that all people
are you.
Remember that you are this universe and that this
universe is you.
Remember that all is in motion, is growing, is you.
Remember that language comes from this.
Remember the dance that language is, that life is.
Remember.[4]

A Mosaic of Traditions

Grounded in a Native Presence

When I first met Vangie in 1984, she was fourteen and living on the reservation ten miles from the bus stop in a complex that included eighteen relatives, a new government home, an older stone home, sheep corrals, and traditional hooghans. The rhythmic swishing of an oil pump on the road to her home was the only sound on the mesa. Pointing to the oil pump, Vangie had said: "My dad had oil royalties from his land in New Mexico. We don't have it from these pumps here. When oil was high we made lots of money, $11,000 a month. But then we had to share that with ten people. Then oil went down and we got a lot less, like half."[5] She threw her head back, laughing. "I only get about $5 or $10 a week. My dad doesn't trust me with money. I just buy everything!" Several new trucks sat outside the main house. "When we had more money we got the trucks. But it seems like every month we spend all the money. On the trucks, repairs, clothes, and food. We still don't have electricity or water. We are still waiting." Over twenty years later when we sat down for an interview in 2006, they were still waiting.

In the 1950s, Bell, Vangie's mother, had responsibilities at home tending to the family sheep and taking care of a grandmother that prevented her attending boarding school. Locally, schools were segregated. Her father, Paul, attended a boarding school until the third grade. Vangie explained: "This is why he understands a little bit more English than my mom. He probably would have finished school, but he was living with his grandfather, and his grandfather wanted to teach him more of the Navajo stuff instead of going to school." Paul was being prepared by his family to be a medicine man.

Vangie's description of her father focused on his jobs with the railroad, in mines, as a hired hand, and his skills as a cook. She and her sisters and brothers delighted in his cooking. "When he was by himself, he learned to cook. We used to always say, 'Daddy, can you please make fry bread?' We liked the way he cooked. He would tell us we needed to learn to cook, but he always cooked for us." Her descriptions of her mother were filled with admiration and strength.

> To me, I want to grow up traditional like my mom and dad, because I think my mom is the strongest woman there is, because she can overcome just about anything. I mean she's just the strongest woman I know. My dad, too. I always think when I get old I want to be like my mom and be able to do all the stuff she does. Even now, she herds sheep and does anything she wants to do. I hope I'm strong like that when I get her age!

Vangie, her sister, and one brother were the only siblings to attend public school. "My other brothers, they went to boarding school, but didn't finish high school. My dad wanted help with livestock. So they stayed at home and helped my dad herd sheep and take care of the horses and cows, just everything around the house. They weren't accepted in the high school anyway." Only in the 1970s were most Navajo people's sons and daughters able to stay in the community for high school. When Vangie started high school in the mid-1980s, the legacy of racial discrimination still permeated the atmosphere of the school.

When Vangie started attending meetings of the Native American Church (NAC) in 1997, she experienced a tremendous growth in personal strength and insight. For her, the morally appropriate practices of putting others and the community ahead of oneself could be realized from this church. Her words here also speak to the Navajo concept of *k'é*, as her family is placed in the center of her social world. This balance is framed by unselfishness, friendliness, peacefulness, and compassion.[6]

> I really like it. I mean it helps you. You pray with the peyote and ask him to guide you. It looks like you are just dreaming about it, but it shows you. I asked him to help me learn to pray like the older people pray. Not always for yourself, to say I want this and that, but they always say the more you pray for other people to have a good life, your life will be as good as theirs. . . . I just want all my friends and family to be happy, and to know that they are okay. . . . makes me happy just to see them happy.

Vangie added NAC practices to her life with a few strategic modifications. "The only thing I can't get out of it, it's just like the LDS [Church of Jesus Christ of Latter-day Saints] church, to be a Mormon you can't drink and stuff like that. You are not supposed to drink with the Native American Church, but when it comes to New Year's you just have to have a drink, you know!" she said, laughing.

When Vangie and I started spending time together during her junior year at Whitehorse High School, I was surprised to find LDS Seminary on her class schedule. Since she had asserted a traditional upbringing and beliefs, I was confused. She explained the seeming paradox. "My junior or senior year, one of them, I had an extra hour in one of my courses so they put me in Seminary, and so I used to go out with a bunch of friends. I never really cared about it actually, but all this stuff in the Bible was interesting. I really got hooked on it because there was so much to learn." She didn't have a memory of being baptized, so she and a friend were baptized at a LDS church. "My mom couldn't believe it. She said, 'Why are you guys getting baptized again? You guys were baptized when you were babies at the St. Christopher's Mission.' I didn't know we were Episcopalian. But I knew we were traditional Navajos." Vangie's path, which led her to join the LDS church, strategically provided her a place in the predominately LDS county. "They [LDS white students] thought you were cool and could be accepted if you were LDS, even if you were an Indian." This acceptance did not require abandoning pleasures in other parts of her life. "They always say if you are baptized you are closer to the angels, because the angel gets your prayers and takes it up. But after we used to go to seminary, we used to all get together on weekends and have a beer party."

Vangie's sister, who had joined the LDS church as a young woman, lived behind Whitehorse High School and was one of her role models. Vangie stayed with her after basketball games and other after-school activities. "She was like the one that started telling me you need to go back to school and college. She just got her degree in nursing or social work at the university. I really look up to her. She's different from the way my other sisters are. I kind of look up to her and think, 'Oh, I want to be like her.'" In many ways, her words spoke of a certain power and resilience that echoed through the experiences of many Navajo young men and women I have met over the past twenty years. In an interview in 1999, Vangie, then twenty-eight, explained:

> I never really did give up my traditional ways, even though I was baptized in the LDS church. After I was baptized, I stayed at home and I got sick. I went to high school, and they told me I had a bad ear infection, and my mom and my dad took me to a medicine man, and I had a ceremony done for my ears. They think it is just hocus

pocus, but it is what I believe. I didn't feel like I was breaking the law or anything because I always think we are praying to the same God, anyway. This God knows how to speak Navajo and all different kinds of languages. If it wasn't for him, we wouldn't have our own language and stuff. I'm sure he understands. It is just one person. It's not like there is an LDS God and a Navajo God. Just think how bad they'd be fighting up there! [laughs] I'm sure he understands what I'm going through. So I never really felt obligated to give up being Navajo.

Religion, many different kinds and spiritual ways of being, played a significant role in the lives of Vangie and her family. "I want to go to church because of Piper. I want her to learn. Maybe I should get her baptized LDS just so we know she is baptized, because with the Navajo culture there is no real baptism or nothing. You are just there to believe." With a giggle broadening into a laugh, Vangie recalled: "Someone just told me, like every Sunday go to a different church and see which one you like, which one really grabs you and have her baptized! We have missionaries that come over, but I just get so tired of them talking about the same old stuff." Some of Vangie's siblings attend Episcopal services at St. Christopher. Others attend LDS services in Bluff and Blanding. Her mother and father practiced Navajo beliefs in their everyday lives. Other relatives were members of the NAC. All family members, however, used Navajo ceremonies for recurring nightmares, health problems, family difficulties, and depression. With a sigh and a broad smile, Vangie told me, "The one thing we know is that we are Navajo. That will never change."

BROWN CHILDREN
By Nia Francisco

See my brown bellied desert sparrow hawks
               said the Earth
listen to cinnamon-brown woman
her children browned from within   her womb

browned   as that of soil
like red mesas and its hidden afternoon shades
like a rusty belly robin

     the shy Sky
who fathered her children
his skin is brown

brown like the bark of towering pine trees
   and like the tiny fuzz
      off a fuzzy caterpillar
   like a red horse with a black mane

dancers of resonating drum songs
we are the children in brown
a brown that can't wash off
it remains a beautiful reflection
   in a puddle of rain water

a brown in twirls of sands
   blown by the winds in the   moon lited nights

listen to this earth woman so bronzed
   her children so bronzed
   her children so reverent they prayed
   whispering to the stars in seasons
She blesses them in these thoughts

Great Grandfathers of the Universe
   You the holy ones
   recognize my daughters
my sons . . . know them by their sacred names
   know their foot steps
let   strands of positive thoughts hang
      from their mouths onward to the future[7]

A Native Gaze: Challenging Surveillance

It was 2001 and it had been almost a year since I had seen Vangie. She had just had her thirtieth birthday, and her daughter Piper was beginning first grade. I turned in my semester grades and drove to her home. We decided to have lunch in Park City [a mountain resort town]; I wanted to do a little shopping, and she had her mother's woven rug to sell. They had just returned from a visit back to her mother's home on the Navajo Nation. She laughed when she told me about Piper's reaction to a traditional forked stick hooghan, which sat next to a small HUD cinder-block house at her parents' home. "She asks me, 'What is that mound of dirt?' It was a forked stick hooghan covered with dirt to keep you warm during the winter. And she didn't know what it was! We are such city slickers! Being that part of Navajo hasn't been part of our lives. We've lived in the city for so long [ten years]."

During the forty-five-minute drive, she talked about Piper's troubles with her teacher. "I knew something was wrong. She didn't want to go to school anymore. I'd ask her, 'What's wrong, sugar? What did you learn in school today?' 'Nothing, it's okay, mom,' she'd tell me. It wasn't like her. To not want to go to school." Vangie decided to visit her daughter's teacher. "She [the teacher] just sat there. Staring at her desk!" Vangie said bitterly. "I said to her, 'I'm asking you if I have offended you. Have I said something that made you mad? Are you taking this out on my daughter? She is just a child. She didn't do anything.'" Vangie tried hard not to express her anger. 'My daughter does not like to come to school anymore. Is it because of you? Have you thought about that? My brother is a medicine man, and he talks to the stars and the creator, and he told me to talk to you when I was concerned about Piper.'" Vangie left unsatisfied by the visit with the teacher. "I think it is because she is Navajo," she told me. "All the others [students] are white."

Our talk took us back to Vangie's own school days. "I faced discrimination in school all the time. I had fights with white girls and us Navajo girls were the ones taken to the office. The white girls lied to the principal." She grinned and recounted one event: "The principal took me in his office because of a fight with a white girl. I got spanked. It was very embarrassing. My brothers and father came to that school and told that principal he was discriminating and treating me different because I was Navajo. My dad told him, 'I can round up Navajo parents and we can spank you first and see how you like it.' It was cool, that principal went and hid in his office!" Vangie turned to me and sighed: "My dad always supported his children in school. Always. Now we are having to do it for our own children. We will always fight so they will not be hurt."

"Sorry I'm late," said Ernie, the newly elected president of the Indian Parent Advisory Committee. "I was out with the sheep today, and you Anglos would say, 'I have a cold.' Us Navajos say, 'I am cold.'" He laughed and turned to write the day's agenda on the portable blackboard. The June 1985 meeting was an important one for several reasons. School officials had agreed to come to hear the parents' concerns about the high failure rate of the Indian students at the high school level. The group would vote on whether to continue bussing the reservation students into town to attend the racially mixed San Juan High

School (SJHS) or bus them to the newly opened Whitehorse High School (WHHS) nearer to the reservation. Plans also had to be made for the end-of-the-year awards banquet. Parent meetings were held in the local elementary school, where Vangie had attended the first six years of her school life. The meetings lasted all day, and participants shared a meal in the school cafeteria. As one parent explained, "If it [the parent meeting] doesn't take all day, then it doesn't mean anything." Childhood experiences involving all-night and many-day ceremonies had taught these Navajo parents the patience and pleasure required for an important event.[8]

Thirty-seven Navajo parents, with children ranging from first through twelfth grades, gathered for the meeting. As the rows of chairs sized for elementary children filled with parents and preschool children, the remaining people stood at the back of the library or sat at long work tables. Young mothers were dressed in blue jeans, blouses or sweaters, athletic jackets, and high-topped basketball shoes. Middle-aged mothers were dressed in cotton or polyester stretch pants or skirts with sweaters and blouses. The three elderly women wore traditional Navajo dress— bright velvet shirts embellished with silver buttons and full-pleated velvet skirts. Men of all ages wore blue jeans, cowboy shirts, athletic jackets, and boots.

The meeting started with a discussion of the need to be involved and responsible. The newly elected officials used themselves as examples of what to do and what not to do. "We can't run off to any squaw dance; we have to come to meetings," and "I'm from a foreign country [the Navajo Nation]. I come all that way for this meeting." Chuckles rippled through the group. The pressure was subtle and then shifted to confront parents on what they must do to help their children in school. Ernie continued:

> I was up at the school and saw the test scores of our children. And it was shocking, very poor achievement. The teachers say, 'I haven't seen some of my students' parents. Maybe they don't care.' The parents must have interest. Parents need to send their children to school. Maybe they say they have a headache. Maybe they are hiding from a test. They must be sent to school.

Many of the parents nodded in agreement.

When the principals from SJHS and WHHS arrived, the discussion of student achievement intensified. The principal from SJHS spoke first. "I will be very frank about the problems your children have in school."

On an overhead projector, he showed the breakdown of Indian and white test scores from 1977–1984 on the California Test of Basic Skills. In both mathematics and reading, the Indian students scored an average of 2 1/2 years behind their white peers. In 1980 at SJHS, Indian students averaged 0.89 out of a possible 4.0 grade point average (almost all Ds, no Cs). In 1990, the student average was up to 1.38 (Ds and Cs). Very little change had occurred. "I wish I could tell parents why scores have not improved much. Possible problems were the long traveling distance to school and the lack of attendance." He then spoke of the "culture shock between these two worlds," a strategic shift that blamed school failure on the Navajo families.

> There is a tremendous shock up there; [it's] mostly Anglo kids, and the students move from different teachers. They are really kinda getting lost. At home they speak Navajo. In the halls they speak Navajo. But in the classroom they speak English, maybe only fifteen minutes a day. Unless students speak the language on a regular basis, they have problems. They need to do homework. Parents cannot be blamed for this; that's not your fault that you have not been able to help. But your grandchildren will have a better time, because your son will sit down with his children to help. It's a slow process. What you do at home and at school are worlds apart. For the most part, your students are doing a good job.

The Navajo parents were not convinced their children were "doing a good job." They were also not convinced that their lives represented "another world." This talk was yet another way to deny their ownership of this very landscape. They persisted in wanting to know why their children did so poorly academically at SJHS. "Our kids are behind; why won't you meet the needs of our kids? If students are having problems, what about people who are on payroll at the school? What are they doing? Why do we still have this problem?" The principal listened sympathetically, and shook his head.

> We are doing everything we can think of. The teachers are faced with classrooms in which Anglo students are two grade levels above and the Indian students are two grade levels below. It's difficult to meet the needs of both groups. That's why Indian students get lower grades, because they are always competing with the whites who always get the As. The teachers get mad sometimes at Anglo students, too. But there is improvement among the Indian students.

We were three and a half hours into the meeting. Navajo parents' speeches had been long, eloquent, and uninterrupted. Navajos respect and appreciate a good speaker. Interrupting a speaker is rude and is referred to as "being like a white person." White participants appeared weary as lunch approached. Anticipating the length of this meeting, a white parent had told me: "I don't bother going up there no more; the meetings are boring. They go over the same thing over and over. And they talk forever. They don't get nothing done. I like to get in there and get things done!" A final comment was made by a Navajo parent, a teacher at the elementary school. "I saw the grades up there, in a teacher's book. This kid had Fs across the book. He wasn't an F student. What is happening? I went home and kicked him in the butt a bit. To work." The room was filled with soft laughter as we left for lunch.

The main issue of the parent meeting—which school they should bus their children to—was the topic of the entire afternoon and also revealed different expectations. This was not a new issue to the district or these parents. In every meeting I attended for five years, from 1985 to 1990, this was a major topic of discussion. On four occasions, straw votes were taken to ascertain which school the parents preferred. The district had been upset over what was seen as "indifference" on the part of the parents, illustrated by their inability to come to a final decision. But to these Navajo parents the communication was clear: they wanted the best educational opportunities for their children at either school. However, the choice of school was their children's decision.[9]

Several Navajo parents supported the proposal for students to attend WHHS because it was closer to the reservation and was more "Navajo," both in student population and parental involvement. As one parent said:

> Fasten your seat belts! I'm going to Whitehorse High School! You don't even have to drive off the reservation to see what your children are doing. I am a full-blooded Navajo. I highly respect my Navajo culture. In this respect, what Whitehorse High School has, we can take advantage of. It is on the reservation. Here I could jump on my horse and ride over the river and see how they are doing. [laughter: the speaker does not have a horse, but a pickup truck] It may be daylight when she gets on the bus to Whitehorse High School. We want all the squaw dances and Yeíbicheii dances to be passed on. They control this at Whitehorse High School; parents control this. They won't be outvoted by Anglos.

Other parents expressed support for SJHS. The experience of interacting with whites embodied important lessons for their children. As one Navajo father explained, "I told her, daughter, you ain't dumb—dumb people go that way. Smart people go up there to San Juan High School." Another parent said:

> Now I'm going to support San Juan High School. It is an experience of a lifetime to interact with other students and have extracurricular activities. If we vote for Whitehorse High School, are we segregating our Indian students? We cannot go back to the past when we were separate. It's important to interact with whites and speak English.

In a powerful moment of insight, a parent added: "I want my kids to get what the white kids get. If they go to San Juan High School, at least they will be exposed to the good academics like the white kids get." However, as the story of Vangie's educational experiences unfolds, this exposure to "good academics," envisioned by the Navajo parent, came with an emotional price and a vocational path.

During the summer between her sophomore and junior years, Vangie decided she did not want to return to SJHS. Going to school year after year in a racially charged context, with little teacher support or interesting curricular experiences, seemed pointless. Vangie explained: "I didn't want to do it anymore because I'd been doing it since seventh grade, but I don't know how I passed my classes to go into eighth grade, and ninth grade, and tenth grade, but I did." She paused a minute before she continued: "I think it was just the way the high school is run. They care more about the white kids than they do the Indian kids. Like my math teacher. He didn't care about if I passed the class or not. I don't know how I passed, but I did. And the principal just yells at you. They just don't care." With dismal grades after her sophomore year, she decided to transfer to WHHS.

For the first time, Vangie encountered a principal who sat down with her and talked frankly about her school record, and what could be done to help her finish high school. "When I got there, they told me I had to repeat tenth grade because I missed classes at San Juan High School. I thought, this has to be it, you know." The principal offered her extra classes for the next two years to put her on track for graduation. "I said, yeah, I can do the classes. When I look back on this, just because I got Cs, I was thought of as no good. It was just someone saying, 'Hey, you are smart. I'll help you out.' I don't think that often happens for the Navajo students at San Juan High School. I think they [Whitehorse High School staff] treat Indians better. You get to be involved in some activities there."

Vangie's last two years of high school were filled with activities in the Indian Club, attending after-school social activities, and playing in basketball tournaments. Although she refused to act in the school plays, she worked behind the stage in all the drama club productions. Her school experiences there were very different from those at SJHS, and racial tension was minimal. For the first time, she was engaged with school. "So, when I got into classes, I went all the time. Every day. I didn't even miss out to ditch school or go anywhere." For her, this choice was a significant decision. "I think if I hadn't gone to Whitehorse High School, if I stayed in Blanding, I would have dropped out, and I would have been probably still living at my mom's house and doing I don't know what." Reflecting back on this move in a 1998 interview, Vangie told me:

> When I got to Whitehorse High School, that's when I thought I'd better straighten up to see what I want to do for the rest of my life. I think that's where I started getting into school and sports and stuff I never tried. I have to do something with my life! I can't just keep ditching school; so I just started kicking ass in junior and senior year and graduated with my class in 1989. I was proud to be in the biggest class that ever graduated from that high school.

Indifference and Invisibility:
Fieldnotes, August 1988 to May 1989

I attended Vangie's classes weekly throughout the year I spent at WHHS. With a mosaic of events, I attempt here to weave the experiences I had in these classes to portray a "day in her school life." Vangie's days were filled with state- and district-required language arts, basic math, reading, information technology/career education, biology, and the electives Shop I and Business Typing. This was a schedule experienced simultaneously by most of the Navajo students. In these classrooms, they effectively blocked teachers' instructional efforts as they claimed control of these spaces. Asserting a Native presence, youth strategically resisted performing the "right" kind of Indian for their teachers, and they chose not to let teachers into their lives. Most of Vangie's teachers had little knowledge of their students' lives as vibrant young Navajo men and women outside the classroom walls. I vividly remember an event that startled me into seeing what this meant for the school experiences of Navajo youth. It was at the end of the school year, right before graduation. Mrs. Ben's vocational class met during lunch time. The center court yard had been carefully set up with two 12-inch Weber grills. Today's lesson was how to grill meat. Compared to her Navajo students' expansive home outdoor cooking ovens for beef and sheep, the Weber grills looked lost and inefficient.

Vangie started her day with an elective, Shop I. "I wanted to learn about cars and all that. And woodwork and typing. So I can do stuff for myself," she had told me. She was the only young woman in a class of eleven young Navajo men. I arrived late, and Vangie and the other students were quietly working on welding vocabulary worksheets. Mr. Troy was a beginning teacher, full of energy and excitement. "When some of the other students in vocational education saw this job posted at Utah State University, they said, 'No way! I would never go down there and teach those Indians.'" He had laughed and said, "I want that job! And here I am."

The classroom was sunny, with windows facing a large, treeless dirt field. On closer inspection, I saw a small garden right behind the school. Seeing the direction of my stare, Mr. Troy came over and explained: "I'm in charge of the Future Farmers of America (FFA) program and that is our garden. You have to take the required course, agricultural science, to be eligible. Last year we had seventy, but this year we really only have about twenty active members." I thought of the area's six-year drought and the necessity of hauling water for gardens and livestock. He continued, "I also started a program to breed the old Navajo Churro sheep.[10] Only a few students had the time for this project." He also taught the required ninth-grade vocational core class. He showed me the text. "The career education class is to teach the students about vocational choices. We teach them a little about all the choices. A little welding, carpentry, plumbing." He then gave me a tour of the shop area.

We left the classroom and moved into a large open room with separate workstations lining the walls. Each was clearly labeled with black stenciled signs proclaiming, "Plumber," "Carpenter," "Electrician," and "Welder." In the center stood large welding tanks, woodworking equipment, and two long worktables. Several sinks lay in a corner, disconnected from the water system. Without windows, the room was lit with fluorescent light, casting an orange glow on the equipment. Mr. Troy stopped at a student's workstation and picked up a thin, flat sheet of metal with curled ends. "This is going to be a candle holder. And the students are also making napkin holders. These are useful items to take home." At another student's workstation, he picked up a small rectangular piece of wood. "This will be a small wooden box. The kids are enjoying making these. To put stuff in at home. Or to give to their parents." Shrugging his shoulders, he looked around the room at the work stations. "We used to have forty of these, but they were expensive to keep up. So we have dismantled most. We don't have many students in vocational education anymore." We walked back into the classroom for his lecture.

The class period was half over, and all the students had finished their worksheets. Most were reading shop magazines or completing homework for other classes. Vangie was working on a reading worksheet. Mr. Troy moved to the front of the room where he had placed two welding tanks. He asked the class, "Now, what do I turn if I want oxygen to come out?" Several students eagerly yelled, "That one! The left knob!" All eyes were on the equipment. The teacher continued, "Now what pressure do I want to put the oxygen at?" "Ten," shouted the class. For the next twenty minutes, he continued a question and answer dialogue with the class connected to the vocabulary from their worksheets. Student enthusiasm was declining. Several students moved their attention back to their homework. Others put their heads down on their desks and closed their eyes. The last attentive students urged the teacher to quit asking questions. "We know the answers. Get on with it! Light it!" Mr. Troy smiled, moved to the tank, and with a whish the flame roared from the tank. All eyes were again engaged in the class activity. Students urged him to increase the intensity of the flame. "Turn it up!" "Close the blinds so we can see the color," "Turn off the light so we can see it better," exclaimed students. He briefly complied with their request, lowered the flame, and spoke, "You have to be careful. I have burned my fingers. And my hair." A safety lecture followed, and as the bell rang, he told the class, "Tomorrow you will all get a turn to light the torch." As students were leaving the class, I spoke to several of Vangie's classmates. "How do you like this class?" I asked. I got similar answers: "He's nice, I like it here"; "It's okay. At least we are learning something that is interesting"; and "He doesn't act like a white person.

He acts like he likes Navajos." The class seemed a pleasant way to start the day. Reading class was next.

Vangie and I walked out behind the school to the temporary portable trailers that housed the language arts and reading classes. The gray and white trailers appeared the second year the school was built and have remained firmly planted on a side of the parking lot over the last dozen years. Students hung out on the dirt next to the stairs, enjoying every minute with friends; the door was within sprinting range for avoiding a tardy slip. The bell rang and students scurried inside. Mr. Smith was bent over his desk, muttering, "Where is it? Where is it?" He looked up. "Sit in your seats, we'll start in a minute. And be quiet." The class rules were spread out in large red capital letters on the wall behind his desk:

ALWAYS BRING A PENCIL/PEN AND PAPER

DO NOT MOVE CHAIRS

RESPECT: SCHOOL PROPERTY—BOOKS/DESK/ROOM—
KEEP THEM CLEAN

RESPECT: FELLOW STUDENTS—LISTEN, DON'T CUT
DOWN

RESPECT: TEACHERS—LISTEN AND FOLLOW DIRECTIONS

Still hunting for his lesson, Mr. Smith raised his head again. "Okay. Let's work on the pen pal letters. For fifteen minutes." Students groaned. A student shuffled papers on his desk and muttered, "I don't care about New Orleans? Or this dumb letter." Another joined him, speaking more loudly, "Who cares about New Orleans. Here on the rez people eat sheep." Students laughed. Mr. Smith moved from the back of his desk to face the class, "Better than mice!" Few students laughed. Most glared at him, expressionless. "Now get to work on your letters." After several minutes, Vangie passed her paper to me.

I get up late on Monday. 'Cause it is the beginning of the week. Get ready for school. Go to school. Go home. Cooking supper, then my homework and to bed. The same from Monday to Thursday. Then Friday I stay around the school till about seven or six and go home with my cousins. If it is cold, I go to my uncles to wait. On Saturday we go to town or stay at home. On Sunday we don't go to church because we have our own beliefs. I won't go into that because it is against our traditions, so I'll say no more about that.

Vangie's best friend wrote: "Well, I'm doing great, I hope! And about school, there are times when school sucks and then again it's alright. So life is just in-between." One young man's letter consisted of one line: "I want to graduate and get out of this school and get off the reservation fast."

After fifteen minutes, students were told to take out their vocabulary list. "You have seven minutes to work on your words. Work together. Legal cheating is what it is called." He looked over at me and grinned. "Work with your neighbors." Five minutes later, Mr. Smith moved to the overhead projector, looked at his watch, and wrote the vocabulary words on a clear plastic sheet. He pointed to the first, "What is a fable?" One student responded, "Short story that teaches a lesson." Looking at a student who was talking to a neighbor, he said loudly, "Do you agree, Fred?" The student looked up and responded, "Yes." "With what?" Mr. Smith snapped. "That you are cute? Is that what you agree with?" The class was silent. Staring at his desk, Fred softly responded, "No." "Then don't agree if you didn't hear," said Mr. Smith as he turned to face the class. "The next word is a complicated one. Metamorphosis. What does that mean?" There was no response from the students. The teacher continued: "What about that program on Sunday night. The werewolf. About the man who changes into a wolf. That's metamorphosis. It's not just a change in emotions, like when a girl says to a boy, 'You are not the same.'" He stopped, hunting for more appropriate words to describe the phenomena. Snapping his fingers, he continued: "Like caterpillars, moths, butterflies. To change into something entirely different." Vangie wrote on her paper, next to the word metamorphosis, "skinwalker."

These students knew skinwalkers.[11] Navajo beliefs paint a picture of individuals who can transform themselves into animals to affect the sickness or death of those they wish to harm. I remembered several years ago when Vangie and her niece Max told me about a skinwalker incident at their home. "We were all alone. It was getting dark. Only us, and my little sister. It was so scary," Vangie said excitedly. Nodding in agreement, Max continued: "It was real dark. It was a cloudy day. We had this big dog. He used to know if somebody was coming a distance away. He just started barking. For about two hours. We were so scared." "Then we heard something on the roof," interjected Vangie, "so we put ash on for protection. Last summer there were skinwalkers over by the river. My uncle saw them." I asked, "What did they look like? Can they look like different things?" Vangie explained: "They hold the evil spirit to go into a wolf or something and tell them what to do. But if they are a person, you know how they are in the movies, they wear those wolf hats or something like that. They are covered in fur and hunchback." Vangie continued the story: "Then the dogs stopped barking. And later my mom and sister came back. They said there was a dog or wolf trail that came to the house. And there were big prints going right over the car. In the dirt. We were so scared." Mr. Smith lacked this knowledge of metamorphosis. And no Navajo student in the class chose to share their knowledge.

Moving on to the next word, he asked, "What is the definition of legend?" One student replied, "A story handed down from the past." Pleased, the teacher repeated the student's definition and explained that a legend is part true, part unbelievable, but that it is based on history, which is different than a tall tale. "Tall tales. They are unbelievable. Like men wrestling created mountains."

The Navajo Holy People are believed to have created mountains.[12] Vangie had carefully explained this fact several times to me. "It's not believable," the teacher continued. "They stretch facts to be humorous. They're made to be funny. Like Pecos Bill. They said he lived with coyotes. You see, it can't be true," said the teacher. Two Navajo students looked at each other and in unison said, "But us Navajo, we live on the reservation with the coyotes." The teacher replied, "Well, I don't know anything about that. Let's talk about parables now." The students, in a high shrill, mocking the teacher, repeated, "Unbelievable, unbelievable." The teacher turned his back, wrote the word "parable," crossed it out, and pulled the lost lesson plan from among the transparencies. "I found it! Now, limericks," he exclaimed. He wrote the first sentence and the students responded:

T: There was once a boy named Bill. Who went with a girl named Jill.
s: Who loved a boy named Phil! [laughter]
s: They went to a Wal-Mart!
s: Then to K-Mart! [students smile at each other]

T: But never did pay any bill.
S: To get a dollar bill.

Students looked at me, rolling their eyes and closing their notebooks. Their rigid bodies spoke volumes about the hostility towards the inference that unpaid bills were the Navajo way of life. Their teacher continued:

T: There was once a boy named Nate.
S: The robbers used him as bait.
S: They called him a snake.

The teacher ignored this last sentence and out loud, brainstormed a more appropriate response, "Great, gate, mate, date?"

S: He raped the girl.
T: Who had a very cool date. They drove all around town.
S: And ended up with a date rape.
T: But they came back with a frown. Because all they did was debate.

This sequence pleased a nodding Mr. Smith. The students, however, were visibly upset. Vangie whispered, "He just doesn't get it." The bell rang. Students slammed their books and stood up to leave. Mr. Smith yelled, "You will not leave this room until we are finished!" Students moaned and reluctantly sat back in their seats. He continued, "You will not leave until Rose and Joe write down the definition of 'parody.'" They both grabbed a piece of paper and wrote, "A funny story about serious literature." Another student grabbed the paper from Rose and read the sentence out loud. "Okay, but you cannot leave until everyone is in their seats." The few students standing sat down. There was a pause and Mr. Smith nodded his head. The students jumped up and ran for the door, six minutes late for the thirty-eight-minute lunch. As he left, one of the students said sharply to me, "It's power, man. He just was showing you and us the power he has. It's the shits, man." We all left for lunch.

Vangie and I went to the cafeteria to stand in line for lunch. As I paid the $1.50 fee for visitors, Vangie pulled out a dollar. "I have to pay ninety cents. Because my parents make too much money, so I have to pay for my lunch. I don't think the food is very good." The metal trays clanked and scratched as we pushed them along the serving shelves.

The faces of the kitchen staff were familiar ones—Navajo mothers and relatives from the community. Vangie greeted an aunt, "Hi! I'll be over after school to get a ride home after practice." Her aunt nodded as she handed up a fork wrapped with a paper napkin. Our plates were filled with folded pizza dough stuffed with a dab of cheese and several chunks of ham, a tablespoon-sized blob of pudding in a white paper cup, a round pineapple slice, canned corn, and milk. None of the faculty ate at the school. As a science teacher told me: "It's terrible. It barely looks like food. But it's the only place for the kids to eat. We leave. They stay."

We joined Vangie's friends seated at long folding metal dining tables. The noise level was lively throughout the cafeteria. Separated boyfriends and girlfriends reunited. Friends huddled together, sharing secrets, hopes, desires, and upcoming plans. Vangie and her friends were excited about weekend plans. "We are going to Farmington shopping. They have a big new Wal-Mart now. I'm hunting for some new high-top shoes. In black!" said Eve. One of the closest towns, Farmington, New Mexico, was 120 miles away. "Will you be back in time for the game?" asked Vangie. "The Harlem Globetrotters are playing at the high school Saturday night. And it is only $2!" "Wow, I forgot," Eve exclaimed. "I'll ask my mom and dad if we can get back in time." Everyone agreed to meet at the school at 6:00 for the game. Vangie turned to me. "They try to have things, like movies or people coming and singing or doing things on the weekends at the school. The school is kinda like a community center. But lots of kids don't come back to the school. They are happy to be away." The talk turned to the "under the bridge place." This is a place known to all the students as a place to hide while drinking. "I was there once, but it kinda scared me. Everyone was really drunk," Vangie told me. "But most are dropped out of school. Or older. It's not a very good place to hang out at. I might even have a beer!" Everyone laughed. It was close to the end of the lunch period. We left and wandered through the halls. Painted industrial gray, the space was not a warm one. None of the hallways had windows to the outside. Brown lockers along the halls added to the dark, uninviting feel of the school. Only one poster was visible—an advertisement from a school catalogue urging girls to try out for the cheerleading squad. The blond-haired, blue-eyed faces of cheerleaders in short skirts seemed out of place in these hallways. We continued past the main office and out into the parking lot. Small clusters of students talked and enjoyed each other's company in the sun for the fleeting minutes remaining before the start of afternoon classes.

I went early to Mrs. Ben's vocational education class. Required of all students, this was one of the easiest—and most boring—classes at the high school. A short, plump woman greeted me with a firm handshake as she showed me around the room. A large stack of textbooks was next to the trash can. Picking one up, she sighed. "These old books used very technical terms about corporations, enterprise, and work occupations— words too complicated for my students." She showed me the new, state-approved text. "Look, it has the objectives that I am supposed to follow right at the beginning. And then the main points are made with 'dots,' so the students know exactly what is important. And a simple description of each thing. And lots of pictures." The glossy pages were filled with smiling African American and white faces, busy working in offices, driving modern trains, in supermarkets, and in corporate boardrooms. Only four pictures were of Asians. No Latinos/as or American Indians were visible. The bell rang and students poured into the classroom.

Clapping her hands, Mrs. Ben began loudly, "Now, start reviewing chapters nine and ten on personal abilities, and images for work." She had the test in her left hand, waving it at the class. "I'm going to review for the test today, but I'll ask the questions in a different order so you can't memorize the correct answers." Vangie and her classmates rolled their eyes. As she started to cover the ten true and false questions, students screamed out, "True! False!" before each question. She shook her head when students gave the wrong answer, to which four boys continually replied, "Yesssssssssss" as they stood up and sat down at their desks. One girl raised her arm and mimicked the teacher's waving hand for each correct answer. The attention by her peers encouraged her to continue to mimic her teacher's every move. Mrs. Ben looked both exasperated and pleased. "Good, you have all gotten As. I knew you could all do it. And it is not just one of you that is shouting the answers. I can hear other voices." Nodding approvingly, she turned and smiled at me. With the grace of a seasoned and organized teacher, she reached for a vocabulary list and wrote the words on the board. As she wrote a word, she asked for its definition and was satisfied with all the students' answers except for the word, "custom." "Listen, you Navajos. This is especially meaningful to you. I know that you all still have customs left." The room was quiet except for a few sharply closed textbooks.

Ignoring the sudden silence, she moved to the last section of the test. "Now, this section is for you to decide what is the best answer to what takes abstract problem skills. What job would take thought or abstract problem solving skills to perform? Carpentry, sports, cosmetology, or journalism?" One boy quickly shouts, "Carpentry!" "No," the teacher replied. "What takes abstract thought? Thinking with the head versus the hands." The student persisted, "Carpentry. It takes math and measuring and all sorts of thinking." "No," the teacher again replied. "It is working with your hands. What takes abstract thought?" One student shouted, "Cosmetology?" followed by another that said, "Sports?" Shaking her head, she replied, "Journalism. It takes thought. The others are working with your hands. You use your hands for cosmetology, sports, and carpentry. You use your head for journalism." The students were not convinced. One boy firmly argued: "Boy, that teacher is crazy. My father is a carpenter. And it takes a lot of thought." There were only a few minutes left in the class. Students started to gather their materials, openly ignoring Mrs. Ben, who still stood in front of the class with the test. Raising her voice over the talking students, she said:

> I understand you all have a science test on Thursday. I was planning on having the test on chapters nine and ten on Thursday. But that would be too much for you. It is too much for you to be thinking about all of this at once. So I will put this test off until Friday. Two chapters and a science test to study for is too much for your brains.

Without a glance at her, students left the room.

Vangie talked about this particular class with disgust. "She is always putting Navajo students down." Mrs. Ben, on the other hand, spoke confidently of her rapport with Navajo students. "Look, did you see how excited they were in my class. They talked! Most Navajo are quiet and they don't talk, because of their culture, you see." The school administration admitted she was one of the weakest teachers, but argued that it was hard to get teachers to move to such an isolated place, and "at least she is certified."

Unlike Mrs. Ben, some of Vangie's teachers realized they connected little with their Navajo students—either with their curriculum or their personal goodwill. Mr. Philips's combined tenth-, eleventh-, and twelfth-grade biology class was located in the main building behind the band room. A new teacher, Mr. Philips was attracted to teaching on the reservation, "I wanted to go to the Peace Corps, but I thought teaching Indian students would be real valuable." A tall, thin man with a short reddish-blond beard, he always wore plaid shirts, blue jeans, and hiking boots. In his small science classroom, he had one sink and three circular workstations at the rear of the room for experiments. Twenty-five plastic chair and desk units sat jammed next to each other in the remaining two-thirds of the room. One set of worn biology and earth science texts was stacked next to the front door. Students, who were not allowed to take books home, bent down and picked up their books as they entered the classroom. Sighing, Mr. Philips spoke of his limited supplies. "I wish I just had half of the science materials the guys have up at San Juan High School. But I guess it's because they have had years to get stuff, and we are just a new school. I have $1,000 for all the science classes, texts, and materials for the entire year. You can't get much with that." He pulled out a new chemistry text he wanted the district to purchase. "It's the best book I have ever found for a chemistry class. It's totally community-based chemistry. Like the first chapter, it starts off with two newspaper articles about poisoned fish. Then it moves into pollution in water and the chemistry of all that. It really deals with social-based reasons for understanding chemistry." The following month, arguing the chemistry book he now used was only six years old, the school district rejected his request.

He moved to the closet behind his desk and pulled out the class's three microscopes for today's lesson. "This is a lab day. It's not your typical teacher-directed class; it is student-directed." As students entered the class, they were directed to the lab stations. "Try to zero in on the cells. Then look for the purple spot in the center. That's the chromosome. Now look for different stages in the division." He repeated this gently yet firmly twenty-seven times during the thirty-minute session. The class was quiet. With texts opened to pictures of cell division, students peered into the microscopes and back to their texts. Half of the students were listening to heavy metal or soft rock on their Walkmans. When Mr. Philips stood next to their lab station, the headphones moved to their shoulders. Students appeared diligent, and bored—but quiet. Many were using the time to finish their math or English assignments. They appeared startled, and annoyed, when he started a lecture.

"Open your text to the next unit. On genetics," said the teacher as he moved to the board. He drew a grid on the blackboard to illustrate how to discover the percentage of dwarfs from the genetic traits of parents. "See, these two are carriers of the dwarf gene. So this one has what percentage possibility of being a dwarf?" A student from the back of the classroom called out softly, "Carriers of AIDs." The teacher ignored the remark. No other student would volunteer an answer. He moved to the next example on the probability of red hair. "Both parents can be dark brown hair and have a child with red hair. It doesn't mean that if the milkman had red hair the husband would think they had been, ah, been together. They can still both carry the red gene." The example distanced him even further from the Navajo students. A student in the front row blurted out, "Mexican red hair!" and another, "Hey, do you have a rubber I can borrow for a while?" Students were giggling. He ignored both remarks. Again, no one provided the correct answer. He turned back to the grid on the blackboard, "This probably doesn't make much sense unless you found eight kids in an orphanage." The same boy taunted, "Who can make eight kids? Probably a dog. At once!" Mr. Philips moved back to the red gene example. "It is possible for someone here in class to be carrying the red gene. It's not a normal thing in [hesitating] in your population." Vangie's friend said with a smile, "He probably has two fathers! [student laugher] Like Navajo!" The resistant class blocked Mr. Philips's last attempt. "There are hybrids and . . . ," he said as he was cut off by a student, "they are white bread!" The bell rang, and students eagerly jumped from their seats and moved to the halls to join their friends. As they left, he turned to me. "I wish I knew more about livestock examples. It would be more relevant to these kids. Make more sense than just the genetics of people. Mr. Jim [Navajo social studies teacher] knows that; I keep meaning to ask him about it. I just haven't gotten around to it."

At lunch one day, Mr. Philips talked to me about the divisions between the vocational thrust of the school curriculum and college-bound classes.

> I had twenty-nine students in my chemistry class. All of them passed last semester. It was a good class, and I didn't water it down or anything like that. I might not have covered as much and in a different way. But I didn't water it down. I think many people think these kids can't make it because they are Navajo. I had almost half of the juniors and seniors in my chemistry class.

Few teachers or the school administration had as high expectations for the students as Mr. Philips. He explained: "I encourage them to go on to college. That is where they will have choices to control their own lives. The tribe needs economists, scientists, and engineers. They don't need these trade schools for the jobs around here. But they should be encouraged to go to college to get control over their resources."

Burned out from the lack of support from the school administration and from dealing with student resistance, a resistance he acknowledged was reasonable, Mr. Philips would leave the school after three years. "The main problem here is the racial issue. We are living here as foreigners in an occupied country. It is clear that there is some dislike for the Anglos here. I don't blame them. I am very radical. From the liberal '60s and '70s. I want to say to them, 'Hey, I'm on your side.' But it doesn't make a difference. They just see Anglos." The school became the shared grounds for racial warfare. He explained: "They see a staff of all whites, and then Mormon. And they feel oppressed. And the students know that they are the bottom of the levels. They feel occupied and pressured and they respond with hostility and cut themselves off from the school." The school district replaced him with another vocational education teacher. Chemistry disappeared from the school's class schedule.

Academic courses opening a path to college were invisible during Vangie's school days. Many teachers were indifferent to the lives of their students. Teachers' knowledge of the Navajo community was framed by negative and limited expectations constrained by racism; manifest manners prevented the students from being "seen." In turn, Navajo youth felt entirely justified in turning classes into carnivals and investing only a glancing connection to what their teachers had to offer.

The Illusion of Opportunities

Education for Work

I pulled into the small paved parking lot in front of Whitehorse High School five minutes before school. The green athletic field stood in sharp contrast to the red dirt and sandstone bluffs. Sheep grazed on the lush lawn, rubbing against the chain-link fence that separated the school from the surrounding Navajo reservation. With ironic grins, the Navajo students call the flock, "Navajo pets." As I entered the windowless, one-story red brick school, Vangie, now a seventeen-year-old senior, joined me. "It's career day, so you can come with me, professor, while I learn about schools!" she exclaimed. It was the fall of 1988, and the juniors and seniors were excused from classes to attend presentations from seven regional colleges and universities, two vocational, or technical, schools, and the Job Corps. The Navajo Nation's Education Office had a representative to explain tribal scholarships. Students moved through four sessions, each lasting twenty-five minutes, in settings scattered throughout the school in the cafeteria, library, several classrooms, and the counselor's conference room.

Vangie and I attended two regional college presentations. Each encouraged students to choose their school. "Some classes are outside and are so much fun. Then there is the choir. You should take that your first year; it is really fun. And you meet all sorts of nice people," a recruiter said. A professionally developed video accompanied the presentation. The second recruiter also showed a polished, upbeat video with smiling white faces, a brief glimpse of a professor lecturing in a large amphitheater, shots of athletic events and a tennis court, and leisurely images of students reading books on rolling campus greens. "If you want to be a policeman, don't come here," the recruiter explained, "but if you want to go into the computer field, or nursing, or in-flight training, come here. It is beautiful and the campus is lots of fun. You can do all sorts of things while you are in school." Students talked excitedly about which college would be more fun.

The representative from a local vocational training school slowly went through a silent slide presentation as he explained the school's program. "And that girl there, she is working at a real good job in a TV station. And that one. She is underemployed. She could get a real good job if she would leave here! See, in all these pictures we have the old and the totally up-to-date equipment. You never know when you will be working in a small place that has old equipment. So we teach with the old and the new." Looking at a student audience of only seven Navajo females, he backed up to a previous slide. "See that computer on that slide. If you are going to work in a big office, you have to learn about computers. And then we have a heavy equipment program. We could use more girls. Because of the Equal Opportunity Program, we could place forty girls a year if they completed the program." The students were quiet and attentive. Vangie whispered, "I'm interested in business college, maybe the one in Salt Lake."

We stopped at the local community college's booth in the library. District school staff and the dean of the college were discussing their success in sending many of the Navajo youth away to school. "Over 60 percent of the graduating class got accepted to college. Some went to the Job Corps. One year later they are all back. Every one of them!" sighed a counselor. A local college administrator explained: "We don't recruit our students. They come to us. Many of the Indian students go to large universities and they fail. Then they come to us. After they have been with us, they all—100 percent who go to larger colleges—will succeed. If we recruited them to start with us, they might think they have missed something. They can get what they need here." Vangie later explained, "This is where they dump all the kids who can't go elsewhere." The booth was full of pictures of Navajo students sitting at computers, building houses, working in hospitals, and sitting in lectures. The recruiter was the only Navajo on the professional staff at the college. Raised by a Mormon family, he had recently returned to work at the college. He spoke softly to several Navajo students. "You can get a good education here. And your Pell Grant will pay for everything. It's close to home so your parents can watch you girls!" The girls laughed and moved to examine the pamphlets in the Job Corps booth.

The last presentation was by the University of Utah, my employer. Two student recruiters stood in front of the small group and emphasized the importance of filling out the applications correctly and getting financial aid forms into the university on time. "It is very important that you do things on time and correctly. It is a huge university. But we also have support for minority students, and we want you to seriously consider coming to the university." The presentation continued with a list of the academic fields offered by the university and the statement, "The classes may be hard, but they are real interesting, and you can get a good education at our university." The presentation was dry, the fun of college life was presented as "getting an education," and the recruiters did not smile.

After the four "periods," students moved into the auditorium for two films by the College Board on financial aid. Students filled the room, talking about the sessions they had attended, boy- and girlfriends, graduation plans and after-school activities. The first film pictured an African American man, one of several individuals interviewed who had "made it." He urged others to attend college. "Anyone can go to college. It is worth it. I am glad I went." The second film, a cartoon on how to correctly fill out financial aid forms, covered topics from estimating summer earnings to who in the household was the legal provider. Students were bored and restless with the films and cheered when the lights came on and they took off for lunch. A counselor spoke to me as we were leaving the auditorium.

> We are the ones that fill out the forms. The students don't do it. About half will go on to some kind of school and almost all of them will be on financial aid grants. And the other half will sit out on the reservation and do nothing.

The images shown to Vangie and her peers during Career Day of youth lounging on green fields, smiling faces in a choir, a class, students using computers, and laboratories, filled the picture window of opportunities facing youth beyond high school. Few Navajo youth realized the life depicted in these tableaux. During the 1980s, almost half of the Navajo youth from Whitehorse High School attempted some kind of post–high school training. Out of one thousand Navajo youth throughout the district, one-third eventually attended the local community college, 6 percent attended universities, and 7 percent attended vocational institutions. Regardless of these efforts, less than one-half of 1 percent completed a four-year degree, only 2 percent completed a two-year degree, and 5 percent received a vocational certificate. None of the youth that attended the community college went on to finish a four-year degree. Over 90 percent of the Navajo youth received no degree higher than their high school diploma. Vangie, however, was an exception. She graduated from high school and attended Salt Lake Community College where she studied business sciences and almost completed a secretarial certificate.

We left school early after the Career Day. As I was driving Vangie and several of her friends home, the conversation turned to what they were going to do after graduation. "I'm thinking about going to Dartmouth. They have a special Indian program. But I don't know if I want to be so far away from home. I might go into the Army. They will pay for my college." Another said, "I'll probably end up with a baby and be stuck here." She laughed. "I really want a baby of my own. I would be really happy, then, at home with my baby. That's what us Navajo do." Vangie jumped into the conversation. "There are a lot of girls that get pregnant. I'm just not going to do it. It will ruin your life if you have a baby. I want to go to college and get away from here so I can get a good job!" One said: "My parents tell me to do what I feel I want to do. I want to go to college. I hear college is a lot of fun. I want to have a business or something and come back to the reservation to live and help my people. I go crazy about thinking about taking care of my parents in the future." Another, who had been silent, softly spoke: "I want to be a race car driver. But my mom thinks it's too dangerous. So I guess I can be a secretary or nurse. She wants me to have a good job like a secretary or something and live at home."

In 1988, the district created the Southern Outcome Based Committee to discuss the unique needs of the schools serving Navajo students. Assigned to the committee were the principals of the three elementary schools and two high schools in the southern half of the school district, the district's Indian Education coordinator, the director of curriculum, and Navajo teachers from each school. I was invited to join the committee. The first meeting focused on school funding and vocational education. The principal from Vangie's high school spoke first.

> Monticello High School [northernmost school] has 80 percent of its students on grade level, and 20 percent off level. It is just the opposite at Whitehorse High School. We have 80 percent of our students off level, and only 20 percent on level. So the gap is widening. We at Whitehorse High School have further to go then the teachers and students at Monticello High School. But we have the same resources at Whitehorse High School. This creates what I call

a 'failure gap.' The richer get richer and the poor get poorer. All schools have the same requirements, schedules, the same per pupil budget. This equals sameness for all schools. But we have greater needs in the southern schools.

Except for the director of curriculum, everyone nodded in agreement. "We should do a different weight for funding, giving schools with Chapter 1 [low income] or Indian students proportionately more," argued an elementary school principal. "Like 1.5, or the National Education Association has proposed a 2.0 for these kinds of language-need students." One of the Navajo teachers suggested, "We need smaller classes, because we are doing a bigger job than other teachers because our students are so far behind." The discussion continued around the difficult task of teaching Navajo children without additional resources from the district. "We are already at a disadvantage because they are behind. I need $12,000 for summer school, six teachers. The school district only gave me $3,000. I managed to scrape together the rest from my budget. But I need district support. They recognize, but maybe they don't want to, the special needs of our students and schools in the south," argued an elementary school principal. After forty-five minutes, the director of curriculum finally spoke: "Many of the classes in the southern schools are very small. The superintendent won't support more money for the southern schools. That would be discrimination. Spending more money on Navajo students. The school board won't support that kind of discrimination."

With the possibility of additional resources silenced and off the table, the discussion moved to the latest efforts in the southern high schools to increase graduation rates and academic success—vocational education. The Whitehorse High School principal explained the efforts at his school.

I'm interested in equal educational opportunity. I have been for ten years. And we have a problem with large academic class size. Some of the classes are thirty or thirty-five or thirty-seven. These classes are too large. Our vocational classes are suffering. They used to be full, but now we don't have enough students. Like auto mechanics only has four students. We used to be 75 percent academic and 25 percent vocational. Now we have 75 percent vocational and 25 percent academic. We need to recognize the needs of the people in this local area. I'm not saying we should ignore the academic classes. But the vocational training is where the jobs are for the local Navajo people.

His vice principal added:

Academics are very important in this world, but we've got to realize that half of the kids or more out of this high school are not going into academic jobs. They are going to go into vocational. In fact, the majority of jobs in the future are still going to be vocational. They're not going to be in the white-collar-type job. But how do you tell them that?

By the end of the meeting, the teachers and administrators had moved away from requesting additional resources for the southern schools, to modifying the curriculum for Navajo students by requiring less difficult academic classes. This realignment of the curriculum was hailed as preparing Navajo youth more effectively for the jobs facing them after high school; a vocational thrust was to become district policy for schools serving Navajo students within two years. The school's vision for Navajo students projected a place for Navajos that was informed by the low expectations set by a discourse of manifest manners; Navajos still had limited capabilities for upward mobility.

In 1990, the district received a 3.5-million-dollar grant to construct a vocational career center at the local community college. In an open letter to the community, an administrator explained the new thrust of the school district into technology and job preparation. Citing state employment statistics that 40 percent of youth in Utah finish college or university training when only 20 percent of the available jobs require a four-year degree, he told of the shock facing graduates who have to be retrained in vocational and technical areas. "Since only 20 percent of the jobs in Utah will require a college degree, the secondary schools must take a more active role in preparing students for employment." The college graduate figure of 40 percent, however, reflected the 97 percent Anglo population of the state, not the local Navajo population served by the district. He explained the necessity for the curriculum to be responsive to employers' needs.

This concept does not mean a lowering of academic standards; to the contrary, most technical jobs now require a strong background in math, physics, and language. Nor does this concept infer that all students should know a specific vocational skill prior to leaving high school. The jobs in our society are changing so rapidly that students will be much better served if they develop certain basic skills and attitudes toward work. Most employers now prefer to train their own employees in specific skill areas. What they want from high schools are students with basic understandings of technology, good basic academic skills, and the flexibility to be retrained as often as the job market requires.

This emphasis in high school served to set the stage for focusing the educational careers of Navajo youth into low-level vocational paths. The district's state-of-the-art vocational school was Whitehorse High School; the predominantly white high school, Monticello High School in the northern part of the district, remained college preparatory. In turn, this assured college-educated white youth a brighter job future in the community.[13] Vangie's path through high school was lined with a vocational curriculum that cut off her path to a university. Her vocational education teacher, Mrs. Ben, saw not a path cut off, but rather a road leading to good jobs for Navajo people. This was affirmed by a counselor at Monument Valley High School who spoke proudly of the "edge" Navajo students had in becoming excellent technicians because of their enhanced visualization skills and manual dexterity.[14] Vangie's education prepared her for "working with her hands."

The graduating seniors at Whitehorse High School were decorating the cafeteria for the evening's banquet. The pale lime green walls of the cafeteria were draped with blue and gold banners proclaiming "Class of 1989." Vangie and friends were covering the long Formica-topped tables surrounded by bench seats with white paper tablecloths. The home economics teacher was directing the scene. "See, put salt and pepper shakers like this around the centerpiece," as she moved from table to table. Small plastic floral arrangements dotted the tables. "It is important to have everything in order. So your parents can be proud of you," she continued as she leaned against the cinder-block wall and surveyed the cafeteria. Satisfied, she released the students to return home to get dressed for the dinner.

By six o'clock, the twenty-four seniors and their parents had returned for the dinner. Moving through a cafeteria line, the diners filled their plates with mashed potatoes, a piece of chicken, canned corn, and red Jell-O. Smiling parents talked quietly to their sons and daughters as they ate. A local Navajo councilman was the evening's guest speaker. He rose from the long table and spoke:

> It is a golden key. For you. Education. You are looking out on the fields of horizon. You can go many ways. Be politicians. Or lawyers. Or doctors. If you are a real good liar, you can be a lawyer! [laughter] I am proud to say I am from here. My great-grandfather, he gave the land for this school. His sheep used to graze here where the school is. This is progress. Now our youth can continue in the world on this same place.

Navajo parents smiled and nodded with approval. Straightening his tie, he continued to talk about how Navajo people must work to strengthen the Navajo Nation. He then shifted into several jokes. The power struggle between whites and Indians lay just below the surface of every laugh.

> There was a group of our people that went to Washington to try to ask for more money. They had learned that when you ate you always had a salad first. You ate the salad, and then you ate your meal. They had learned that eating with whites. So they were in Washington, and they sat down to have dinner with the congressmen. And they were sitting there, and they said that there was a very pretty salad in the center of the table. They had put flower decorations on the tables. So the Navajo people saw it and thought this must be our salad. Like when you eat with white people. So they started to eat the flowers. The congressman couldn't believe his eyes. He said, 'They must really be hungry! They need to have this money for food.' So right there he said, 'I am going to give you the money you requested.' See, us Navajo people have learned how to make things work for us in the government!

After the laugher died down, the awards part of the ceremony started. A total of twenty-four awards were given to the top twelve seniors. Awards came from local companies who drilled and mined on Navajo land. Utah Power and Light Company presented scholarships of $500, to be used at the local community college, to five students. The Mobil, Phillips, and Texaco oil companies each gave $750 scholarships. Local tribal chapter houses presented $200 scholarships, and the Navajo Nation gave a $500 scholarship. The principal ended the three-hour ceremony:

I am very proud of all of you. Half of you will go on to college. It will be hard, but I will pray for you. The rest of you will stay here. And I hope you won't come in and vandalize our school! [laughter] Seriously, life is up to all of you now. We have enjoyed having you in school, and we look forward to educating your children. I will personally shake all your hands at the graduation ceremony on Saturday.

Over seven hundred people packed the high school gym for the graduation ceremonies. Mothers, fathers, aunts, uncles, brothers, sisters, cousins, and friends squeezed into the stands. The air quickly became hot and heavy as the crowd awaited the entry of the graduates. Surrounding the graduating seniors were local officials from both the Navajo tribe and the school district. After prayers from a Mormon bishop and a Navajo medicine man, the ceremony started.

Speeches went on for over three hours. Navajo dignitaries told jokes amid optimistic predictions for youths' future job and school successes. The assistant principal addressed the graduating seniors: "If you take God with you, you will also be getting God's support as you struggle against the two biggest problems facing you on the outside world—drugs and alcohol." A parent leaned over me and whispered, "What about jobs? What they need is God to help them find jobs!" Another parent laughed. "Is God Navajo? That might help!"

At the conclusion of the ceremony, a Navajo speaker urged youth, "Don't take just a bite of the cake. Take it all. Reach out and learn as much as you can. And then you can decide where you want to go. Back here to help your community or out there somewhere."

After the ceremony, students and their families crowded into the interior courtyard for an informal reception. Pride filled the enclosure. Youth had graduated. Their families and community embraced their success. There was little talk about the future. Laughter and smiles reaffirmed the day's honors. As Vangie said, "They respect me. They know I finished high school. Now I can go on with my life."

Family and Work in the City: 1990–2006

The phone rang around ten in the morning on a crisp winter day in 1998. Vangie was calling from her job with Advantage Parking in downtown Salt Lake City. "Hi, I'm in my booth. It is a slow day. I've been reading novels. Just a minute. 'Yes sir, it will be $2. Thank you.'"

She laughed, "Look how polite I am! This is an easy job." I didn't know about her new job. "It's not too cold, and I can listen to music if I want. And the pay is good. I make $7.25."

For the first time in almost ten years in the city, Vangie started a job above the minimum wage. "By the time I left there, when I did my regular job, I was like making $7.25 an hour, and then when my boss wasn't there and I would step in for him, I was making $9.25 an hour. So I had like two wages." Vangie rated this job as her easiest.

> I really liked that job. I mean, it was the easiest thing you could ever have, just sitting there and pushing the buttons on the gate to let people in and out. [laughs] And I would sit there all day just reading a book. In the morning, you'd get there at the parking and pick up cigarette butts in the elevator and clean the elevator, and that was it. And that takes about thirty minutes, and then the rest of the day you would just sit there, but it was tiring, though.

The historically rooted gaze of many white employers was layered with assumptions about Navajo workers as undependable, somewhat problematic in their work habits, and undeserving of wages they would demand for their sons and daughters. Embedded in these layers were also experiences with Navajo men and women as honest, skilled, conscientious citizens who worked seriously to gain the respect of their employers. Vangie, Jan, and Mary, like other Navajo women moving in and out of low-paying jobs, claimed employers were not dependable because they cared little about their lives and families. These women worked hard, but put little of their hearts into their jobs. Within the discourse of manifest manners, these efforts at being good employees and demanding conscientious employers were dismissed. The economic and social slot for Navajo people was low and narrow.

Vangie and I met at her high school the year she had her first job in 1985. "I started working in the summer at the Recapture Lodge. I used to work there every summer since my sophomore year. No, my first one was at the Sunbonnet Cafe. When these two couples opened it, I used to be their dishwasher." While still in high school, she also wove her first rugs for sale.

> I asked my mom what can I do to make up my art class, and that's when she taught me how to weave a rug and how to do a sash belt.

That's when she taught me how to do that. And through the summer, I sold some rugs to Recapture Lodge, and they would buy it for so cheap and then sell it for so much.

Her jobs, restaurant and motel service, mirrored those of most of the other young Navajo women in the community. All of the Navajo women I have come to know over the past twenty-five years worked at the Recapture Lodge at one point in their lives. It was also where I stayed when I visited.

Vangie had spent the year after she graduated at home with her parents, siblings, and relatives. It was then that she started dating Gordon. He lived in Salt Lake City, was going to Salt Lake Community College, and urged her to try college. "He goes, 'You should try it at the college level,' and he sent me an application, and I mailed it back. He told me to go to Shiprock to the Bureau of Indian Affairs office, because they help you with a grant. The only thing they would pay for was vocational [a one-year certification program], and so I thought, well I'll try word processing." With a grant for a year's support, she moved to Salt Lake City to attend the community college. "So, they helped me out for a year, but I needed one more quarter to get my certificate, and they said, just one year. I had no money. So, I started working." Her first job in the city was at Taco Bell.

"Taco Bell was right down the road from the college. I made lots of friends at college, and so we used to always go to Taco Bell because their tacos were just forty-five cents." She talked about the eventful day. "They had applications there, and then we all filled out one, and I was the only one that got in there," she said, laughing. "My other friends, they were just like, 'How did you get in?' and I said, 'I don't know. I just got in.' I think I worked there for a year." She started working at the minimum wage in 1991, $3.75. By the time she left, she was making $4.50 and working forty hours per week. "They used to be so strict about overtime and stuff like that. They didn't want you to go over so they would have to pay more. And we had no benefits. Except we could eat tacos at half price." She grimaced, "I ate a lot of tacos that year!"

Vangie described taking her job seriously. "I think wherever I go, I put in my 100 percent, and they just like the way I worked. And so I really got along with all the managers." Although the managers liked her work, saying she would be getting a raise, Vangie remained underpaid. "So I waited, and they were just giving me a quarter raise, and I thought that's not worth it. I work too much for you guys. Like when they had a manager's meeting, they would always put me in charge of everything. But they didn't want to pay for your work." During this time, Taco Bell had a productivity competition between all the Taco Bells in Utah. "They said if you keep the times down in the drive-through and up front, we'll buy you guys jackets with Taco Bell logos. So we worked our butts off. I mean this was the first time we were competing with other Taco Bells, too." Vangie threw up her arms and angrily continued: "Out of that whole thing, guess what? The managers and everybody up there got jackets. We only got sports bottles that were this small," her hands closed together to about six inches, "and it said 'Taco Bell.' And I'm like, you guys said jackets, what is this? And I said, 'That's it. I'm sick of this.'" Vangie quit and found work, again as a hotel housekeeper.

Vangie's friends told her about a housekeeper manager who organized women to drive from Salt Lake City to Park City to work in a variety of hotels. "Our friends were working up there at Park City and were making $6.00 an hour doing housekeeping. The housekeeper manager was looking for people to join the team to work in a different hotel. Max [her niece] and I, and my sister-in-law, and Max's friends worked for the same company. There was like six of us plus the housekeeping lady and her son." With the recommendation of her relatives, Vangie was hired. "They gave me an application, and I filled it out, and they gave it back to her [housekeeper manager], and then I just said, 'That's it folks. I'm going to Park City!' They are going to pay $6.00 an hour cleaning up after white folks. At Taco Bell, I served white people and cleaned up after them. If I have to clean after white folks, I might as well get more money." She laughed, and grew weary as she talked about the day's work. "Remember in 1992 or '3 they had that big storm where the snow was real big, that's when we used to work up there. We used to take the Blue's Brothers, that work bus, that picked up a lot of people. We would get picked up by the freeway. It used to pick us up at 5:00 in the morning; we had to be over there by at least 4:30 to be picked up at 5:00 to get to Park City at 7:00. It was like $2.50 a day going back and forth on the bus, because we used to get our discounts from the hotel." Although she talked about how tired she was at the end of the day, Vangie liked the job. "They paid overtime, and they had benefits and everything. The people were real nice. I worked there for maybe a year and a half, and then I got pregnant with Piper. When I was seven months, I stopped working up there, and I just stayed home."

Vangie gave birth to Piper on September 3, 1993. "I stayed home, up until December, just me and Piper and Gordon. And then I applied at Food 4 Less, probably January, I think it was, and then I got the evening position." Juggling two jobs and a new baby, without the extended family support on the reservation, was demanding. Working at Food 4 Less also meant a drop in pay from her housekeeping position in Park City. "Minimum wage was $5.25, and they started me at $5.00. By the time I left I was making $5.75." Vangie spoke of the pleasure of meeting new people at her various jobs, as well as the struggles. "I used to work at Food 4 Less, and people would come through your line, and they had all these coupons, and they would expect $50 to be taken off their grocery list. And they yelled at you. I would just stand there letting them finish. And then I called the manager to take it. I wasn't paid to take that kind of abuse."

Over the next decade, Vangie moved around the job market. "I just started applying here and there, just putting applications in wherever I wanted to. I didn't want to put them in at the fast food places like McDonalds. I thought, 'I know how it is working in a Taco Bell; I don't want to go through that again!' You work so hard and you get less pay—it 's not worth it." Vangie landed a job with the newspaper agency at $7.25 an hour driving a van delivering bulk newspapers to home deliverers. After three months, she quit to take a job as a supervisor and booth attendant for Diamond Parking. Two years later, a head teller position opened at Loomis, Fargo & Co; she stayed for three years. In 2000, she took a job with UPC Discover Financial Services as a reconciliation clerk. Working there on the night shift, she spoke of an easy job, and the time away from her daughter. Vangie decided to stay at home to support Piper through elementary school. During our interview in 2006, Vangie had just returned to working at a Chevron gas station to save for their return to live on the reservation.

In a thoughtful and final assessment, the possibilities of material wealth and economic security in the city could not compete with the pleasures of the family. Again, although unspoken, the Navajo concept of k'é seemed to provide her guidance. "Oh, I live so far away, I hate it," Vangie said emphatically. "So the family is more important than the house. Because I think the family is always going to be there for you. And when you tell your job that you have a situation that's come up, they don't care. They are like, if you don't come back, you are fired." She grinned broadly, "And, all right, I quit then!"

Mrs. Ben's career education class did little to help Vangie along her employment path. Neither did her shop classes. She was skillful with her hands, but had few of the networks that lead to caring employers with upward career possibilities. With ironic insight, Vangie's counselor at Whitehorse High School had told me: "The Navajo kids around here just work to get money. They don't think 'career,' like you or I would. It's just the money." I remember disagreeing with him, seeing his comments as demeaning, and dismissive of Navajo students' integrity and career commitment. In an interview in 2006, I asked Vangie to reflect on her jobs over the past seventeen years and the counselor's comments. She, too, claimed that the purpose of a job was for money, not self-esteem, a way out of the house, or independence. "I think it was mainly the money. Some paid differently, and some less without experience. But it was mainly for the money." In my reflections, I think I better understand the counselor's comments. Given the kinds of limited career opportunities faced by most Navajo men and women, caring primarily about the money one got from their labor investment was a wise and sound decision.

HARD TO TAKE
By Luci Tapahonso

Sometimes
this middle of the road business
is hard to take

Last week in Gallup,
I was in line at Foodway
one checkstand open and
a long line of Navajos waiting
> *money and foodstamps in hand*
> *waiting to buy food and pop.*

My turn and I fumble
dropping the change
> *Sorry, I say, sorry*
> *The cashier looks up smiling*
> *first smile in 20 minutes of Navajo customers*

Oh—that's okay. Are you Navajo?
I swear, you don't have an accent at all!

She's friendly too quick and I am uneasy.
I say to the people behind me
Ha' 'at' íí sha' ní?
Why is she saying that to me?
We laugh a little under our breaths
and with that
*   I am another Navajo*
*   she doesn't greet or thank.*

My change is dropped in front of me
*   and we are not surprised by that.*

Merle Norman offers a free make-up job
*   just the thing for a new look*
*   I say to myself and stop in*
*   for an appointment.*

For 15 minutes, I wait for a saleslady
then I ask for an appointment outright
*   Just a moment, she says,*
*   someone will be with you shortly.*

I wait some more while the salesladies
*   talk about a great hair dresser,*
*   General Hospital and Liz Taylor.*

So I just leave, shortly is too long,
seeing as I'm the only customer in the place.

I guess I can do without a new look
but this kind of business
*   sure gets hard to take.*[15]

2006: Returning Home, Coming Back

We meet at my home in Salt Lake City to talk about the draft of the chapter I had given Vangie the previous winter. Faced with escalating heating, gas, electrical, food, and credit card bills, the family had chosen to give up the burden of the house mortgage, and their home was repossessed. Gordon was remaining in Salt Lake City with his drafting job, and Vangie and Piper were moving home to the reservation. Vangie explained their decision: "I don't mind living in the city. There isn't really anything bad about it, but I'm to a point that my mom really needs my help. And I want to be down there for her." And then there was Piper.

> I don't know, it seems like she has missed so much, from being here, from growing up here in the city. Like when I was little, my mom and dad used to take me to my aunt's where there was a ceremony. And they would say, 'This ceremony is for this. Let's go in so you can watch, and see how it is done.' That was how it was done. The next time, if you were going to talk to somebody, you already knew how to help that person, because you had seen it get done. Piper doesn't know this stuff.

I asked about her feelings on leaving life in the city. "It's not fulfilling," she said softly. "At first, it used to be our thinking that we were working for the house, and we got the house, and everything was working good. And then, all of a sudden, I was tired of being here. I wanted to see my family. I don't want to be here." Leaving the city and returning to live near the reservation was a move grounded in enriching relationships to create a more fulfilling life. Middle-class life in the city had a sort of emptiness embedded within the lifestyle. Vangie and Gordon wanted more for Piper. "It's like we have put Piper in a place where she was brought up around white people. And she needs to be around Navajo people to see what it's like to be Navajo."

Thirteen-year-old Piper was excited about leaving city life. "I wanna live back down where my grandma lives," she carefully explained to me, "cause it's not really busy as it is back here. Even though there's no electricity or water down there, it's still a great place to be. It's quiet, it's loud up here, and then there's a lot of cats down there." Life closer to more family was good. Animals also were good. "I think when I was in first grade I liked animals, and I thought I wanna be a veterinarian, so I can learn how to take care of pets, help them get better." As we were talking, she was organizing her set of Japanese comic books. "My mom and I found these in Blanding. You read them backwards, and they are exciting adventures, kinda like *Star Wars*. Very cool." Adventures also happened on the pages of her own experiences near her grandparents' home.

My cousins and I used to climb on those rocks near Montezuma Creek and hunt for quartz. And one time we were up there, and we were getting really thirsty. I was like, 'Man, let's go back down to the house, 'cause I wanna go get a drink of water.' And there was this bell cactus—it was full of water. My cousin points to it and says I should drink it or be a alien. I was like, 'Please!' [laughing] He said, 'You'd rather use a white man's way?' I said, 'Yes!' Better than getting sore lips or just big lips from that cactus!

When Vangie reflected on what it means to her to "be Navajo," she spoke of her childhood. "When we were little, we'd end up in the sand dunes. We'd tell my dad not to cut the horse's tail. And we'd hang on to the tail, and the horse would drag us around. We'd do crazy things like that." And she spoke of what her parents gave to her. "I think I'm proud to be who I am. Growing up with my mom and dad who were telling us all these stories of Coyote and the animals in the winter. Where we came from." Knowledge of place, or "where we come from," is what Vangie and Gordon wanted for Piper. "We buy books for her," Vangie explained, "but it's not real explanatory. You can catch the point here and there, but it's not how the Navajos do it. Everyone has their own story, and they all relate to each other. And it is easier to explain it in Navajo." Piper shared her story of Coyote and Skunk Woman with me in English.

This Coyote was hot and said, 'Rain, rain, cover me. Rain on me.' And then he goes, 'Rain, rain, cover my feet. Rain, rain, cover my legs,' and he kept saying it, and then he said, 'Rain, rain, cover my bones. Rain, rain take me to the river, and rain, rain, leave me here.' Then Skunk Woman came along. She and Coyote made up a deal, to get those animals and to trick them and eat them. 'We tell them I am dead,' said Coyote. And so Skunk Woman went to get them, and then they got that stuff in their eyes, I don't know what to call it [laughing], and then she killed them. They cooked them, and then they had a race to go all the way from the camp to that mountain, the mesa, and then come back. Coyote gave Skunk Woman a head start, and she hid in a hole, and she ran back and took out the animals, and she ate them. She put the tails back in the ground and ran back to her hole. And then Coyote was running back over there, and Coyote's a trickster, he was going to eat them and didn't let her have them. And then he pulled the first one and there was just the tail. Then Skunk Woman came up and goes, 'I ate them. There's still the tails and the bones,' and she gave them to him. And then Coyote had all of that to eat. It's really funny. The other animals always beat Coyote. You never want to be Coyote!

Vangie expressed the concern that her younger relatives do not see the importance of family knowledge. "They think it sucks to live on the reservation! And that it doesn't really help to get a medicine man. That's how younger Navajos living on the reservation see it. It's important, later on, down the road. But to them, it's nothing. But when you move away and realize how bad you need help, you go back." Vangie leaned back and shook her head. "It's a lot different than what some whites think." She paused, then grinned broadly. "One of my co-workers said, 'Do you Indians dress like that, in leather buckskins with a feather in your hair?' I said, 'No. Indians are dressing like cowboys. And it's the whites who are dressing up like Indians.'" We both grinned at the image. At that point, I reached over and pulled out a July 2, 2005, *Salt Lake Tribune* newspaper clipping on the centennial celebration in San Juan County. A color picture's caption read, "A local theater group rehearses a play that incorporates not only the past one hundred years but the hundreds before that, when generations of American Indians lived in the Blanding area." On stage were five young Ute and Navajo actors, dressed in the clothing of their ancestors, including moccasins. Behind an "1880" sign, at the center of the stage, stood a white man. He was dressed in a long cotton shirt with a Ute-styled apron and sash, over Levi's slacks and leather shoes, and appeared to be deep in thought, with closed eyes and outstretched arms. Sticking out from a bandana were long black braids like those worn by Italian actors in old westerns. Even today, whites don't look good playing Indians.[16] We laughed until we cried.

IV

(Re)sculpturing Belonging

From Yeíbicheii to Hip-Hop

Mary Sam

The Surveillance of the Body
Yeíbicheii and Youth

The cold cobalt sky was star studded when Mary, her mother Carol, and an aunt arrived in their Chevy Blazer to take me to the evening's Yeíbicheii dance. This was an unexpected honor and pleasure. I had run into Mary and Carol at the trading post when I was in Bluff for a school district meeting in the winter of 2000. I was happy to see them. We were close in a way that gave ease to our sporadic visits over the past twenty years—Carol (like me) was an educator, and Mary, as a twelve-year-old, was the first young Navajo who befriended me when I started my fieldwork. At that time, she and her family lived in a mobile home across the street from my rented home in Blanding. Mary, a socially and racially marginalized break-dancer, and I, a non-LDS outside ethnographer, became friends.

We arrived at a relative's home on the Navajo Nation for the Yeíbicheii dance after 10:00 P.M. Our early arrival guaranteed a prime spot at the front of the dancing area. Several other families had already begun to form the loose lines of supporters that would surround the elongated earthen dancing area. We quickly moved our lawn chairs into position. Within minutes, Carol dashed to a pile of cut firewood and returned to build a fire in front of our seats. "Hey, you need to be a strong woman to do this," Carol teasingly called out to the other men and women around us preparing their places for the evening's ceremony. "We know you are," softly returned with the breeze. Chuckles echoed through the red sandstone landscape. Soon, large forked fires dotted our visions as we formed two rows of hunched figures draped in blankets and silhouetted by flames.

On the other side of the dancing area, slightly out of the fire's light, sat a customized food wagon. Attached to a King Cab pickup truck, the aluminum-sided, four-wheeled wagon reminded me of many of the trailers I had seen over the years modified and adapted to house families on the move, handle extra water barrels, provide temporary cooking facilities, add a bedroom at the home complex for a daughter's new family, or provide winter hay storage for livestock. A wooden frame extended beyond the trailer to form a covered and enclosed dining space which snugly fit two wooden tables and four benches. Flickers of firelight danced off shiny plastic red and white tablecloths, and a carefully worded menu advertised Navajo hamburgers (ground beef on fry bread), hamburgers, Navajo tacos, mutton stew, hot chocolate, and coffee. On the other side of the dancing area stood a rectangular, plywood, windowless building with a door-less entry. A paper plate nailed to the side of the entry read, "Open." The dim light from the surrounding fires illuminated a figure cooking over a two-burner propane stove by a kerosene lamp. Before the evening was over, both of these food stands would be busy.

As the sky darkened almost to black and the temperature dropped, between two hundred and three hundred people gathered, forming concentric rows of cars surrounding the dancing area. The young and the old, near and distant relatives, and strangers came together from throughout the northern part of the Navajo Nation for the ceremony. Crisp black Stetson cowboy hats, Wrangler jeans, and pointed cowboy boots appeared on some of the older men. Others wore athletic shoes, blue jeans, flannel shirts, and bandanas around carefully braided hair. Throughout the crowd, young men, women, and children wore warm baggy pants, tennis shoes, and sweaters. I wore two sweaters and a down jacket in an attempt to stay warm in the single-digit-temperature winter night.

The dancers started close to midnight. The drumbeat reverberated around their bodies' movements as they came into the dancing area. To the north was a brush corral for the gods, and to the south was one for the Earth People. The patient remained in the ceremonial hooghan. The first set of dancers moved slowly past us. Long, diamond-shaped sequined sashes reaching to the ground trailed behind each masked dancer. Carol leaned over to me. "This is the last night, and so they are wearing masks. They are the young ones. They got their start at the elementary school. That is where they learned to dance the Yeíbicheii. That is how Jim learned to dance, too." Mary added, "Last night they were dancing in their baggies. And their jackets." She looked at her mother and giggled. Carol added: "Sherry [her adopted daughter] would be here at the dance if she was not pregnant. They say you shouldn't go

if you are going to have a baby. It will hurt the baby, or the patient."
Everyone nodded. Carol continued, "Look at her," pointing to a young
woman whose belly was protruding from her black leather coat, "She
just wanted to be here." Everyone laughed. No one dismissed her presence. Carol and her sister talked about one of the dancers that had just
passed us. "That was a wonderful Yeíbicheii. The tall, thin one. He was
the lead dancer at the last dance I saw. And he is a rapper. He is a real
good rapper. And a real good Yeíbicheii."

The Holy People, supernatural beings, are called to ceremonies by
prayers and offerings to help "set things right" or restore health to the
patient and reestablish harmony in the universe. Some of the Holy People, known as Yé'ii, are led by Talking God in dances during the nine-
day Night Way and Mountain Chant ceremonials. These, along with the
Enemy Way, are the Navajo ceremonials best known to non-Navajos
because of the spectacular dances on the final night, and because they
are among the few dances that are performed in public, outside of ceremonial practices, in places such as the Shiprock Navajo Fair. The Night
Way was the ceremony I attended with the Sams.

Historical translations of Navajo oral texts paint a picture of the
universe as a complex interlocking and unitary system. Not seamless,
but clearly connected. And within this whole system, both good and
trouble exist as different states of being; one can live life with situations of orderliness and harmony, or one can slip into situations that are
uncontrolled and unharmonious. Navajos have developed an intricate
system of ceremonies to deal with establishing and maintaining a har-
monious balance, or hózhó. Roughly translated as "pleasant," "beautiful," or "blessed," this concept represents things that are good or favor-
able, as opposed to things that are harmful or cause trouble. Trying
to describe this concept in the 1950s, Leland Wyman explained: "It
expresses for the Navajo what the words beauty, perfection, harmony,
goodness, normality, success, well-being, blessedness, order, and ideal
do for English speakers. It is the central idea in Navajo religious thinking and their basic value concept."[1] Philosophically, the central aim of
Navajo ceremonies, then, is to restore this balance or hózhó. Reflecting
on the experiences he saw by the 1970s, Wyman wrote that

the practical-minded Navajo if questioned would say that ceremonials are carried out first, to restore and maintain health; second, to

obtain increase of wealth, the well-being of home, flocks, and fields, the security of himself and his relatives; and, perhaps, third, to acquire certain ceremonial property, such as the white shell or turquoise bead token to wear as protection from lightning and snakes. Unspoken benefits would be the prestige value of giving costly ceremonials and the opportunity for social gatherings.[2]

Falling "out of balance," and becoming ill, is the result of an individual's conscious or unconscious acts of inappropriate behavior; illness is not caused by the Holy People. Rather, according to James Faris, "It is violation by humans of prescribed order and proper ceremonial observances and attitudes, conditions of balance, beauty, harmony, and peace that brings about illness. This order, these ceremonial observances, these proper social relations have been set down by the Holy People in Navajo history."[3] It is the individual's responsibility to live in beauty and harmony, but in times of illness, one can turn back to historical memory and practices to regain harmony. "In Navajo terms, the Night Way is a healing practice undertaken for stricken people. It is a healing practice by which human beings attempt to re-harmonize and re-order and re-balance their relationships with one another and with a Navajo universe."[4]

The Night Way we attended was used to cure all sorts of head ailments, eye and ear diseases, and mental disturbances, but in this case, the patient suffered body pains. Teams of masked dancers, Yé'ii, impersonating Holy People, moved up and down the dance area during this final night. The leader of the dancers, Talking God, wore a whitened buckskin mask with outlined circular holes for eyes and mouth, a fringe of hair, a spruce collar, and a fan-like head ornament of radiating eagle plumes. He is also called Yé'ii Bicheii, or Grandfather-of-the-gods, which has been Anglicized to Yeíbicheii. Locally, as Carol did, all of the dancers, as well as the Night Way itself, were spoken of as a Yeíbicheii.

A BIRTHDAY POEM
By Luci Tapahonso

This morning, the sunrise is a brilliant song
cradling tiny birds and brittle leaves. The world
responds, stretching, humming. The sunlight is Diyin,
sacred beams as the Holy Ones arrive with prayers.
They bring gifts in the cold dawn. Again, as a Diné
woman, I face east on the porch and pray for Hózhó

one more time. For today, allow me to share Hózhó,
the beauty of all things being right and proper as in songs
the Holy Ones gave us. They created the world,
instilling stories and lessons so we would know Diyin
surrounds us. Our lives were set by precise prayers
and stories to ensure balance. Grant me the humor Diné

elders relish so. No matter what, let the Diné
love of jokes, stories, and laughter create some Hózhó.
Some days, even after great coffee, I need to hear a song
to reassure me that the distance from Dinétah is not a world
away. I know the soft hills, plains, and wind are Diyin
also. Yet I plan the next trip when we will say prayers

in the dim driveway. As we drive, Kansas darkens. Prayers
and memories protect us. In the tradition of Diné
travel, we eat, laugh, refuel, sing. Twice in Texas, Hózhó
arose in clear air above the flatness. The full moon was a song
we watched all night. We marveled at how quietly the world
is blessed. After midnight, Lori asks about Diyin

Diné´é who dance in the Night Way ceremony. The sacred Diyin
Diné´é come after the first frost glistens. Their prayers
and long rhythmic songs help us live. This is a Diné
way of communion and cleansing. At the Night Way, Hózhó
awaits as we come to listen and absorb the songs
until they live within. It is true that the world

is restored by the Holy Ones who return to the Fourth World
to take part in the Night Way. They want to know that Diyin
still exists amongst their children. Their stories and prayers
guide us now. At times, the Holy Ones feared the Diné
would succumb to foreign ways. For them, it is truly Hózhó
to see us at the Night Way gathered in the smoky cold. Songs

rise with fire smoke. I tell Lori we Diné are made of prayers.
At times, the world may overwhelm us, yet because of the Diyin,
each morning we pray to restore Hózhó, Hózhó, Hózhó, Hózhó.[5]

As we huddled near the fire that winter night, talk drifted to the importance of family, the struggles Navajo youth faced in schools and with friends, and the difficulties of raising children. These were topics

that were repeated in numerous conversations and formal interviews
I had with Carol over the years. In 1992, she had described her own
upbringing.

> I came from a poor traditional family. So I worked. When I was
> fourteen, I had a job cleaning. I was buying my own clothes. Because
> we didn't have money. And the traditional homes were more into
> school. They kept saying to go to school and learn the white way;
> you might need it someday. That's what my parents said, and I did.
> To get an education and be a service to others, and get a job and
> have a nice home. But kids are different now. Like the ones that come
> from homes in town. With TV, all sorts of things the parents buy for
> the kids. They just sit at home and watch TV. They don't care about
> school or nothing. They only care about their friends. And many
> of their parents don't help them. They can't help them with school,
> and they don't tell them about being Navajo anymore.

This particular night she spoke with satisfaction about her children.
"Jim is up in Moab building hooghans for retired people, white people.
And Mary here, she is doing real good. She has been substituting at
Bluff Elementary. She has substituted for me, and has done real good.
They are encouraging her to go to school and become a teacher. Like
me. Can you believe it? Both of us would be teachers." Twenty years
ago, when I had first met the Sams, this seemed an unlikely scenario.

Breaking as Performance: Visibility and Hope

It was mid-September in 1984, and I had just returned to Blanding from
a three-day weekend visiting my family in Albuquerque, New Mexico. I
was into my second year as an assistant professor, and this was my new
research site. As my car pulled into the driveway, five of my new neighbors, Navajo students at the high school I was researching, came over
to help me unpack. Mary, a tall, slightly built fourteen-year-old ninth
grader with shoulder-length dark hair, grabbed my briefcase and a bag
of books. "Is this full of gold?" teased Jim, her brother, as he lifted my
Macintosh, the first of its kind—a 128K—from my truck. I laughed: "I
wish it was! It's a glorified typewriter called a personal computer. And
it cost me $3,800. I need another job to pay for it!" None existed yet
in the district's classrooms. They helped carry my suitcases into the hot
and stuffy living room, and we moved back outside on the porch to
catch a breeze and talk.

"Where did you go?" asked Mary. "To my mom's birthday party," I explained, "and what did ya'll do this weekend?" One of the boys replied with little enthusiasm: "I went to Cortez with my dad, to visit my uncle. And then we went to a bunch of stores to get stuff for the week." Mary interrupted: "Jim and I went to the reservation. Our grandmother's house. She lives over that suspension bridge that goes across the river. She needed our help." "Yeah," Jim inserted, "we went to hunt for porcupines. They were eating her watermelons. She has a big garden down by the river. We found one, a real big fat one and killed it. We saved it for the quills. Our grandma is going to teach us how to make things with it. Like they used to do. But it's kinda hard, because she doesn't speak English. And I don't know much Navajo. But I do know a couple of words." Several of the others nodded. Mary, with a shy smile, added: "We want to learn. But Navajo is real hard. And our grandma makes fun of us when we don't talk right." Heads throughout the group nodded, as the children grew silent. The sudden creak of a metal door opening and an adult's voice calling several children's names broke the silence. As they ran across the street, Mary turned back and yelled, "See you at school tomorrow!"

For the rest of the fall, I spent a lot of time with Mary, in the school's hallways and out of school. She was a bright, cheerful, and shy young girl. She rarely talked about her classes, but was quick to talk about friends and music. "I'm in that group that hangs out at the end of the hall. We are like, into break dancing. And a lot of my friends are Utes. We aren't snobs like the jocks and those other white kids." Although Mary herself did not break-dance, "I'm too shy," she could always be found watching her brother and friends perfecting their moves. Such was the case during the homecoming football game the first week in October.

As in many rural communities, the townspeople turned out for the football game, and the stands were crowded as they cheered for their team. All but one of the players were white. Off to the side, next to the concession stand, were the break-dancers. A large circle, two to three people deep, formed around individual break-dancers. Three large portable stereos, propped on shoulders, provided the sound system. Mary and I crowded into the front of the circle. A young Navajo on the ground spun gracefully on his shoulders, moved upright with one arm, moon-walked in a circle, and pointed to challenge an opponent in the circle. The crowd cheered. Another Navajo took his place, executed several shoulder spins, failed a head spin, sprung upright, and moved with undulating arm and foot movements around the circle as he teased and taunted several Navajo girls next to us to move into the circle with him. The crowd laughed and clapped. For over an hour, the young people performed well and enjoyed themselves. Suddenly, the word spread that someone had managed to gain access to the school. The group of breakers cheered as they ran for the gym to continue the break dancing. The game continued, few missed the Indian students, and the home team won.

As I left the game with the high school librarian and a high school teacher, I asked about the group of break-dancers. In a discourse of manifest manners, Navajo youths' resistance to colonization practices was dismissed. "I see them in my library; it's mostly the Utes and the town Navajos. You know, the kids who aren't doing well in school" and "I can't understand how they can learn with their arms always moving like that in class. They look like they are working, but their arms are always moving. I don't understand it," they replied. As I would come to discover, few white adults understood these youth, who were dismissively labeled "bad Indians" and "poor students." One teacher explained it this way: "It's their attitude. It's defiant. They walk around with their head in the air." With a hint of critical insight, the librarian described the break-dancers: "It's like being a kind of warrior." A Native gaze frosted the air in this community, refusing to succumb to the surveillance of the white community.

Christmas vacation was just around the corner when Mary and Jim invited me over for a dinner of Navajo tacos and to watch their favorite movie, *Breakin'*. The warm smell of fry bread and pinto beans filled my nose as I stepped into their living room. "Welcome to your first real Navajo meal," called out Carol. She wiped her flour-covered hands on a towel as she reached to give me a gentle handshake. The room was full of her children and several of their friends, all stretched out on overstuffed chairs, couches, and the floor. They were at the end of the movie. "We'll rewind it in a minute so you can watch it," said Mary. After dinner I settled into a soft, burgundy, velveteen Lazy Boy chair to watch my first break-dancing movie. The plot was simple but powerful, and Jim and Mary had memorized much of the film's dialogue. The main characters were serious, sensitive young men and women who were not given a chance because they were poor, young, and black or brown. In one dramatic moment, the main character got into an argument with the "good" white dancer.

Hey, you don't know how I feel. You don't know nothing about me. Your friends are all snobs, man; they are just like you. Up there in your tights being told what to do. We don't care if we don't step on our right foot. We do what feels good. And we don't do it in the classrooms, either. We do it on the street. We don't fit into your world. 'Cause we don't have the right credentials.

They cheered, and Jim's younger brother said to me, "It's cool. They win over the dumb straight white guys." Jim added, "It used to be cowboys and Indians. Now it is breakers and cowboys." The film ended with the following rap epilogue:

> Now you know breaking can't be beat.
> It's the sound, it's the culture that's out on the streets.
> It's the life of our city youth,
> 'cause they are so talented
> and now you've seen proof.
> You've got the talent.
> We've all got the talent.
> All of us have our dreams.
> And though as impossible as it might seem,
> you can make it with true motivation.
> Hard, hard work
> From graffiti, spinning, rapping, breaking, and dance
> for most city youth it's their only chance.
> To gain recognition and make a name,
> and possibly a chance for fame.
> So when you see them try,
> stop and watch, don't pass them by.
> 'Cause they're just people like you,
> trying to make their dreams come true.

As I left at the end of the evening, Jim was rewinding the film in preparation for the third showing. Not one person, including Carol, showed any signs of boredom.

It was a few minutes before first period when Mary and I walked into the school. Around the trophy case, down the steps, and in the lower foyer hung the "popular" group—jocks and cheerleaders from prominent community families. Mary whispered: "To be some of those [the popular group], you have to be born into them, and the only way an

Indian can fit . . . is if he is good in sports. And I still think that would not work." Navajo students' descriptions of the popular group were not flattering, "This is where the preps, who wear pale colors that don't match and letter jackets, hang out. Funny cut hair, bright makeup, and striped pants and different patterned tops." The boys leaned, one foot up against the wall, facing the trophy case. A few students sat up on the banister. The tightest cluster of popular girls was up against the corner next to the front glass doors. The homecoming queen and her friends were dressed in jeans and pale pink and blue sweaters. Their long blond hair was secured in ponytails with large multicolored ribbon bows. They were talking about Saturday's dance. "It was great until they started break dancing. It's always like that. The Indians start that, and it ruins the dance." This space was occupied by the popular group between classes, before and after school, and during lunch, where they talked in small, tight, same-sex groups about social, rather than academic, subjects.

Adjacent to this area, still in the main foyer, was a set of wall heaters. This was the standing territory of tenth-, eleventh-, and twelfth-grade Navajo boys who were bussed to school from the reservation. They, too, leaned with one foot against the wall, but rather than talking, they were silent observers of the activities around them. Although their time was restricted before and after school due to the bus schedule, they were always in their place at lunch. Mary explained: "They are the reservation kids. They stay together in the school. With their cousins. They stay together."

Down the main hall, underneath the Indian display case (containing photographs and articles about the Indian students) on one side and an open announcement case on the other, were hard wooden benches occupied by the "middle" groups of students. Some of Mary's friends hung out here. One described the group: "Us normal kids, we do all sorts of different things and have different small groups of friends, Indians and whites, but we aren't the preps, and we sure aren't the lower-class kids." Here, small mixed groups of students faced each other. Benches were always packed at lunch, expanding like an accordion to contain additional friends, and at the same time dropping off students at both ends. Although many Indian students hung out there, they were more often Navajos from the town than from the reservation. The space between the benches was small, making this a public area with high visibility and contact. Students reached out to hit or touch passing students, moving in, out, between, and back to the benches as they talked of friends, enemies, and social activities.

The remaining large gathering area in the school was at the far end of the main building in the foyer in front of the auditorium. By no coincidence, this was the farthest location from the administrators' offices. In the words of a Navajo student who hung there, "Lower-class kids hang out there. And sometimes us breakers 'cause we can break and listen to our ghetto blasters [large portable stereos]." These youth were the most "invisible."

Many of the students in this area, Indian and white, seemed almost transient in the school. They moved in and out of the building in small, quiet groups, often quickly leaving the school at lunch time to wander downtown, then slowly making their way back to their classes through this school entrance. Mary was often with this group of Navajo students.

The principal recognized the racial divisions in his high school: "I've got two schools here, Indian and white. They just don't seem to fit together. It has always been like this." Racial disparity was presented as a normal fact of history. The school's 1985 yearbook bore out this image. White students are shown lounging around cars, leaning against motorcycles and 4 × 4 trucks, walking on the school grounds, and in homes around the community. Over a three-year period, 1985–1987, only ten candid photographs showed Indian students, and they were all in schools, classrooms, or hallways. The double-page pictures of "School Favorites" showed no Indian faces. There were no Indian students in the National Honor Society, on the Student Council, or as cheerleaders. A few Indian students were in band, the Future Farmers of America, and Future Business Leaders of America. One Ute student was on the football team, and a few Indian students were on the track, wrestling, and basketball teams. No Indians were class officers or "Dream Dates." Framed with neo-colonialism, these yearbooks exemplified the place for Indians in the school.

I was sitting with Mary and her friends on a hallway bench during lunch one day when they were signing each other's yearbooks. "Look," Mary said assertively, "here on the first page is the homecoming queen." The full-page, glossy color photograph showed a smiling blond wearing a crown and a pink formal. "Now look at us." She flipped to the last page of the yearbook. A matte black-and-white photograph showed a smiling "Indian princess." "It's still the Indians at the back of the bus. That's what they think of us." The next year, the faculty advisor for the yearbook, who openly expressed contempt for Indian students, resigned. That year, the Indian princess smiled in color across the page from the homecoming queen. The following year, it was back to the back of the bus. Although in color, the Indian princess' photograph had shrunk by half and appeared on the next to the last page. In 1992, I asked the faculty yearbook advisor about the Indian royalty, whom I could not find in the yearbook. He smiled and enthusiastically pointed to one tiny picture on the general page titled "Indian Club": "Look, here it is. Great looking, isn't it?" I was speechless. He went on: "Isn't it great? Look at all the Indian graduates we have. Five, no, six in all." Almost thirty-five Navajo and Ute students had started out as freshmen.

Over the following year, Mary, Jim, and their friends appeared and performed at all of the home football games, and when the weather turned cold and the sport changed to basketball, the breakers moved inside. Out of school, the breakers continued to practice, carrying their dance floor—pieced together from cardboard—from house to house to perfect difficult head and shoulder spins with their friends. They performed at school dances; a small group of students did a routine for the school alumni assembly; several of the students performed at community dances; and two gave break-dancing lessons to younger children at the community spa. Like Mary and Jim, a majority of the breakers were from the town or nearby areas, where they were almost invisible to the white community surrounding them. They saw school as having little relevance for their lives and ranged from average to poor academically. One day, I showed the high school principal a picture of a group of break-dancers performing inside the school—where the use of boom boxes was prohibited—and he exclaimed, "That doesn't even look like my school!" A few told me they break-danced as a tribal competition; others did so because it was different and "cool"; and some wanted to "show those whites." Break dancing was a performance that asserted the very physical existence of these youth.

Within this context, these breakers danced to communicate cultural solidarity, skill, and self-worth and to affirm assertive resistance to their subordinate social position. The group was tolerated by the administration as a passing youthful fad or explained away as normal "because Indians traditionally dance." Breakers were accepted by socially marginal white students and disliked by the jocks and the more prestigious social group of white students. These students saw clearly the resistance behind break dancing: "They are always breaking to look different from us. It's something they do that we don't do." For these Navajo youth, break dancing provided an arena in which to compete for success that would stand in direct contrast to the repeated failures they experienced in classrooms. And if one believed in movies and the heroes they produced, there was a chance for success, fame, and money, even for break-dancers. Their Native presence proudly set them apart from their white peers.

The image of the power surrounding break dancing also was not ignored by the younger Indian students. By the end of the first year of my research, many of the Navajo children from the elementary school nearer to the reservation were also break dancing. Teachers told me, "It's hot down here, too." This was beautifully illustrated in the school literary magazine in a story with the theme of break dancing in a witch tale written by a thirteen-year-old Navajo girl titled, "The Tree Who Wanted to Break Dance." The story was about a tree that wanted to break-dance but couldn't because its roots kept him immobile. A witch, dressed as an old lady, came by and agreed to turn the tree into a boy if he would then teach her how to break-dance. The witch went home and concocted a special liquid to feed the tree. The next morning the tree drank the mixture, and within minutes, a boy emerged with a cap on. At his side was a big box-shaped stereo. The witch was delighted and demanded to be taught how to break-dance. The boy was reluctant and asked for a history—he wanted to know what his name was and where he came from. The witch was upset, but finally gave him the name of a friend. In the words of the young writer: "So they both went home. 'Cupcake' taught the witch how to break-dance. Every minute they got, they would put 'Beat Street' in the stereo and start to break-dance together. They challenged all the other breakers and lived happily ever after."

For most of these Navajo and Ute break-dancers, success—money and fame as valued in a discourse of manifest manners—was illusionary. Jim and several of his friends left school before graduation and found only temporary semi-skilled employment. The unemployment rate for high school dropouts was over 60 percent. With resilience, they started families and remained in the community. Mary also left high school, in 1985, but shortly after, she attended the Job Corps to work on a general education diploma and a certificate as a heavy equipment operator. Within the year, she returned to raise her two children in her mother's home. As they grew older, these youth turned toward heavy rock and heavy metal as a medium to continue to express their challenge to a system that provided few rewards for Indians.

Alongside the Yeíbicheii: Heavy Metal as Resilience

Both Mary and Jim grew up through elementary school attending "Navajo Culture Days," and Jim became a Yeíbicheii dancer. As he moved into high school, his performance changed to claim a different kind of social space in a white context—as a break-dancer. With emancipatory hopes for performing their expertise as break-dancers, as well as the insight and ambivalence in this hope, Jim and his friends thought they would achieve validation through competitive performance. As their disillusionment increased, their performative stance shifted to heavy metal and hard rock. In Jim's words: "We don't do that anymore. It didn't work. We got tired. We listen to heavy metal now. And hard rock. It's tough music. We don't dance. We just listen." Suggesting a growing wisdom on their part, the romanticism of proving themselves in an authentic manner gave way to the protest stance of heavy metal. The move to heavy metal—a music genre that screams with anger, distrust, sadness, powerlessness, and alienation—still represented a stance of resiliency against the violence of colonization. Mary, Jim, and their friends' voices spoke of the continued struggle to assert their rights and presence on the landscape.

The entire high school was required to attend the Dress Assembly. The hall was full, as a group of parents, teachers, and administrators explained the new clothing rules. A counselor spoke first. "First of all, we feel that we have had a lot of things that have made us feel bad this year, sorta put down. We want to kind of upbeat the school a little bit." She moved her arms above her head and exclaimed, "This is a great school!" Students clapped and whistled. She continued: "We want to be positive about this new dress code. We want others to look at you guys and say, 'Look, this looks like a great group of kids,' instead of looking at you guys and saying, 'What a bunch of bums.'" She read the first line of the code: "Dress and grooming of students should be within the limits of generally accepted good taste, modesty, and cleanliness." The principal stepped to the microphone: "We are asking you not to wear clothing that advertises alcohol or drugs or heavy metal rock groups. We will ask you to take those clothes off. I know some heavy metal groups are RAD [Rockers Against Drugs]. Figure out who is RAD and who is not. Then don't wear those tee shirts with those bands on them."

Students groaned, several complaining loudly, "This is a prison!" The principal responded: "No, it is not a prison. It is not the faculty against the students. Guys, no society can survive without rules. And we are talking to only a few of you, maybe twenty or thirty. The rest of you are fine." The counselor added: "It's just the general idea that we're all really neat around here; we need to express the fact that we are the best. The only way we can do it is by walking around with the best on. We are trying to establish a nice institution for learning for you guys. We want to avoid prison for you."

The Only Good Indian
By Janet Campbell Hale

'White people respect good Indians,' my mother said rather casually as she sat darning socks and mending small tears in our clothes. I was about four at the time. I sat on the floor beside her chair, coloring in my (probably Carmen Miranda) coloring book. 'Good Indians are clean and neat, hardworking and sober,' she said. I wanted to get away from her. I hated it when she talked like that, and I could not, even to myself, articulate my feelings because I was too young. I couldn't get away because it was raining. She wouldn't let me out. No escape. 'White people look down on the other kind, the bad one, the drunken, lazy louts.' I stopped coloring and went to a window and watched the rain pour. Mom's voice droned on.

She would often instruct me on being a good Indian, the kind white people approve of (and sometimes, when I was a little older, on being the kind of woman men respect). I would feel the resentment rise in my blood. Why should I care? Why don't they worry about being the sort of person I respect? Why should I have to be the one to live up to someone else's expectations? Anyway, trying to be a 'good Indian' was a futile endeavor. Several years before Gram Sullivan was born, General Sheridan had made his famous remark regarding the only good Indian being a dead Indian. I didn't care to be a good Indian.[6]

When I reflected on Mary and Jim and their friends' performances, I saw and heard a consistent message in their reactions to schools, the white community, and their own standpoint—a resistance to the coupling of "goodness" with "whiteness," and the resilience and survivance of being Navajo, however they wished to define this. The insistence on living their lives as Navajos—albeit in many different forms—was at the core of their actions. These acts of survivance were expressed in a variety of ways. Some were mundane everyday performances such as maintaining silence in the classroom. Others were more overt: wearing black, performing public dances, withdrawing from the white community, and choosing to refuse to move to cities. These performances represented not only a reluctance to accept white colonization, which was exemplified with the folk belief "the only good Indian is a non-Indian," but also, more assertively, these were acts of the desirability of being Indian (whatever this might look like), rather than becoming white.

With a Native gaze, jokes and moral lessons mocked whites as rude, loud, disrespectful, immodest, selfish, uncaring, and shallow.[7] Navajo youth were cautioned against the influence of whites. As one parent told me about a relative, "I hear he is seeing a white girl. Watch out, it's dangerous!" This danger was also an insult. At the swimming hole one day, Elizabeth and Ernie Begay's youngest son, who was swimming with me, was scolded by a group of Navajo men: "Is that white woman your wife? Why aren't you with Navajos?"

White surveillance, on the other hand, insists that imitating whites is a goal desired by all groups and refuses to acknowledge that Indians are happy being who they are. From this viewpoint, the insistence of Navajo youths on "being Navajo" cannot be relegated to the margins and viewed as a sign of failure, but rather must be seen as an act of courage. The life paths they desired were ones that need not lead them from their Navajo-ness to whiteness. I chuckle as I am reminded of a folk story that was told frequently by Navajos throughout the Navajo Nation. A white tourist asked an elderly Navajo man as he pointed to a road in front of them, "Where does this road go?" He replied, "The road doesn't go anywhere. It stays. The tourists go."

Young Mothers: "I Didn't Like the Way the Teachers Looked at Me"

As Carol and I drove to Blanding on a crisp, sunny fall day in 1986, the cottonwood trees glowed gold against the burnt red earth, and the shrub oak added a brilliant red to the landscape's earthen palate. Mary had decided to drop out of school for the time being—she was a junior and had just had her first baby. "She should quit. I was paying for a babysitter, and she would go out to the lake with friends instead of going to class! I wasn't going to pay for her to play," Carol said sharply. "She said she wanted to keep the baby. Her father and I have tried to help her as much as possible." Carol turned to face me in the car. "With us Navajos, we don't give babies away. We keep them in the family. There is always a place for another baby in a family."

Young Navajo women left school for a variety of reasons, including feelings of rejection from their teachers and racial hostilities in schools. But the primacy of family responsibilities and networks was at the core of many of these reasons. Over 45 percent of the young women I talked to said they left school because they had to work at home or at a job.[8] Expressing disinterest toward school, 44 percent said that they did not see the importance of school in relation to what they wanted to do in life. Although 50 percent expressed difficulty with the academic work, specifically reading, they insisted that it did not influence their decision to leave school. Mary, however, was academically a good student. Almost 40 percent of the women who dropped out of school, like Mary, did so because of pregnancy or to care for children. Ninety-five percent of the young women who left school stated their parents wanted and encouraged them to stay in school and graduate. Parental encouragement, however, was not enough. Although their motherhood was accepted in their homes, it was unacceptable in school.

Teenage pregnancy confirmed racial beliefs that whites held about Navajos, and these young mothers felt "pushed out" of school. As one young mother told me: "The teachers, you know, they look at you differently. They know you have had a baby, and they stay away from you. I didn't like the way they looked at me." Mary echoed these feelings: "I thought about it for a month, and then I just said, well, I just wanted to stay home, and I did. That time I was pregnant again; so I decided just to stay home because if I go back to school, them kids [whites], they're really ignorant. They really start saying stuff to you. 'Oh, look at that girl. She's pregnant.' I didn't like that." Her counselor, shrugging his shoulders, had told me simply, "These Navajo girls get married young."

For many Navajo women, schools were hostile or boring and disconnected from their lives outside of school. Almost half dropped out of school. Mary was no exception. Within some groups of friends, educational success was even more elusive. "There were seven of us. From preschool all the way through high school. And only two of us graduated. One just dropped out and four had kids," explained Jan Begay's cousin. With or without a high school diploma, over two-thirds continued to live their lives in their homes on the reservation. For most of these young women, matrilineal networks, which provided a successful place in life on or near the reservation, provided roles that schools did not. High school was often viewed as something to "get over" and was rarely seen as critical to these women's lives. This transparent connection with school was still faced by Mary's, Jan's, and Vangie's children and other Navajo youth from the next generation. The experiences of Navajo students with school, as I have seen, remained disconnected, sometimes disrespectful, sometimes hopeful, but too often only fleetingly connected to the lives Navajo youth desired to live.

"I just felt out of place," Mary told me when she explained her reasons for leaving school when she was fifteen. "Because I'd just be home all the time. There's hardly anything to do except to watch TV. I had the baby when I was a junior, and I stopped because of the baby when he was sick." Mary's baby developed a brain virus when he was six months old, and she spent six weeks in Salt Lake City while he recovered at Primary Children's Medical Center. "The doctors said he could have a seizure anytime, so I can't just leave him with any babysitter," she explained, "And the teachers. Some of them treated me nice, but some of them didn't. Do you ever have that feeling when people look at you all weird? Give you real dirty looks? That's how some of the teachers are." Mary tried returning during her senior year, but left school for good when she became pregnant with her second child. The Job Corps was her next attempt to complete her education.

During fall break at my university, I decided to drive to Bluff to visit friends. I stopped by Carol's house and found Mary preparing to leave to attend a Job Corps program. "I decided to go to the Job Corps in Montana, Anaconda, then I changed my mind to South Dakota. Because there's a whole bunch of nice cowboys up there!" she grinned broadly. Several of her friends had already left for various Job Corps centers. "They pick you up in a bus from Cortez or Durango. They pay for your meals. Like if you stay in Salt Lake or in a town, they pay for your motel." "How have your friends liked the Job Corps?" I asked. "Just the same old thing. They just mess up drinking, drugs, and just get homesick and come home. I'm not. I'm going to stick it out as long as I can. I don't want to come back and make nothing out of myself." Carol nodded. "We can take care of her kids while she finishes her education." The counselor for Indian students at the high school had encouraged Mary to leave town to continue her education. "She told me the Job Corps will help you get a job and finish your schooling. You go into school for a year and you get your high school or GED diploma.

After that, if you're planning on going to college, you have more years. But you get a job faster in the Job Corps because you finish it in one year." Mary wanted to work in professional business organizations as a receptionist or in another staff position. Her mother encouraged her to study to become a heavy equipment operator, an occupation that had few women, but paid nearly twice the yearly salary of office occupations. Pleasing her mother, she decided to be a heavy equipment operator. In an interview twenty years later, she elaborated on this decision. "I wanted to go into the office occupation. But I went to the heavy equipment area. I liked the classes, but my instructor was rude, ignorant, sexist, and discriminated against Indians. He says it was to toughen up women for men's jobs. It pays good money. So I kicked ass for my mom." Before the year was up, Mary decided to return home. Two years later, in 1989, she completed a GED, and was awarded a high school diploma.

Teachers, school administrators, and counselors viewed young Navajo women's career goals as limited and vocational in nature. "The girls want to be nurses, dental assistants, secretaries," explained a counselor. "Their expectations for themselves are very low. There is very little interest in the professions." My interviews with thirty-five young women preparing to graduate, however, revealed that many of them wanted the jobs the counselor saw as male jobs. Mary and many of her peers did not view their occupational desires as being restricted because of their gender. Over one-third, 34 percent, said they wanted to become heavy equipment operators or welders or to work in electronics. Only 17 percent indicated that they sought secretarial, nursing, or cosmetology jobs. Over one-third, 34 percent, expressed desires for professional-level work in education, social work, architecture, and in the medical field. Regardless of these desires, very few young women moved into any of these kinds of jobs. In fact, most openings that these young women encountered on the job market required little, if any, schooling.

An Outside Gaze

Contesting Unequal Opportunities

In late August 1997, I drove to the district offices for the first meeting of the court-appointed Curriculum Committee. The previous April, the U.S. Department of Justice, the Navajo Nation, *Sinajini et al.*, and the San Juan School Board again came to a court-approved agreement. In a unique agreement that combined three different lawsuits against the school district, four committees—heritage language, curriculum, finance, and special education—were formed to develop new school district instructional plans. Each committee consisted of three school-appointed and three Navajo Nation– and Justice Department–appointed educational experts. One issue was that the district was accused of denying American Indian students the same educational opportunities and services (such as equal access to certain academic programs) provided to white students. My research had been used in the court case, and I was appointed by the Navajo Nation to serve on the Curriculum Committee.

As I drove the 350 miles, I thought of what little improvement in educational achievement had occurred since the case against the district started in 1974. As measured on the California Test of Basic Skills (CTBS), Indian students at the eighth-grade level had made few gains in a decade from 1977, when the average was a 5.0 grade level equivalent, to 1987, when the average was 5.6. In 1990 and 1991, eleventh graders at Whitehorse High School scored in the 15th percentile in reading. In 1997, the district switched to the Stanford Achievement Test. Achievement scores were still dramatically low; eleventh graders designated FEP (Fully English Proficient) averaged in the 23rd percentile in reading, while their PEP (Potentially English Proficient) peers scored in the 9th percentile. From 1984–1990, Whitehorse High School graduated only 63 percent of its Indian students, and San Juan High School graduated fewer than half of its Indian students. In a 1992 "Report Card" sent to all post office box holders in the county, the district reported that the dropout rate for non-Anglo students was four times higher than for Anglo students. The district also reported the dropout rate had increased from 1989 to 1991. The average Indian graduate was reading at only the seventh-grade level. Most of the dropouts were at least six grade levels behind the national average. Over twenty years, from 1977 to 1997, Navajo students showed few real gains in academic abilities. In September 1997, the Utah Taxpayers Association rated the district as the worst in the state based upon school testing results. The district got an F+ for its 1996 SAT scores, a C for its 1995–1996 test improvement, an F+ for its test scores with a poverty index, a D– for a 1996 final grade, and a cumulative grade covering the previous five years of a D+. Some school district personnel blamed this dismal record on Indian students and their families. One white woman bitterly explained:

> It's so cultural! As soon as one of them bobs above the water a bit, they pull him back down. It's innate! It's so destructive. They [Navajo families] pull everyone down if one tries to succeed. Some people give me that line, 'They walk in beauty stuff'—it is certainly a good part of the traditional stories and culture—but this other is so negative. They are such a negative people. They make sure most don't succeed.

Navajo families blamed low academic achievement in part on racism and inadequate schooling. A Navajo student's description of her experiences in high school illustrated what this looked like.

> The teachers really don't listen to the Indians much. Like an Indian would raise up their hand. These white teachers don't want to take the time to work with Indians. Then they just look at them, and they ignore their hands and stuff like that. But when a white person, a white student, raises up their hand, they'll go to them first. So, it's like whites, they get served first and then the Indians last . . . Probably because they want the Indians to be dumb . . . They probably think that the Navajos don't know much.

In many ways, these different perceptions and experiences were at the heart of the lawsuits against the district. These issues were on our minds during our first meeting.

The six of us from the consensus committee sat across from each other in a conference room in the district's main office. One retired superintendent, an assistant superintendent, and the district's assistant superintendent represented the school district; a thirty-year educational expert for the Department of Justice, a bilingual expert from the Navajo Nation, and I represented the Navajo plaintiffs. The district assistant superintendent opened the meeting.

> Let's go over the purpose of the committee. The 1997 Agreement of Parties listed the following outcomes as mandatory: The district agrees to continue to incorporate a Native American cultural awareness component into its curriculum and to formulate a more formal cultural awareness plan. The district shall make educational programs available so that all students are offered an equal educational opportunity and shall use its best efforts to provide equal access to educational services and courses that are substantially similar.

An examination of the district's four high schools' course offerings was the first action item of the meeting. The Justice Department expert provided handouts for the committee. "I compared the offerings of the courses in each school. I was really shocked. I haven't seen anything so bad since the '60s in the South." Bodies stiffened from across the table. The committee silently read the charts. Of the district's twenty-one offerings in social studies, only three were offered at Whitehorse High School—U.S. history, world geography, and U.S. economics. Of the thirty-two different kinds of English/reading courses offered in the district, only the basic Language Arts 7, 8, 9, 10, 11 appeared on the list of possible course choices for students at Whitehorse High School, along with eleven different sections of Basic Reading. Math 7, 8, and General Math Review were offered in ten different classes, and only two classes were offered in any higher math course—a combined algebra/geometry class. These Navajo students did not have the opportunity, like students at the other district high schools, to take Algebra I, Algebra II, calculus, or trigonometry. Earth systems, physics, and chemistry were also missing from the schedule. Due to a lack of math and science courses, high-achieving students from this school could not gain admission to the University of Utah, even with a diploma. The educational expert finally spoke again, "Any high school that has to have eleven reading courses tells me the schools are simply not doing their job. I have never seen anything as bad as this." In a nervous and defensive stance, the assistant superintendent quickly inserted, "The district recognizes the problem. We are devoting our efforts this year to reading for all the Navajo schools."

My colleague and I left Bluff shortly after sunrise on November 1999 to drive through Monument Valley for the first Curriculum Committee evaluation meeting of the school district's reform efforts of the previous two years. For forty-six miles, the two-lane road undulated up and down and across the red sandstone landscape. The road seemed small and out of place as we drove between the monoliths scattered around the road. We climbed up a small pass and descended into the shimmering red valley. The high school sat alone, surrounded by stunning mesas, monoliths, and buttresses. A lime green playing field established the boundary between the Navajo Nation and the school district.

We gathered in the faculty room just before first period for coffee, juice, and donuts. Most of us had been with the committee from the start. The directors of secondary education, elementary education, and special programs now represented the district. The tensions of earlier years were subdued, although we were cognizant that we represented different constituents. We reviewed our evaluation sheets. "We have streamlined the observation forms. Teachers have been confused and want to know what we are looking for," explained the director of special programs. The principal, who had shared the forms with her teachers, added, "My teachers have seen the form and agree good teachers should be doing this." We focused on four areas. One, we wanted teachers to have lesson plans with assessable behavioral objectives of what was to be taught. Simply put, we felt teachers should know what they were going to teach when they stood in front of a class. Two, we wanted teachers to be able to identify the students most in need, the limited-English speakers, and show how they were addressing their needs. Simply, the youth most at risk should not be ignored, even if they are sitting quietly in their seats. Three, we wanted teachers to have a plan that promoted cognitive and academic interaction, rather than simple nonverbal seatwork. And fourth, in Navajo classes, we wanted teachers to teach in Navajo, using English only in a limited way. In reviewing our vision, everyone agreed we were asking for what any outsider would consider good instruction.

We divided up and spread throughout the school to observe. I went to Algebra I, a course recently added to the school's curriculum. When I entered the classroom, students were working alone at long rows of desks facing the front of the classroom. The teacher was working at his desk computer. Two problems were written on the board as examples of the steps the students were expected to follow. The topic for the day was rational numbers. I sat in the back of the classroom, apparently unseen by the teacher. After fifteen minutes, a student asked the teacher a question. He moved to the board to work out the problem and quickly moved back to his desk. There was a general "feel" of a traditional math class—math problems on the board, students working individually and quietly on problems in their text. One Navajo boy worked with a white girl on several of the problems. The two Navajo girls in front of me filed their nails, talking and reading Scholastic magazines. The teacher remained seated at his desk for the next twenty minutes.

Almost forty minutes into the class, he noticed the Navajo girls' lack of attention to the math problems, and an absence of calculators. Moving over to them, he said: "Now you know you are supposed to have calculators. Move up front to share with the other students. Get your books together and move up to someone with a calculator." He returned to his desk. The girls stood up from their desks but did not move. Several minutes passed and the bell rang. As I left the room, he came over. "I didn't see you in here. I don't have my lesson plans. I left them at home. But I could go get them for you." I told him not to bother. "The next time I visit I will look at your lesson plans for the year." He didn't smile as he shook my hand.

Moving to another period, I was joined by two of the district administrators. We observed an English enrichment class. On the shelves surrounding the room were stacks of student folders from the last several years. Student manuals and reading text filled several bookcases. The writing on the front board read, "Things to do today—Review KWLS, Work on bib/note cards, Record research reading in logs." All available wall space was filled with posters of American Indians, Navajo stories, and pictures of Monument Valley. Next to the door was a large poster of Navajo values, "The Beauty Way of Living and Learning." A smiling, confident face of a young Navajo woman claimed your attention. There were seven students in the room, three of whom were resting their heads on the large center table. They didn't bother to look up when we entered the room.

Cheerfully, the teacher hurried over to explain the day's activities. She has been the ESL teacher since 1984. I remembered what she had said to me when I had observed her class during my first year of fieldwork, "The students hate me, but they don't mind the classes." Jan, Vangie, and Mary had all passed through her classes. She fumbled in her blouse pocket to find a bathroom pass for a student. "They are working on their level. Each of them has a portfolio. They do research and things, and then record their findings in their log. And then they take a test, on the computers, to see if they can move to the next level." She walked us over to the computers in the center of the next room. "Only eight of the twenty-two computers in this ESL lab are working. But we are working on this." Back in the class, she moved from student to student, bent over them, quietly asking if they needed assistance. Most shook their heads. Few were working on their assignment. If they remained quiet, she moved to the next student. I looked at their papers. I could not describe this as an enrichment class. Short worksheets did little to promote critical thinking or reflective thought. Boring lessons. Bored students. At the end of the evaluation, all of us agreed this class, or "type" of class, was failing students; it was not the other way around. We left this class disturbed. And we had begun with such high hopes.

Right before lunch, I decided to attend a biology class. The lesson was on "living parameter," specifically the pH level of solutions. With a graphic organizer on the board, the teacher explained H_2O, acid, and base. Energetically, but quietly, he moved throughout the class. In an evenly divided class, the Navajo and white students sat side-by-side in the teacher-planned seating chart. Students were attentive as he wove around the classroom. An observer could see youth reaching out to correct a chemical equation on their neighbor's lecture notes, or hear soft verbal exchanges about each other's notes. The air felt comfortable and pleasant. Pre-arranged partners for lab experiments assured face-to-face interactions. During this day there was much laughter and task-engaged behavior. I walked through the classroom during the experiment asking about the class. One Navajo student explained: "It's a fine class. We get along. And he makes this biology real interesting. He teaches us." His white partner grabbed his pencil, "He gives me all the answers!" They both laughed. It was an excellent, well-prepared class that engaged both white and Indian students. I saw engagement in a science lesson that on the surface might be seen as "not connected to Navajo lives." It was excellent instruction, nevertheless. And, isn't this a key issue? I went to lunch with hope.

The hope soon faded. It was a disappointing afternoon. After lunch, a district administrator and I attended an eighth-grade U.S. history class. When we entered, the teacher, who was an American Indian, was sitting on a stool in front of the classroom reading a newspaper. Half of the students had their heads down resting on their desks. The others were quietly reading. No lesson plans were in sight. Seeing us, he turned to the class: "Listen here, in the paper it says, 'Indians urged to support census.' This means you guys should all get counted." A few students moaned. "Okay, let's start." He folded the paper and moved to the front chalkboard. He had written, "Veterans Day: What's it about. Remembrances and Respect." He asked the class, "What is November 11? At 11:00?" No one answered. He persisted, "What's this date?" Several of the students yelled out, "Cool," "Style!" The teacher sighed, looked at us and then back at the class, "It's the 'V' word. Veterans Day," Students again yelled out, "Vegetables," "Veterinarian," "VD." Gentle laughter rolled through the room.

The teacher moved to the back of the room and read from a report stapled to the bulletin board. "This is about the Navajo code talkers. They are credited for winning the war because they used Navajo and none of the Japanese could understand Navajo." This topic was filled with difficult considerations of both the pride in the contribution of Navajo people and of white colonization. I was surprised to see that this did not pique the students' interest. Half of the class still had their heads on their desks.

Ten minutes had passed since the beginning of class. The teacher seemed nervous with our presence. "Ok, let's do this worksheet. Get into your groups." Students slowly turned their desks to form groups of three. The handout had one question, "Why do we have Veterans Day?" with three subsections, "History, Clinton's Letter, and Demographics." He said, "Now the seventh graders wrote almost a page on this assignment, so you should do more." One student responded, with a grin, "Ours is in invisible ink." Several students laughed. "Yea." "For us only." Ignoring this comment, the teacher said loudly, "And this is the day that you should all find a veteran and thank him. For saving our country." Students spent the next thirty minutes thumbing through their 1978 Merrill Publishing Company text, *American History*, for answers to the question. The administrator and I almost fell asleep. When the bell rang, relief showed on the teacher's, as well as the students', faces. Along with the students, we quickly left the class.

I went out of the main building to the temporary trailers, where I found the reading classes. Reading Right was a class required of all students. The bell had just rung, and students were slowly entering the room. Clusters of round tables and chairs filled the room. Nothing covered the light green walls. A large plastic book display case next to the front door stood empty. There were no chalkboards in the room. The teacher was finishing writing the assignment on the freestanding white board. It read: "Mural: Picture painted directly on a wall or ceiling. Intimacy. Silhouette. Curiosity. Spasmodically. Petrified." Students entered the classroom, put their books and notebooks on the tables, and went to pick up their reading folders. The teacher explained: "The folder tells them what level they are at. They go to the library and get a book at their level in the reading series. Then they come here and read it and take a test at that level on the computer."

Everyone knew the routine. Young men with oversized blue jeans and unlaced athletic shoes moved to claim their folders with little interest. Three young women, in blue jeans, sweaters, and athletic jackets, sat comfortably on a couch. They were reading well-worn romance novels. Within the first ten minutes, half the class left to check out books at the library. Several failed to return. The others returned with less than half the period remaining. None seemed to acknowledge either the teacher or the assignment board. By the end of the period, all the students were reading. The class was quiet. The teacher remained at her desk, grading and recording student papers. The class was devoid of interactions between students and the teacher the entire time. The students seemingly passed the time in silence, protectively disconnected from the school around them. I had no confidence this was helping with their reading. Over the past fifteen years, I had seen many reading classes similar to this one. I thought about the "flatline"—little visible improvement—of reading test scores over the past two decades, and I sighed as I left the classroom.

At the end of the day, the committee gathered to talk about our shared observations. In general, we were disappointed with the quality of the teaching we had observed. All the teachers had been told we would be in the school that day, and still many did not have their required lesson plans. Most teachers' in-class instructional time was for only a few minutes during each fifty-minute period we observed. The vast majority of students' time in class was working individually on projects, worksheets, or question assignments from the end of chapters. Attempts at "question and answer" sessions were only marginally successful in most of the classrooms. An overall picture from the discussion of what we had seen showed students sitting unengaged in lessons that were uninteresting and disconnected from their lives. For the most part, they were letting the day pass around them. Life in classrooms could be tolerated, and in a few cases even enjoyed, because of an excellent teacher. Life with friends, however, was good. Nothing seemed to have changed from when Mary was a fourteen-year-old student in her ESL classroom over twenty years ago.

During the four years of monitoring schools and teachers across the district—regardless of their teaching assignment or cultural affiliation—the team saw many wonderful instructional lessons, and many depressing classrooms. Due to the *Sinajini* lawsuit, heritage (Navajo and Ute) language classes were now available to all students, in all grades, in all appropriate schools. Elementary schools required thirty minutes of language instruction in Navajo per day and fifteen minutes of a content area in Navajo per day. Secondary schools offered two levels of Navajo language classes. All English and Navajo teachers became English-as-a-Second Language (ESL) endorsed and certified. Navajo and Ute language teachers were hired at each school site. All the courses needed to get into post-secondary institutions in Utah were now available to Navajo students.

Our intervention to enhance the educational experiences of Navajo youth was not without criticism. With the belief that Navajo language was the pedagogically sound curriculum choice, we designed a curriculum that included Navajo language classes in all schools at all grades. Many Navajo parents supported the program. Some did not, questioning once again the intent of white educators. All of the Navajo parents I knew never believed in the commitment of the white community to treat who they were, and what they said, with justice or respect. History supported their disbelief.

A Voice for San Juan County Navajos
Mark Maryboy, San Juan County Commission

San Juan County Budget Hearing, December 11, 1989

The issue today is fairness. Is it fair that 50 percent of San Juan County's residents receive 5 percent of the county's budget? Is it fair that 50 percent of the county's citizens are denied equal access to the budget process? Is it fair that half of the county lives in terrible poverty, while black gold has flowed from the reservation for thirty-five years?

I was elected to the county commission in 1986 because the U.S. Justice Department ordered a re-districting plan to ensure Navajos a voice in county politics. Navajos are 50 percent of the county's population. Most of my constituents reside on the Utah portion of the Navajo reservation within Utah's richest oil field.

My people are viewed as a minority who do not contribute to the tax base. In fact, we are a majority which has contributed a major portion of the tax base. I have received information which shows that for the past ten years, San Juan County received $140 million in revenue; $28 million came from taxation on the reservation, yet only $7 million was spent for services to reservation residents. In other words, San Juan County spent only 25 percent of reservation revenue for reservation residents and only 5 percent of its total budget for 50 percent of the county residents. In the same ten-year period, non-reservation residents received a benefit of $21 million from taxation on the reservation. . . . I will no longer be silent about the discrimination in the county's budget. I am the voice for San Juan County Navajos in the county budget process. I say all San Juan County citizens must be treated with fairness.

November 2002 was the last monitoring visit by our team. We spent a tense week observing in classrooms, seeing some excellent instruction and many teachers still struggling. At the end of that week, at the "debriefing meeting" usually reserved for our meeting with principals, we were told the school district would no longer allow us into the schools for observations. An administrator moved to the board and wrote two dates: December 7, 1941, and August 8, 1945, and asked us what the dates represented. After a period of silence, he responded, "The beginning and end of World War II." He then wrote April 7, 1997, and that day's date, November 8, 2002. "We have been at this longer than WWII. And now, on January 8, 2002, No Child Left Behind was enacted, and we will have to answer to that. Our new board members do not agree with the consensus plan. We have to move forward, and get this lawsuit behind us to serve the needs of our students." We were presented with the district's new direction, and a letter sent to the U.S. Justice Department was shared with the team. In it we were accused of "burdensome program and process requirements" that were forced on the district by our "high pressure negotiation tactics" and "outlandish interpretations of broad legal requirements" in the original 1997 consensus agreement. Our twice-a-year monitoring visits were "highly intrusive" and resulted in "disruption to our staff and programs." In general, the district argued that the curriculum plan caused an "adverse effect on students." In addition, the district argued that they could not adequately teach the state core curriculum because of the "loss of class periods to obligatory Navajo language classes." At the elementary level, due to "inflexible Navajo language requirements," fine arts, PE, health, science, and social studies programs had suffered. At the secondary level, the district argued they had to "abandon or de-emphasize" Sterling Scholar, the Science Fair, and the Academic Decathlon because of the demands of the monitoring team. In addition, required curriculum and heritage plans were responsible for causing the district to lose several faculty members, and over $200,000 of vocational funding, and made it difficult to recruit teachers. The final assertion stated, "The plan requirements and the monitoring activities are impeding our ability to respond to the No Child Left Behind legislation."[9]

We received a new Language Development and Curriculum Plan—a plan we called the "non-consensus plan." This plan moved Navajo language from a required curriculum offering at each southern school (majority Navajo schools) to one that would be optional, dependent on an adequate number of students registering for the class. In a district that had a history of reducing Navajo teachers and Navajo language and culture classes, this was an ominous echo of the past. The full circle put us back where Navajo language and culture were seen as frills capable of being deleted during times of budget tightening or when more time was needed for PE, health, technology, social studies, or extracurricular activities.

During the 2003–4 academic school year, the San Juan School District and the Navajo Nation again came to a consensus over the revisions of our original plan. In the final plan, at the unwavering insistence of the Navajo Nation, Navajo language was again a mandatory district-wide course offering. Monitoring efforts in the district, however, were narrowed to evaluations that only focused on Navajo language and culture teachers. These Navajo teachers now bore the brunt of the workload required to continue the curriculum changes. This shift of surveillance—removing white teachers and 95 percent of district classrooms from evaluations—also created a transparent place for Navajo teachers in schools; teachers could be "looked at" to see what kind of "Indian" they were presenting in classroom. "It makes me so nervous when you would come in with that team," Carol had told me. "Navajo teachers were being judged on how good we teach Navajo, and those white teachers sit in their classroom and do nothing. I know our clans, but the language is a challenge to teach when you don't have materials."

The success or failure of the reform efforts centered on the least powerful educators—Navajo teachers—in the district. In effect, school officials and non-Native teachers could continue with a vision that rendered Navajo youth invisible beyond language and culture classes. The imagined Indian again took center stage, shadowing a critical Native presence.

Growing Up

"I'm a Modern Indian"

"I consider myself a modern Indian," Mary told me during an interview in Blanding on September 18, 1987. "And my mom is half and half. Part traditional and part modern. And my grandparents were traditional." We were sitting in the small town park having lunch with her two-year-old son. We talked about music and concerts; she was no longer listening to heavy metal; it was still Jim's favorite music. Our conversation continually returned to "being Navajo" in a predominately white community. "I just think of myself as an Indian. I don't really think of myself as a Navajo. I'm not saying that I'm not a Navajo, but I just call myself an Indian because I don't know the language." She pulled her little boy into her arms, gave him a hug, and smiled. "We are all human, you know. Because I don't understand all about the ceremonies, I'm not traditional. I'm a modern Indian." She paused. "I had my Kinaaldá. You live up here in Blanding, and then you go down there and it is all in the Navajo language. I don't really talk Navajo. Just mainly English." I confessed that I had been totally unsuccessful learning Navajo. "Yeah, it's hard. My grandma just barely spoke English. My grandpa just a little bit. But when you talk in English in front of him he kind of understands." Several young Navajo women pushing strollers passed us and waved. "That's Wanda. She has a baby Jeff's age. In the future I would like someone teaching my children different kinds of traditions. Wanda is doing that. I wouldn't mind letting them talk in Navajo or Ute either." When she spoke of her children's future, her words echoed the desires of many of the Navajo youth I had come to know. "I want to have a nice home, furniture. Nice vehicle. Have the best for my kids. Let them come up with nice things, go to a good school, live in a good area. I want my kids to know about Navajo stories and ceremonies. That is who they are. I would like that. Not only for my kids, but for all Native American kids to know who they are."

99 THINGS TO DO BEFORE YOU DIE
By Nila Northsun

cosmo mag came out with a list
of 99 things to do before you die
i had done 47 of them
or at least my version of them like make love on the forest floor
spend a day in bed reading a good book
sleep under the stars
learn not to say yes when you mean no
but the other things
were things only rich people could do
and we certainly know
we don't have to be rich before you die
things like
dive off a yacht in the aegean
buy a round-the-world air ticket
go to monaco for the grand prix
go to rio during carnival
sure would love to but
no maza-ska
money honey
so what's a poor indian to do?
my list included
go 49ing at crow fair
learn of 20 ways to prepare
    commodity canned pork
fall in love with a white person
fall in love with an indian
eat ta-nee-ga with a sioux
learn to make good fry bread
be an extra in an indian movie
learn to speak your language
give your gramma a rose and a bundle
    of sweet grass
watch a miwok deer dance
attend a hopi kachina dance
owl dance with a yakama
curl up in bed with a good indian novel

better yet
curl up in bed with a good indian novelist
ride bareback and leap over a small creek
make love in a tipi
count coup on an enemy
bathe not swim in a lake or river
wash your hair too and don't forget your pits
stop drinking alcohol
tell skin walker stories by a campfire
almost die then appreciate your life
help somebody who has it worse than you
donate canned goods to a local food bank
sponsor a child for christmas
bet on a stick game
participate in a protest
learn a song to sing in a sweat
recycle
grow a garden
say something nice everyday to
     your mate
say something nice everyday to
     your children
chop wood for your grandpa
so there
a more attainable list
at this rate
i'm ready to die anytime
not much left undone
though cosmo's
have an affair in paris while
discoing in red leather and sipping champagne
could find a place on my list.[10]

There was a knock on the door of my motel room. I opened the door and saw no one. Puzzled, I started to close the door when Mary bounded out from around the corner with a broad grin. We both laughed and hugged. It had been four years since I had last seen her. She still had the same slight figure and long shiny dark hair as when we had first meet in 1984. It was now the fall of 2004, and she had come to my room to talk about her chapter. We settled around the small wooden table, and as I turned on the tape recorder, the first words Mary uttered were about her sons. Her oldest had just graduated from high school. "My middle one lives with my aunt on the reservation, and he knows about the language and lifestyle, how it is not to have electricity or water. He speaks Navajo. My youngest is a real good Yeíbicheii dancer; he learned this in elementary school. My oldest has to have his electricity and his water running 'cause that's a lifestyle that he knew all these years. He sings hip-hop. He and his friends have a CD out. They are real good, and they talk about the stuff they had to go through with those Anglos in school." She smiled as she handed me a picture of her youngest. "And then my smallest in middle school. I think he's kind of in-between. He has to have his Xbox, video, or TV. But he can rough it out there in the reservation by being dirty and doing whatever he wants without taking showers." She paused before she continued. "He doesn't know much Navajo. But he wants to be a powwow dancer. He wants to be a traditional men's dancer with the huge bustle of eagle feathers. I think he likes it because of how graceful an eagle is."

I asked Mary to talk about youths' experiences growing up in the community today.

> Nowadays? It's like until a few years ago they didn't want to be Navajo; they wanted to be a different kind of minority like Mexican, black, or something else, but now there are all of these logos on tee shirts and bumper stickers saying 'Stay Native' and 'Be Proud of Who You Are.' Like the Navajo code talkers in films and Tony Hillerman books gave young people a lot of respect for those guys that fought in the war, and it seems like they're more proud of who they are, and they're Native and they're Navajos.

In an interview the day before, Mary's oldest son, who was eighteen, had spoken very similar words.

> In the past, some Navajo were ignoring who they were. They were pretending to be like other minorities. Not Navajos. They were like into gangs like some minorities are into. We are more into like 'Native Pride,' 'Be Native.' They sell those kind of tee shirts in that magazine, Native Peoples. We are into being proud of who we are like other Indian people around the country.

Towards the end of our interview, Mary switched to reflect on her own sense of identity. "Back then, when you interviewed me when I was fifteen, I talked like I didn't care about being a Navajo. I was still in the teenage world." She shook her head and sighed. "So now I'm thirty-five years old, and I'm proud of who I am and where I come from. I'm glad I got to experience how to speak some Navajo, and my mom really pushed knowing your clans, which is very important." She smiled when she spoke of her mother's teachings. "She did that to me because she wants me to say that to my kids when they grow up so it won't die. I was just a young teenager thinking I knew it all." She then spoke excitedly about her youngest son's middle school experiences with the new Navajo language and culture teacher. Coyote (re)emerged in his teenage world.

> My son has a bilingual teacher, and he tells me all these traditions about the Navajo, like what are do's and don'ts. One day I ran over a coyote. It was like one hundred yards from where I was driving. It ran across from the east to the west and then back to the east, and it circled around. I thought, 'What the heck's going on?' I honked my horn and that critter wouldn't leave, and then it went under the truck and I ran it over. My son goes, 'Why did you do that? Now we are going to have bad luck.' And I was like, 'You think so? ' 'Yeah, that's what my teacher told me. If a coyote crosses your path, according to which way it goes, it tells you a story behind it, and you have to do your corn pollen and pray and go see a medicine man to remove the hex.' I told my sister-in-law about what happened, and she told me it was a fox and not a coyote so I didn't have anything to worry about. But I even had to ask a friend about it because I didn't know, and he said the same as my son. He goes, 'If you run over it, the coyote committed suicide because he didn't know which way to go to either. Listen to the sender, whoever sent that coyote out to get you. Or else he's like in a place where he can't do what the sender's telling him to do. But you just had no choice but to run him over. So when you do that, it's like an automatic, um, freedom for him, cause he made the right choice. I guess in a way that way the hex won't work on you.'

Living on the reservation for Mary and her sons meant moving into a landscape where learning what is or is not appropriate behavior occurred daily. In this context, "city Navajos" were not at an advantage. Having a softer context growing up made for an ease that almost cheated oneself from the pleasures of a tough and meaningful life. As Mary explained, they were called "cheap Indian"—a phrase implying inauthentic, not expensive, low status.

Like if you live on the reservation, you're more proud of who you are because of the things you got taught by your grandmother, grandfather, or aunts or uncles, mother, and father. But in the city, it's like there wasn't much teaching. You just get up, take a shower, everything was there for you when you needed it. You just live like anybody. You know what I mean? You're spoiled. And that's how we got looked at when we lived in town by some of my friends that lived across the river. They didn't have what we had; even though we were up there, they looked down on us. 'You guys are too cheap to go out and get water and use it for a bath and wash dishes,' they would kind of come down on us, and 'You guys can't live without electricity, you always have to have that, you guys are cheap Indians.' They called us 'cheap Indians' because we lived in town and they lived on the reservation.

"My middle son, he can talk in Navajo pretty good," Mary said with pride. Discussions over the years about life in the community always revealed the ideal of speaking the Navajo language, even if the person was a non-Navajo speaker. Mary spoke of her family's efforts to use Navajo in their home.

They don't use Navajo very much because in our household we're speaking English all the time. Two or three years ago we would have a 'Navajo night.' Me and my mom, we'd go, 'Okay, it's Navajo night; you can't talk in English. Everything you hear is going to be in Navajo, so if you can't speak it or hear it, don't even talk at all.' [chuckling] We tried it for almost a month; it was hard. But, my little one, he can understand Navajo, and he's twelve years old! Not very many twelve-year-olds can understand Navajo.

This brought forth a set of admonishments Mary felt from her grandmother. "My grandmother would get mad at us; in Navajo, she'd say, 'What's wrong with you? You're a Navajo but you don't even understand Navajo. You need to talk it.' And she'd get after her daughters. This is how my mom has also helped me. She would tell me, 'You need to talk to your kids in Navajo all the time; that's the only way they will learn their Navajo language. Or, they just act like they're like white people.'" That last bit of advice was important to Mary, and she pulled her son's schools into the task of following this advice. "My youngest has been in school in Bluff, and he has learned a lot from his bilingual teacher. This has helped him learn his Navajo. And he has learned a lot from his paternal grandparents. A real bilingual program will get more kids involved with Navajo."

OUR TONGUES SLAPPED INTO SILENCE
by Laura Tohe

In first grade I was five years old, the youngest and smallest in my class, always the one in front at group picture time. The principal put me in first grade because I spoke both Diné and English. Because of that, I skipped beginner class.

All my classmates were Diné, and most of them spoke only the language of our ancestors. During this time, the government's policy meant to assimilate us into the white way of life. We had no choice in the matter; we had to comply. The taking of our language was a priority.

DICK AND JANE SUBDUE THE DINÉ

See Father.
See Mother
See Dick run.
See Jane and Sally laugh.
    oh, oh, oh,
See Spot jump.
    oh, oh, oh,
See Eugene speak Diné
See Juanita answer him.
    oh, oh, oh,
See teacher frown,
    uh oh, uh oh

In first grade, our first introduction to Indian school was Miss Rolands, a black woman from Texas, who treated us the way her people had been treated by white people. Later, I learned how difficult it was for black teachers to find jobs in their communities, so they took jobs with the Bureau of Indian Affairs in New Mexico and Arizona in the 1950s and 1960s.

Miss Rolands found it difficult to adjust to living in a mostly Diné community, connected to the outside world by only a dirt road that was sometimes impassable in the winter.

See Eugene with red hands, shape of ruler.
   oh, oh, oh
See Eugene cry.
   oh, oh, oh
See Juanita stand in corner, see tears fall down face.
   oh, oh, oh

In first grade, we received the first of our Dick and Jane books that introduced us to the white man's world through Father, Mother, Dick, Jane, Puff, and Spot. These and other characters said and did what we thought all white people did: drive cars to the farm, drain maple juice from trees, and say oh, oh, oh a lot.

Oh see us draw pictures
   of brown horses under blue clouds.
We color eyes black, hair black.
We draw ears and leave out mouth.

   Oh see, see, see, see.

Miss Rolands, an alien in our world, stood us in the corner of the classroom or outside in the hallway to feel shame for the crime of speaking Diné. Other times, our hands were imprinted with red slaps from the ruler. In later classes, we headed straight for the rear of the classrooms, never asked questions, and never raised our hand. Utter one word of Diné, and the government made sure our tongues were drowned in the murky waters of assimilation.[11]

Balancing Faith and Healing:
Linking Mothers and Daughters

"My religion would be Episcopalian and traditional," Mary told me during an interview in the fall of 2004. "I started going out to the mission in 1998 because they don't conflict with your traditions like the Pentecostal church. In that church you have to get rid of your traditions so that you can be more at peace with God, but the Episcopalians believe in the word of the Lord and also they believe in the traditional." The challenge over control of the Navajo body moved from break dancing, to Yeíbicheii and heavy metal, and to Episcopalian, Evangelical, and Navajo beliefs of being on the landscape. The place in which she was now grounded located her at St. Christopher's Mission. She could be Navajo there, like her mother, who was pictured, along with Jan Begay's father Ernie, in a late 1940s picture in front of the mission titled, "A group from first school."

Mary's spiritual journey was strengthened at a revival with her mother in 2001. "I was having trouble with my stupid man again and was depressed. My mom started watching this religious TV show called Benny Hinn. And the next thing you know I was sitting down watching it too, and it made me feel good." Within a week, Mary and Carol decided to travel to Las Vegas for one of his revivals at a large stadium. "It was breathtaking, hearing about the word of the Lord and the Bible. It was a healing ceremony; that's why we went down. Because my mom had problems with her body too." She stretched out her hands. "Because I'm a beader and a pottery painter I have problems with my hands. I think I might have early carpal tunnel syndrome, and so I thought maybe my hands will get healed." Her face lit up with a broad smile. "He was a really powerful man. And at the end he prayed that if anybody had health problems and believed in the Lord they would be healed. And, you know, on the way back to the motel my hand stopped hurting. It was pretty awesome."

I reflected back on the first summer I spent with Jan Begay and her family. Hand-painted signs identifying the locations of Christian revivals were sprinkled throughout the northern portion of the Navajo Nation. One day, a sign for a Pentecostal revival appeared on a dirt intersection near the Begays' home. Jan asked me if I would like to attend. "We could go over there tonight," she had said. "I have never been to one, and us Navajos don't know if we believe that stuff. But I'm curious." I, too, had never been to a revival, and I quickly agreed to join her. The walk was a little over a mile, and when we arrived, about a dozen people were moving under the white tent to take their places on the metal folding chairs. Jan and I took seats in the back. Over the course of the next two hours the crowd grew to almost fifty people. A few of the older women wore skirts and blouses of crushed velveteen adorned with silver buttons; most women wore slacks and collared blouses. Men were modestly dressed in western shirts and blue jeans. Very few teenagers or children attended the event. Two preachers, one white and one Navajo, from the Born Again Church of Christ led the audience in prayers and songs. The different movements of bodies struck me. The few white people lifted their hands high in the air as they sang with eyes shut, heads tilted upward, and bodies moving sideways. Most of the Navajos sang and prayed with arms bent lightly at their sides, hands facing sky forward, heads slightly bent forward, and bodies moving like a slight breeze. Jan and I talked about these differences. "Like, I think it is because that is how you act when you do traditional ceremonies. Quiet like. It's how you show respect. I don't know if everybody can give that up, even when you are in a church meeting like this."

After Mary's healing ceremony in Las Vegas, she decided to make some significant changes in her life. She had worked as a substitute teacher for a year in the school her mother taught at, and was then hired as a preschool aide. "I got that job and was working with the preschool program for two years, and that's when President Bush came in with that license you had to have because of No Child Left Behind." The teachers praised her teaching abilities, but without certification, she could not continue working at the school. A hard worker, she returned to beadwork, painting pottery, and part-time housekeeping work at $5.95 an hour to support her household. "I want to go back to school, move out of Bluff. I have looked into it, and they are building a new hospital at Red Mesa. I figure they will need dental assistants. So that is what I am going to study. Then I can make a better life for me and my son. And move back home." Several weeks after our last interview, Mary moved with her son to the city, and applied to the local community college.

Mary ended our conversation with advice for young Navajos. She was mindful of her own choices. "I think even though I messed up when I was young, dropped out of school and had kids, there's still a chance for other young people to better themselves by getting an education and going away to college to become something." She laughed: "Instead of being a baby machine! Write that down for the book! Not just staying home and taking a bunch of shit from your old man who is drinking and running around." She paused:

> Nobody deserves something like that. You can be a better person seeing what the world can offer you while you're single. Nowadays it's like a lot of young people just wanna hurry up and get into a relationship, like 'jumping in the sack' and think it's love when it's just lust. You can write that too! By better person I mean you can be away from home for a short time becoming something, getting a job, and helping your own people.

PERHAPS THE WORLD ENDS HERE
By Joy Harjo

The world begins at a kitchen table. No matter what,
we must eat to live.

The gifts of earth are brought and prepared, set on the
table. So it has been since creation, and it will go on.

We chase chickens or dogs away from it. Babies teethe
at the corners. They scrape their knees under it.

It is here that children are given instructions on what
it means to be human. We make men at it,
we make women.

At this table we gossip, recall enemies and the ghosts
of lovers.

Our dreams drink coffee with us as they put their arms
around our children. They laugh with us at our poor
falling-down selves and as we put ourselves back
together once again at the table.

This table has been a house in the rain, an umbrella
in the sun.

Wars have begun and ended at this table. It is a place
to hide in the shadow of terror. A place to celebrate
the terrible victory.

We have given birth on this table, and have prepared
our parents for burial here.

At this table we sing with joy, with sorrow.
We pray of suffering and remorse.
We give thanks.

Perhaps the world will end at the kitchen table,
while we are laughing and crying,
eating of the last sweet bite.[12]

I pulled up to Carol's and Mary's homes on the west side of Bluff.
Several well-fed, mixed-breed dogs bounded off the wooded porch,
moving through the dust cloud, to intercept me as I stepped out of my
car. I paused to wait to be greeted. Mary's old trailer was moved to Bluff

when Mary and her sons left her husband's family home on the reservation. Sitting perched on cinder blocks, next to Mary's double-wide trailer, mother's and daughter's homes were almost touching. I turned to look south to the San Juan River and was filled with the view Mary and Carol faced every day they opened their doors: lush cottonwood trees lined the light brown river, the main source of water in this arid semi-desert landscape, and soaring red buttes marked the northern boundary of the Navajo reservation. Wild turkeys, reintroduced in Bluff by students from the elementary school, scurried through the tamarisks along the riverbanks. An occasional blue heron could be seen in flight against the red sandstone cliff walls. Twenty miles across the river was Mary's grandparents' home and grazing area.

We settled into chairs around the kitchen table. The surrounding walls were full of family photographs. Sons, daughters, and grandchildren in graduation photographs from Head Start, elementary school, and high school were interspersed with group photographs of the family. Patterns of Navajo designs intermingled on pillows, chairs, wall designs, and coffee cups. The air smelled of warm comfort from the roast in the oven. The Sunday dinner would gather the family together for a claimed moment before people moved away to the week's work schedules.

The most exciting news was Jeff's high school graduation. Two rolls of film captured the happy event: three buddies with arms around each other beaming to the camera; Jeff in his cap and gown holding his diploma; Mary and Carol smiling next to Jeff. "It was a real good graduation. The family was there. And his friends. He was real happy to graduate," said Mary softly and proudly. I asked what he was going to do next. "He is going to Salt Lake City. With his uncle in West Valley. To hunt for a job. There is nothing here for him. So he wants to try to find work in the city." Carol nodded and added, "A lot of the kids leave here. There is not much here because of the way Indians are treated." The conversation turned from Jeff's graduation to race relations in the county. "It's all the same. The same as it was twenty years ago. They [whites] think they have changed, but it is the same." Carol sighed. "They are all so prejudiced. You have been coming down here for twenty years, Donna, and it's the same. You saw what they did to my kids, and now they are doing it to my grandkids. It's all the same." We talked about the lawsuit and the struggles still facing Navajo youth. "My grandson said the teacher told him no Navajos get As. What does he mean by that! It's that Navajos are no good. They can never get As," she said bitterly. I remembered the school district's attempts to make sure no student in the district would receive a failing grade. Rather then giving a student an F, teachers gave NGs, for "no grade," to encourage the student to redo assignments and retake tests rather than accept failing grades. Students called the NGs, "Navajo grades."

The delicious smells and warmth from the oven drew our attention to supper. Carol stood up from the kitchen table and moved to the stove to prepare tea. "It's Navajo tea. My mother taught me how to gather the tops just at the right time. And then dry it." She handed me a small, lightly fragrant brown-green bundle of the tea. "You can take that home. You won't be able to buy it at Smith's grocery store," she said, laughing. "And they call this Mormon tea, those white. I don't know why they call it that! We know what it is, and it is Navajo tea." She returned to the table with large mugs filled with the steaming brew. It was delicious. As we ate roast, steamed corn on the cob, fry bread, and green salad, we continued to talk about our families, work, life, and play—and gossiped just a bit.

Epilogue

Sheepherders on the Landscape

Doing Research

I started my research as a stranger to both the school and home communities of these young Navajo women. As I moved in and out of the field site over the past twenty-five years, I have assumed different roles with different groups of people. Some of these roles overlapped. Others conflicted directly with each other. Teachers, administrators, political leaders, parents, students, and community members answered my endless questions within the context of formal interviews and casual conversations throughout this time. When my work was focused on the study of the high schools, I became involved in extracurricular school activities, including athletic games, plays, dances, and carnivals, and "hanging out" at local fast food restaurants. I attended school and community meetings with Navajo parents, and was invited to participate in discussions to help develop strategies to intervene in school district decisions, such as disciplinary codes, attendance regulations, bussing schedules, equal band equipment, and bilingual education. I trained teachers in University of Utah graduate courses, and I became involved in the *Sinajini et al.* lawsuit against the school district. From the beginning, my role has shifted back and forth between that of friend, participant, observer, scapegoat, outside expert, "Indian lover," foe, and sheepherder.

When I first started my fieldwork, I began herding sheep with Jan Begay and her sister and brothers. It seemed a natural context in which to spend time with them and see what their life was like out of school. Herding sheep was their job. We had rich and pleasant talks, but were always eager to escape the relentless sun and return to the shade of their mobile home and the background hum of the television. I was not taken seriously as a sheepherder, and my efforts were greeted with points of laughter that would last for decades. Relatives asked continually, "Was she crying out in pain? Was she tired from all the hard work?" followed by gentle laughter. At my wedding, Ernie teased: "Donna was in our family. She hasn't been herding sheep, so we wondered where she was, so we came to find her and we ended up here at her wedding." My colleagues and family laughed heartily. And district educators countered me with, "I need to start herding sheep to be a real researcher like Donna." The oddness of my role as a sheepherder has provided grounds for either humor, wonder, distrust, admiration, or insanity for almost everyone I have known. The outsider putting on the sheepherder's clothing never works as a disguise.

On the other hand, growing up around the community involved serious sheepherding responsibilities for Jan, Vangie, and Mary. They, too, spoke of the performance of sheepherding as what "traditional" Navajos did. Sheep had been, and still were, a part of their lives. In a trading post one afternoon after school, Jan had picked up a postcard of a Navajo woman herding sheep. "Take that one," she had told me. "It is a real traditional example of Navajos. But my mom and her sister use the truck for some herding." She had winked and said, "But I don't see any white people doing this." Over the years, sheep herds decreased, then increased, then decreased again—but never vanished. Elizabeth, Jan's mother, once told me: "We have very few sheep left. We go away to the city for work, and they die without us. But we can never leave them. They are my mother." Jan, Vangie, and Mary became young women either away from the landscape dotted with sheep, or living on the reservation with children of their own, assuming the responsibilities of herding the family's sheep and goats. Over the years, my talks with all of these women have been sprinkled with memories of herding sheep. A symbol on a postcard capturing a manifest manners portrait of "traditional practices" can be used by youth with a Native gaze to reinscribe and claim a way of being Navajo. Even as youth and their parents travel in pickup trucks to herd sheep, and in sports cars as they move across the landscape, the gentle and persistent ties to place work on young Navajos.

Early in the fieldwork, I systematically asked youth what they knew about Navajo ceremonies, and deities, such as Changing Woman, First Woman, Spider Woman, and Salt Woman. I remembered being disappointed when youth responded vaguely about the importance of Navajo culture, but with little detailed knowledge. In my notes from 1984, I wrote: "Oh, no! They know so little. It is true that much of Navajo culture is being lost. They say they don't talk much with their grandparents because they don't speak Navajo. They seem to have lost so much." My (mis)perspective represents a consistent stereotype and misunderstanding of what being Navajo is all about, as well as my own manifest manners when I had frozen their images in an unchanged frame of history to then be judged authentic or real. I had ignored what I knew intuitively had been my own experiences growing up. As one travels complex and messy life paths, one is always learning and becoming—one never completely "arrives."

I started the writing of this book with concerns of (mis)representations of Navajo youth in educational discourses as well as in ethnographic texts. I end with similar concerns. At points, I found myself sliding into yet another romanticized portrait of Navajo peoples in my text. At other points, my representations seemed harsh and critical—or at least narrow—of youth who were producing new ways of being Navajo. As I tried to peel back the layers of history, race relations, contested landscapes, and educational experiences to understand their stories, I saw how historical memories lightly clung to their skin and shaped their practices of "being Navajo."

In the beginning, I had intended to write a more traditional educational ethnography with chapters clustered around the research findings, such as chapters on schools, communities, jobs, and families. This changed through my relationships with Jan, Vangie, and Mary who helped me see these categories as lived and historicized experiences that can only be understood when we look at their daily lives on and off the landscape of the Navajo Nation. They chose to have their lives presented as stories, rather than interweaving their stories together along topic or theoretical themes. As Vangie said, "My life is whole, so I want my story to also be whole."

During the past three years, we have worked together in the thinking and writing of each of their stories. This began with their reading of my interviews with them, from as early as 1984, and has continued with their reading of not one but two drafts of this book. We had line-by-line discussions of their individual stories, but they chose not to talk about each other's stories, for, as Jan said, "I don't know their lives so I shouldn't speak of them." They were delighted with my stories of their experiences, but also had suggestions for changes. Things started sliding off the pages. Some were embarrassed by their youthful actions, so we worked to soften the image in the text or eliminate painful events. Others were sensitive to the use of labels, such as "traditional" or "modern," which did not reflect who they were. And, all three spoke with amazement and pride at their accomplishments, specifically their families, as they traced the growing complexity of their identities as Navajo women over the past twenty-five years.

Highly problematic were the names I had given them. "Too boring," said Elizabeth, who asked that middle names be used in Jan's chapter. "Even if people know me, I want to say this is mine." Vangie's daughter wanted a name change for a different reason, "I want to be called Piper. She is a witch on the TV show *Charmed* that fights demons." Even though I had used different names in my past publications, without hesitation I made these changes. By claiming a family name, a name from a Japanese comic, a name that sounded soft and pleasant, or rejecting a last name that, although common throughout the Navajo Nation, was connected to a local family with a problematic reputation, these women asserted their Native presence. I hope that what has slid off the pages has been replaced with a richer and more respectful presence.

The Final Words

Reflections from a Navajo Presence

The sky was a crisp blue with temperatures just below freezing—making the deep mud a swimming rather than sinking adventure—when I drove to Vangie's in-laws' home on the Navajo Nation in December 2007. We settled into the kitchen of the spacious trailer, began preparing meatloaf for Gordon's father's birthday dinner, and talked about her decision to return home. "The main thing was to help my mom. Over at her house, about an hour and a half away, she has running water but no electricity. We do the laundry. I'm glad I came back. Since my dad passed she needs our help." She pointed to a Navajo basket hanging on the wall. "My mom is weaving baskets now. She needs three to have the ceremony." I asked her to explain. "It is a Navajo tradition. It is to keep the spirit from coming back. To block it off. My sister passed. And my dad passed. The ceremony is really to release their spirit." Like so many times in the past, noticing my wrinkled forehead, she continued. "It is for the whole family. But she is head of the household so the ceremony is for her. It is her blood that runs through all of us. So it helps us, the family, too." Piper was also a reason for returning home. "I want her to understand herself and her culture. I want her to live here. And to talk Navajo." Shaking her head gently, she exclaimed, "She only knows how to say 'hi' and 'bye!' But she is learning a lot from my mom. My mom teaches her. Piper really likes school. I tell her to do real good, for her future." She stopped, looked at me, and grinned. "I tell her, 'I want a good nursing home!'" We both laughed. Piper's plans differed from her mom's. "She wants to move back to the city. 'Cause I think she grew up in the city. But, when she gets older, she might realize how good it is to live here. And, like it here."

I asked Vangie what she wanted people to learn from her story. She took a long time before responding. "That it is a whole different world. White people wouldn't know what to do. The nearest store is about fifteen miles away. They don't know about our lives." There was another pause, and she continued. "Money. It is an issue. You see it everyday on the TV. You are selling yourself for this. Buying things. Getting new cars. The elders are talking about getting our horses back. But, we still need the cars to go to the store to get the hay to feed the horses!" She shook her head at the impossibility of returning to life as it was one hundred years ago, smiled, and asserted: "I really want to stay here. But the only thing I miss is all of the fast food restaurants I see on TV. You can't have Pizza Hut delivered way out here!" Teasingly, I questioned, "Changing Woman misses Taco Bell?" She grinned, "Yeah, I do miss that."

During that same visit to southeastern Utah, I was able to spend time with Jan and her family. As I drove to their home, I thought of the support and friendship they have offered me through these years. On the way, I stopped at the Begays' family cemetery. Ernie's grave was covered with bright plastic flowers. I smiled at the care and love given to this place, and cried for a lost friend. As I left, I straightened a small flag bent by the windswept mesa.

I was lucky, and found Elizabeth and two, of her now twenty-two, grandchildren at home. The afternoon was full of chatter and laughter as we caught up with the past several years. "Ernie would have loved the book," Elizabeth assured me. "And excited to have our book in the trading post out here. This way my grandkids will know about our life. What it was to be Navajo back then. All those hard days out herding sheep!" Elizabeth laughed. Elizabeth seemed tired, caring for two preschool children, but proud of her family. "Everyone came home for Thanksgiving. Everyone." We walked out to the hooghan Ernie and his children had built. "We put a long table around here," she said with a brush of her hand around the centrally placed wood-burning stove. "We put a tablecloth out, and candles lit all around the hooghan. We had wine, turkey, mashed potatoes, and salad. And pie. It was real beautiful. We were all together." I had no problem imaging the beauty of that night.

Home from for a weekend from a work site, Jan and I got together the next day for a final interview. I asked her, first, how she felt about having a book about her life. "I think it's kinda neat! My dad would have been very happy with our story. When I read it, I was like, oh my gosh, I'm always moving to a job! And I then had to go back to LA for another job, but I told my mom, 'I'll be back. Be patient.'" I want to live here," Jan had said firmly. "I want my foundation to be here."

During the last two years Jan worked as a pipe fitter's helper, safety inspector, and welder in work sites from California, to Oregon, Nevada, Colorado, New Mexico, Wyoming, and Utah. She specialized in sub-contract work at industrial plants undergoing safety two–three-week shutdowns. Her wages vary from $19.75 to $28 per hour, with $75 to $100 a day for food and lodging. Jan's four children stayed with Eliza-beth. "When my dad passed away, I had to work to pay for all of this. I give my mom half of my check to take care of her needs. I buy her food. And she takes care of my kids. That's how we all make it with help-ing each other." There were, however, struggles with Navajo neighbors over Ernie's grazing permit, and work accidents. "I think there is some witchcraft going on. Because I had a coyote come close to me at work. I wasn't paying attention, and I had an accident. Sometimes a coyote can be a messenger of when bad things are going to happen. So I guess that is what he was trying to warn me." Paying attention to traditional knowledge helps in daily living.

I asked Jan to reflect on her life. With little hesitation, she spoke about the importance of family and her excitement for her children's developing lives. "My kids are doing well," she said with a broad smile. "The girls had their Kinaaldá. It was beautiful. Everything was good. They loved it. And they dance traditional. Their grandma is where they are learning things. They go to fairs, and hang out around Navajos. That's where they get to hang out with their relatives and friends. And, she encourages them to go to ceremonies. They know a lot." Jan is par-ticularly proud of her daughter's visions for their futures. "They are both learning a little Navajo. Tosha wants to be a designer of Native clothes. And Tisah wants to go into computers. They don't go to break-dance, or hip-hop. But they do like Navajo comedians." Jan works hard to provide for her children. "They need access to the Internet. To talk to the world. And, they do love to download music and play video games. With a better job, I'm going to get them wireless Internet here at home." And, as always, she spoke of the struggle to position her children to attend good schools. "My daughters are into track and volleyball. They like competing with those whites. But they are not doing too good in school. They are in a weak school down here. I'm waiting to see what is happening this year in school. We might have to move to Flagstaff. But, not far. I want to be near my mother."

Jan also spoke about the enduring racism she faced almost daily in San Juan County. "When I was young I used to think, 'I can do it. I can do it.' But it is hard. Life is hard. Learning the Navajo traditions and being around the white people is really hard." Jan surprised me when she put her head in her hands, and took a pained breath. She looked directly at me. "It makes you feel uncomfortable. That was what it was like growing up. 'Who are you?' 'We don't want you here.' My mom and I are going up to Blanding to do our laundry today, and I know that I will run into someone who will treat me like crap. It has always been that way." After a reflective pause, she continued: "When I am out there [work sites out-of-state], I get respect. But here it is like they don't want you to have anything. They don't understand you. They push you away. Or, push you down." Jan looked at me, sighed, and shook her head. "Here it is all negative. Because of race relations. I feel like, why did they come here if they don't like Navajo people?"

Mary and her three sons moved from Bluff to a small town almost three hundred miles south of Salt Lake City in 2004. In the spring of 2008, I drove to her urban apartment for our last interview. I thought of those early days in 1984 when I moved across the street from her home in Blanding and had attended her classes, spent long hours talking after school, and watched break-dancing performances and movies together. I would soon learn that my fond memories were not always shared. I asked how she felt about having her story in this book. She paused slightly. "Kind of excited, and also bashful. Because of the things I did when I was young. Like break dancing! And having a baby. I was thinking, geez, how stupid can I be?" She laughed. "But I'm glad I have my kids; 22, 21, almost 16, and one year."

Her two oldest sons shared a two-bedroom apartment a few minutes away, and worked for the same contractor during the past two years installing insulation. "He's a white guy and he is real good to us," said Jeff. His brother agreed. When they weren't working, they spent time playing music and enjoying the time with their girlfriends. Her other son, still in high school, was a critical reason to move to this small town. "I moved to the city because I wanted my son to have a different lifestyle. To be around people other than his relatives and to get away from some of those bad friends' influences in San Juan." She had also moved here as a possible site to continue her professional training. "I came to go into a dental assistant program, so I could get a job back at the new hospital they are building at Red Mesa, or to go into counseling to help young Indian teenagers with their problems. I now have had to wait a bit, because of my new baby, but I'm still going to pursue my dreams, no matter what." In the meantime, Mary brings income into the family by working part-time cleaning and preparing apartments for new renters in the complex where they lived. She liked the woman she worked for and felt trusted and respected. "I have the master key to this whole place," she said as she led me to the complex's conference rooms for our interview, opened the door, and we settled into comfortable chairs.

As in with my conversations with Jan and Vangie, I asked Mary to reflect on her life growing up as a young Navajo woman. Her first words were, laughingly, "I wish I never lived in San Juan County! I'm just kidding," she quickly inserted. "When I think back on it and think about schools, I wish those teachers had helped us Native American kids. With our work. Not to ignore us. Not to be ignorant. And what I hear now, from relatives, is that it is still going on! It is so sad." This led us to talk about some disturbing experiences Indian students were having. "I hear that teachers say to kids in the hall, 'Speak English. Not Navajo.' That is ridiculous! It's because they don't like the Navajo students, and it's because those teachers don't understand Navajo, and they are afraid the kids are talking about them." I found myself grinning as Mary confirmed the teachers' fears. "Remember that Old Crow guy? It was like that." I had no problem remembering the critical gaze the students used to mock their vice principal, who had a rather prominent nose, and whom they judged as uncaring and non-relevant to their lives. Mary was clear about who she was. "Me, personally, I like being a Indian person. Because it reflects a lot about my generation, my heritage, and my traditions. And that I owe to the influence of my grandfather and my mother."

As she spoke about her sons, their relationships with their grandmother, Carol, continually emerged. "I'm really thankful for my mom helping my oldest kids to graduate. She really pushed education on them. She has very high expectation for my kids. I'm glad I have a mom like that!" Carol, also, provided the path to the experiences of many generations of Navajo peoples before her for her children and grandchildren. "Right now, we are about six hours away from home on the reservation. When we go back home and there is a ceremony, like a Yeíbicheii or a fire dance, or something like that, my mom would say, 'Hey, so and so is having a ceremony, let's go check it out.'" Mary laughed and looked at me, the inquiring friend and anthropologist. "It was a healing ritual, I guess you would say! To me, it makes you feel real good. To be Indian, again."

Notes

Preface

1. Pseudonyms are used for all of the people I write about, with one exception. Mark Maryboy was the first Navajo County commissioner in the state of Utah, an accomplishment not easily hidden with a pseudonym. The locations I write about—the Navajo Nation; San Juan County; cities, towns, and schools in the Southwest—are accurately named and identified in the historic and public records I have used throughout my research, so I have chosen to also identify these locations correctly. By not naming individuals and carefully altering some identifiable characteristics, I hope to protect the confidentiality of those who shared their thoughts and words with me over the past twenty-five years.

2. Vizenor, *Manifest Manners*, quoted at "Our Lives: Contemporary Life and Identities" (ongoing exhibit at the National Museum of American Indians on the National Mall, Washington, D.C.).

3. There is a rich body of research critiquing colonialists' educational practices and asserting American Indian survivance—claiming cultural and linguistic rights—by Indigenous scholars. See Lee, "If They Want Navajo to Be Learned, Then They Should Require It in All Schools"; Wilson and Yellow Bird, *For Indigenous Eyes Only*; Vine Deloria and Wildcat, *Power and Place*; Swisher and Tippeconnic, *Next Steps*; McCarty et al., "Indigenous Epistemologies and Education."

4. For a discussion challenging the expected "place" for American Indians in America's landscape, see Philip J. Deloria, *Indians in Unexpected Places*.

5. See Foucault, *Discipline & Punish*.

6. For more detail on research methods, see Deyhle, "The Role of the Applied Anthropologist"; and Deyhle, Hess, and LeCompte, "Approaching Ethical Issues for Qualitative Researchers in Education."

7. This term and the visual image of Indians wrapping themselves with blankets has been historically used in films, literature, and public discourse to describe Indians as uneducated, unassimilated, un-Christian, resistant to progress, and undeserving. In a letter to U.S. Congressman T. C. Pound on January 28, 1880, Pratt used this term as a means of laying the grounds for the necessity of boarding schools. "I send you today a few photographs of the Indian youth here. You will note that they came mostly as blanket Indians. A very large proportion of them had never been inside of a school room." Pratt, *Battlefield and Classroom*, 248.

8. Standing Bear, *Land of the Spotted Eagle*, 189–191.

9. Deyhle, "Constructing Failure and Maintaining Cultural Identity"; Deyhle, "Empowerment and Cultural Conflict"; and Deyhle, "Success and Failure."

10. For debates on these positions, see Erickson, "Transformation and School Success"; Ogbu, "Variability in Minority School Performance"; and Trueba, "Culturally Based Explanation of Minority Students' Academic Achievement."

11. Malkki, "National Geographic," 37.

12. Deyhle, "Navajo Youth and Anglo Racism."

13. Iverson, *Diné*, 248.

14. In Navajo creation stories, there were four worlds before this fifth, "Glittering World." Filled with technology, non-Navajo influences, and life experiences outside of the four sacred mountains, this world offers opportunities, as well as challenges for Navajo youth. See Irvin Morris, *From the Glittering World*.

15. Vangie explained that her statement needed to be understood on two different levels. One level, as practiced by following traditional Navajo beliefs, is when after her birth her umbilical cord was buried near her mother's home. The other level is beyond this physical point where she sees this as a metaphor for the connection she feels in her heart for her place on the Navajo landscape.

16. Archaeological evidence supports this prior occupancy claim. The success of this struggle is evident in the expansion of the Navajo reservation. The current Navajo majority population in the county also speaks to the success of Navajo peoples' efforts to remain on their homelands. See McPherson, *Northern Navajo Frontier 1860–1900*, 2.

17. Historically, this rationale that Indians were not "using" the land has been used frequently to justify the removal of Indians from their homelands. This "mastery of nature" ideology appears in early settler diaries from San Juan County.

18. Holland and Lave, *History in Person*, 1–2.

19. Nagel, *American Ethnic Renewal*, 63.

20. Vizenor and Lee, *Postindian Conversations*, 93.

21. Ibid., 85.

22. Vizenor, *Manifest Manners*, 16.

23. Ibid., 8.

24. Nagel, *American Ethnic Renewal*, 71.

25. House, *Language Shift among the Navajos*.

26. Vizenor and Lee, *Postindian Conversations*, 84.

27. Owens, "As If an Indian Were Really an Indian," 117.

28. Norla Chee, "Tonto Is My White Name," 70.

29. Tedlock, *The Beautiful and the Dangerous*, xiv.

30. Foley, "On Writing Reflexive Realist Narratives," 114.

31. Ibid., 114.

32. There now exists a rich set of ethnographic writing that represents this new theoretical position. I use these two ethnographers as explicit examples that, in particular, inform my own writing because two Indian Nations—the Zuni and Masquaki—are the focus of their research.

Place and Boundaries

1. Navajo chapters are community and political organizations first started by the Bureau of Indian Affairs in 1925. Following the American political tradition, chap-

ters elect local council members to the Navajo Nation's Tribal Council, lead by an elected president and vice president. There are three chapter houses adjacent to San Juan County. See Wilkins, *The Navajo Political Experience*.

2. In my past publications I used the term "Anglo," which more specifically referred to peoples of Northern European heritage, to avoid the essentialization implied by the term "whites." Throughout this book, however, I will use the term "whites" most often to describe the European American population in the county. I am fully aware of the essentialized nature of using this term to describe all "non–people of color," but this is the term used by the groups I describe. First, historical documents, almost exclusively written by European Americans from this area, and contemporary interviews I conducted used most frequently the dichotomous terms "Indian" and "white." Second, almost all the Navajo and Ute people used these terms in daily life. I use "Anglo" here when this was the specific term used, such as in a legal court document or newspaper article. "Pioneer" was the term used in historical documents to describe the first European Americans from the LDS church who settled in San Juan County. This presented an image of one arriving onto an open and vacant place as the "first people." I use the term "pioneer" when it appears in documents, and in the context of how white people describe themselves. In an attempt to represent these newcomers from a Native perspective, I have chosen to refer to them as "settlers." This term paints a picture of a group moving onto a landscape and claiming, or settling, a place that might already be the homeland of other peoples. As Charles Mills explains, "The United States itself, of course, is a white settler state on territory expropriated from its aboriginal inhabitants through a combination of military forces, disease, and a "century of dishonor" of broken treaties." My use of the term "settler" is a strategic one and more appropriate given the contested landscape I write about. See Mills, *The Racial Contract*, 28.

3. This Navajo word means "a place where there is living." Traditional hooghans were round log-style homes.

4. McPherson, *History of San Juan County*, 55.

5. Maryboy and Begay, "The Navajos," 274.

6. Ibid., 279.

7. King, "The Utah Navajos Relocation in the 1950s."

8. Large fairs have a history of over seventy-five years throughout the Navajo Nation. Annual fairs are held at Gallup and Shiprock, New Mexico; at Tuba City, Arizona; and now in Bluff, Utah.

9. Associated Press, *San Juan Record*, September 12, 1990.

10. In a mud-bogging contest, competing trucks with huge tires drive through mud trenches in a race to the finish line.

11. Racial discrimination in San Juan County accounts for the presence of federal election monitors. As late as 1956, Utah prohibited Native Americans residing on Indian reservations from voting. *Allen v. Merrell*, 305 P.2d 490 (Utah 1956), vacated 353 U.S. 932 (1957). Referencing this long history of discrimination, a federal court found the rights of two Navajo candidates for election to the San Juan County Commission had been violated and ordered them placed on the general election ballot (*Yanito v. Barber*, 348 F. Supp. 587, 591–595 [D. Utah 1972]). In 1984, the federal government brought two lawsuits against San Juan County, alleging violation of federal voting laws in *United States of America v. San Juan County*, United States

District Court for Utah, Docket Numbers C-83-1286 and C-83-1287 (1984). In one case, the court ordered the county to institute election reforms, including bilingual election procedures for Navajo voters. In the other, the court ordered the county commission seats apportioned by district. This resulted in the election of the first Navajo to the county commission, Mark Maryboy.

12. McCarty, *A Place to Be Navajo*, 22.

13. DeGroat, "My People."

14. Associated Press, *San Juan Record*, September 12, 1990.

15. The Native American Church (NAC), or the Peyote religion, is a pan-Indian, semi-Christian, nativistic religion. Appearing in the United States in the 1880s, the NAC was practiced by Utes and Navajos north of the San Juan River as early as 1914. Many Navajo NAC members also follow traditional Navajo practices. See Aberle, "Peyote Religion among the Navajo."

16. "Treaty between the United States of American and the Navajo Tribe of Indians," 21.

17. McPherson, *History of San Juan County*, 281.

18. Helen N. Shumway, *The First Forty Years*.

19. Robert McPherson explains that his choice of terms is connected to popular beliefs in the United States that create the ideal of "civilized" and its opposite, which is captured in terms like "wild," "savage," and "heathen." From this popular perspective, "civilization" means "city-dweller." This, of course, chooses to not privilege the first "city-dweller" and builders in this area, the Anasazi. See McPherson, *History of San Juan County*, 95.

20. Benally, Wiget, Alley, and Blake, *Dinéjí Nákéé' Nááhane'*, 60–61.

21. Hurst, "Bluff City, Utah," 19.

22. Iverson, *Diné*, 245.

23. Mark attended the Highlander Folk School in rural Tennessee. Started in 1932, the school was an adult educational center committed to achieving economic, political, and racial justice in the South and Appalachia. See Adams and Horton, *Unearthing Seeds of Fire*; and Glen, *Highlander, No Ordinary School, 1932–1962*.

24. The Enemy Way ceremony, originally intended to protect warriors from the ghosts of enemies, has been broadened to be a cure for sickness caused by the ghosts of a non-Navajo. For a description of the Enemy Way and other Navajo ceremonies, see Wyman, "Navajo Ceremonial System."

25. The term "squaw dance," although used by both Navajos and non-Navajos, is a derogatory term used to describe a sacred ceremony. I use this term only in direct quotes.

26. Edson, "Hold-Out," 36.

27. The Posey War, the last formal Indian war against the United States, occurred just south of Blanding Town in 1923.

28. Associated Press, *San Juan Record*, July 25, 1990.

29. McPherson, *History of San Juan County*, 97.

30. Hurst, "Bluff City, Utah," 15–30.

31. Ibid., 17.

32. Ibid., 17.

33. Ibid., 17.

34. Lyman, *Indians and Outlaws*, 39.

35. Leland Chee, *The Twin Rock Times Literary Magazine.*

36. Jones, "Preface to the Writings of Kumen Jones," 23.

37. Ibid., 23.

38. Lyman, *Indians and Outlaws*, 38. Stories such as this, with a moral of Indians "doing bad" to Mormons, being the "wrong" kind of Indian, and paying for it by falling ill and dying, appeared in personal journals and travel diaries throughout the regions colonized by early Mormon settlers.

39. Peterson, *Look to the Mountains*, 59.

40. Associated Press, "Fee Waiver: Equality for Everyone?"

41. Throughout Arizona, Utah, and Idaho, predominantly LDS communities built religious schools, LDS seminaries, next to public schools so their sons and daughters would have daily access to religious training while receiving high school credit. The Utah ACLU challenged this close connect as a violation of the Establishment Clause of the First Amendment. By the early 1980s, high school credit for religious instruction ended, although release time has continued.

42. For a series of articles on the relationship between the LDS church and American Indians, see *Dialogue: A Journal of Mormon Thought* 18, no. 4 (1985).

43. Ulrich and Fox, "L is for Indian: An Alphabet for Little Saints."

44. This was from an open letter put in all the faculty and staff mailboxes on November 15, 1984.

45. Tonya Morris, "Posey: A Leader of the Witapunuche Utes," 20.

46. Ibid., 20.

47. Ibid., 19.

48. Ibid, 16. Interview with Stan Bronson, Oct. 14, 1987.

49. McPherson, "Paiute Posey and the Last White Uprising," 8.

50. Cited in McPherson, *History of San Juan County*, 67.

51. McPherson, "Canyons, Cows and Conflicts," quote on 257. See Iverson, *Diné*, chap. 4 for additional examples of white ranchers grazing livestock on Navajo lands. In 1918 these problems lead Samuel F. Stacher, Superintendent of Indians Affairs in the region, to complain in frustration, "Too bad that all these greedy white stockmen from around the state wish to freeze out two or three thousand Navajos for the benefit of less than a dozen white Stockgrowers" (107, fn. 25).

52. Lyman, *The Outlaw of Navajo Mountain*, 231.

53. McPherson, "Paiute Posey and the Last White Uprising," 7–14.

54. Tonya Morris, "Posey: A Leader of the Witapunche Utes," 18.

55. Ibid., Interview with Stan Bronson, 4.

56. McPherson, "Paiute Posey and the Last White Uprising," 10.

57. Lefler, "Memories of the Ute Roundup," 28.

58. Lyman, *Indians and Outlaws*, 193.

59. Ibid., 193.

60. Ibid., 194.

61. McPherson, "Paiute Posey and the Last White Uprising," 13.

62. Bronson, "Posey," 46.

63. Tonya Morris, "Posey: A Leader of the Witapunche Utes," 20.

64. Dr. Beth King is a cultural anthropologist who has conducted ethnographic research in San Juan County and throughout the Navajo Nation since 1980. These quotes come from interviews she conducted in 1995–1996.

65. Tew, Journal. Referenced in Tate, "Elk Mountain."
66. King, "The Utah Navajos Relocation in the 1950s."
67. Ibid.
68. Ibid.
69. Ibid.
70. This incident is also discussed by Maryboy and Begay, "The Navajos," 301. They write that Navajos speak of a roundup of over one hundred horses by government officials that were sold for dog food. The authors report that it was the first time American Indians in Utah had successfully sued the government for intentional wrongdoing.
71. King, "The Utah Navajos Relocation in the 1950s."
72. Smith, "State Asks That Grave-Robbing Charges Be Reinstated."
73. Smith, "Baffled by Burial Decision."
74. Ibid.
75. Iverson, *Diné*, 63.
76. Basso, "Wisdom Sits in Places," 87.
77. DeGroat, "My People."

Traversing Landscapes

1. The figures from the U.S. Department of Education in 1986 showed an average attrition rate (data that show the proportion of a given entering high school class that does not graduate four years later) in the state of Utah for the class of 1984 to be 21 percent. The dropout rate of Indian students in my study was almost double the state average. See Deyhle, "Constructing Failure and Maintaining Cultural Identity."
2. Tapahonso, "For Misty Starting School."
3. In 1974, Navajo parents and students filed a federal court class action alleging deprivation of equal educational opportunities by the San Juan School District. A consent decree and injunction was entered in 1975. The court ordered the construction of elementary and high schools on the Navajo Reservation; equality in financing, equipment, supplies, and other resources; and the provision of educational services and programs beneficial to Indian students, including bilingual and bi-cultural education. There was further litigation in the 1990s in *Sinajini v. Board of Education* and other cases. One case resulted in the construction of a high school in an isolated area known as Navajo Mountain. Another lawsuit involved the district's special education programs. Various legal matters were combined into one consent decree. See *Sinajini v. Bd. of Educ.*, 964 F. Supp. 319 (D. Utah. 1997). In the Navajo Mountain case, the court rejected the district's argument that it had no obligation to educate Indians on reservations. See *Meyers v. Board of Education*, 905 F. Supp. 1544 (D. Utah 1995) and Baca, "*Meyers v. Board of Education*." This case has been hailed as a landmark in Indian education. Scholars look to these cases as examples of how conflicts over government services on Indian reservations are resolved. The court has kept the Sinajini and Meyers cases open for continued monitoring and enforcement of education services to Indian students in San Juan County. Over three decades after the lawsuits began, the cases continue to produce benefits for Navajo children. In 2007, the school district announced it

was building an elementary school in Monument Valley to comply with one of the court decrees.

4. The *Lau v. Nichols* court case decision required school districts to provide some kind of alternative educational program if students did not speak English, the language of instruction. To neglect the language needs of students, however, amounted to denying them equal educational access to school instruction. In response to *Lau v. Nichols*, the Department of Education issued a decree for districts to follow. See U.S. Department of Health, Education and Welfare, Office for Civil Rights, "Task Force Findings Specifying Remedies Available for Eliminating Past Educational Practices Ruled Unlawful under *Lau vs. Nichols*."

5. Lurie, "Relations between Indians and Anthropologists."

6. The first laugh celebrates the child's first expression of emotions through laughter and tears. The individual with whom the baby first laughs is obligated to sponsor a ceremony to honor the event. See Schwarz, *Molded in the Image of Changing Woman.*

7. Tapahonso, *Blue Horses Rush In*, 37.

8. Kinaaldá is a coming-of-age and puberty ceremony which ushers a Navajo girl into adult society. The four-day ceremony, following the example set by Changing Woman (also known as White Shell Woman or White Bead Woman), is used to bind the community together with a Navajo woman's physical, moral, and intellectual strength. See Begay et al., *Kinaaldá*; Frisbie, *Kinaaldá*; and Roessel, *Women in Navajo Society.*

9. Roessel, *Women in Navajo Society*, 105.

10. Zolbrod, *Diné Bahane´*, 58–59.

11. In 1954, the LDS church officially adopted, as part of their missionary activities, the Indian Student Placement Program, in which American Indian children were "adopted" by a Mormon family. American Indian youth lived with foster families during the year, went to public schools, and were educated into the LDS Church. Home visits occurred for a few weeks or months during the summer. By 1980, approximately twenty thousand Indian students from various tribes had been placed in LDS foster homes. The program is no longer expanding, placing only 1,986 children in 1980, and in the future will be focusing on high-school-age children. This program has touched almost all of the Navajo families in this area. In every family, close or distant clan members have experienced LDS foster homes. For some, the experience was positive; for others, it was disastrous. This program was ended in 1996. See Birch, "Helen John"; and Topper, "Mormon Placement."

12. Tohe, "The Names."

13. Liebler, *Boil My Heart for Me.*

14. Ibid., 45.

15. Ibid., viii.

16. Ibid., 145.

17. Roberts and Hurst, "Indian Education," 72.

18. Gary Shumway, "Blanding," 149.

19. Smith, "The Integration of the San Juan County School District," 33.

20. Roberts and Hurst, "Indian Education," 72. This is still the case in 2009.

21. Smith, "The Integration of the San Juan County School District," 33.

22. Ibid., 33.

23. McPherson, *Navajo Land, Navajo Culture*, 230.

24. Among those Navajo young women who dropped out, 44 percent failed to see the importance of school in relation to what they wanted to do in life.

25. This and the subsequent quotes in this section are from a taped interview with Sam reconstructing his comments the day after the meeting.

26. Ration, "Smith Lake, New Mexico."

27. The name Inuit is now used by these Indigenous peoples.

28. Compiled statistics provided by the Comprehensive Economic Development Strategy Plan of the Navajo Nation for 2005 and 2006 revealed 42.9 percent of Navajo individuals, 40 percent of families, and 53.1 percent of families with a female head of household live below the federal poverty level. Reid, *Navajo Women*, 80.

Changing Woman at Taco Bell

1. Stephen Trimble, *The People: Indians of the American Southwest* (Santa Fe: SAR Press, 1993), 122. Changing Woman (*Asdzáán Naádleehé*), also known as White Shell Woman or White Bead Woman (Yoołgai Asdzáán), is an important and beloved figure in Navajo history and epistemology. As the daughter (or granddaughter) of First Man and First Woman, she is central to the connection between the Holy People and Navajo people. According to Farella, *The Main Stalk*, 63: "She is the nurturer, the giver, the provider. One feels primarily warmth, trust, and safety in her presence . . . The births of human beings started with her as she created them, and one still refers to her as "my mother" or "my grandmother." Changing Woman is the first Kinaaldá; a "Walking into Beauty" ceremony that marks a young girl's passage into womanhood. Young Navajo women today, like Vangie, "become" or follow the path laid out by Changing Woman as they themselves have Kinaaldá. And in doing so, they ensure the survivance of Navajo beliefs, practices, and values as handed down by the Holy People to Changing Woman. In using Changing Woman's name for Vangie's life story, she and I are respectfully trying to show the power and place for Navajo women today that reflects "the embodiment of goodness" that connects them to the teaching of the Holy People. Even when they work in cities at places like Taco Bell, their presence as Navajo women began with Changing Woman. See also Begay, *Kinaaldá*.

2. Tapahonso, *Blue Horses Rush In*, 35.

3. This Navajo house blessing incorporated elements of the Native American Church with the use of coals and the cedar smoke blessing.

4. Harjo, "Remember," 40.

5. Vangie's father lived on allotted land, off the reservation, where he was able to collect royalties directly from the oil companies. Very few Navajos are in this advantageous position.

6. Lamphere, *Weaving Women's Lives*, 42.

7. Francisco, "Brown Children," 3–4.

8. Deyhle, "Empowerment and Cultural Conflict."

9. For specific information, see Deyhle and LeCompte, "Cultural Differences in Child Development"; and Lamphere, *To Run After Them*.

10. The Spanish introduced Churro sheep to Navajos in the 1700s. This sheep is strong, endures in dry environments, and produces a fine long fiber.

11. For a discussion about Navajo beliefs about skinwalkers, see Kluckhohn, *Navaho Witchcraft*.

12. For a rich picture of the Navajo Holy People and their relationship to the landscape, see Beck, Walters, and Francisco, *The Sacred*; Yazzie, *Navajo History*; Zolbrod, *Diné Bahane'*; and Reichard, *Navaho Religion*.

13. A local county report revealed that two-thirds of the jobs in the county were located in the northern portion of the county, where almost 75 percent of the Anglo population lived. Government ranked as the number one employer, the school district the number two employer, and the county the number three employer. These three provided a total of 750 jobs. A majority of these jobs required either a college degree or some college education.

14. Associated Press, "School Board Reviews Pilot Program."

15. Tapahonso, "Hard to Take," 17.

16. Philip J. Deloria, *Playing Indian*.

(Re)sculpturing Belonging

1. Wyman, "Navajo Ceremonial System," 537.

2. Ibid., 537. Also see the following for a discussion of Navajo beliefs and religion: Farella, *The Main Stalk*; Kluckhohn and Leighton, *The Navaho*; Reichard, *Navaho Religion*; and Witherspoon, *Language and Art in the Navajo Universe*.

3. Faris, *The Nightway*, 15.

4. Ibid., 235.

5. Tapahonso, "A Birthday Poem."

6. Hale, "The Only Good Indian," 126–127.

7. For example, see Basso, "Portraits of the 'Whiteman,'" and Foley, "The Silent Indian as a Cultural Production."

8. The statistics derive from a set of 168 questionnaires I conducted in 1989–1990 with Navajo youth who had left school.

9. The No Child Left Behind Act was signed on January 8, 2002. The controversial act was proposed to improve school performance and enhance accountability by increasing standards and requiring the certification of all teachers. Critics have argued that the act relies too heavily on standardized testing and outcome-based education, which is thought to stifle student learning and critical thinking.

10. Northsun, "99 things to Do before You Die."

11. Tohe, "Our Tongues Slapped into Silence."

12. Harjo, "Perhaps the World Ends Here."

Bibliography

Aberle, David F. "Peyote Religion among the Navajo." In *Handbook of North American Indians*, edited by A. Ortiz and W. C. Sturtevant, 558–569. Washington, D.C.: Smithsonian Institution, 1983.

Adams, Frank, and Myles Horton. *Unearthing Seeds of Fire: The Idea of Highlander*. Winston-Salem, NC: John F. Blair, Publisher, 1975.

Associated Press. "Fee Waiver: Equality for Everyone?" *San Juan Record*, March 31, 1993.

———. *San Juan Record*, September 12, 1990.

———. *San Juan Record*, July 25, 1990.

———. "School Board Reviews Pilot Program." *San Juan Record*, March 13, 1991.

Baca, Lawrence R. "*Meyers v. Board of Education*: The *Brown v. Board* of Indian Country." *University of Illinois Law Review* 5 (2005): 1155–1180.

Basso, Keith H. *Portraits of the "Whiteman": Linguistic Play and Cultural Symbols among the Western Apache*. Cambridge: Cambridge University Press, 1979.

———. "Wisdom Sits in Places: Notes on a Western Apache Landscape." In *Senses of Place*, edited by S. Feld and K. Basso, 53–90. Santa Fe, NM: School of American Research Press, 1996.

Beck, Peggy V., Anna Lee Walters, and Nia Francisco. *The Sacred: Ways of Knowledge, Sources of Life*. Tsaile, AZ: Diné College Press, 1977.

Begay, Shirley, et al. *Kinaaldá: A Navajo Puberty Ceremony*. Rough Rock, AZ: Rough Rock Demonstration School, Navajo Curriculum Center, 1983.

Benally, Clyde, Andrew O. Wiget, John R. Alley, and Garry Blake. *Dinéjí Nákéé' Nááhane': A Ute Navajo History*. Monticello, UT: San Juan School District, 1982.

Birch, J. Neil. "Helen John: The Beginnings of Indian Placement." *Dialogue: A Journal of Mormon Thought* 18 (1985): 119–129.

Bronson, Stanley. "Posey." *Blue Mountain Shadows* 23 (2000): 46.

Chee, Leland. *The Twin Rock Times Literary Magazine*. Bluff, UT: Published by the Bluff Elementary School's Fifth Graders, 1992.

Chee, Norla. "Tonto Is My White Name." *Blue Mountain Shadows* 11 (1992): 70.

DeGroat, J. R. "My People." *Diné Be'iiná: A Journal of Navajo Life* 1, no. 1 (1987): 33.

Deloria, Philip J. *Indians in Unexpected Places*. Lawrence: University Press of Kansas, 2004.

———. *Playing Indian*. New Haven, CT: Yale University Press, 1998.

Deloria, Vine, Jr., and Daniel R. Wildcat, eds. *Power and Place: American Indian Education in America*. Golden, CO: Fulcrum Publishing, 2001.

Deyhle, Donna. "Constructing Failure and Maintaining Cultural Identity: Navajo and Ute School Leavers." *Journal of American Indian Education* 31, no. 2 (1992): 24–47.

———. "Empowerment and Cultural Conflict: Navajo Parents and the Schooling of Their Children." *International Journal of Qualitative Research in Education* 4, no. 3 (1991): 277–297.

———. "Navajo Youth and Anglo Racism: Cultural Integrity and Resistance." *Harvard Educational Review* 65, no. 3 (1995): 403–444.

———. "The Role of the Applied Anthropologist: Between Schools and the Navajo Nation." In *Inside Stories: Qualitative Research Reflections*, edited by K. B. deMarrais, 35–47. Mahwah, NJ: Lawrence Erlbaum Associates, 1998.

———. "Success and Failure: A Micro-ethnographic Comparison of Navajo and Anglo Students' Perspectives of Testing." *Curriculum Inquiry* 16, no. 4 (1986): 365–389.

Deyhle, Donna, Alfred Hess, and Margaret LeCompte. "Approaching Ethical Issues for Qualitative Researchers in Education." In *The Handbook of Qualitative Research in Education*, edited by M. LeCompte, W. Millroy, and J. Preissle, 597–641. Burlington, MA: Academic Press, 1992.

Deyhle, Donna, and Margaret LeCompte. "Cultural Differences in Child Development: Navajo Adolescents in Middle Schools." *Theory Into Practice* 33, no. 3 (1994): 156–166.

Edson, Edith McDowell. "Hold-Out." *Blue Mountain Shadows* 15 (1995): 36.

Erickson, Frederick. "Transformation and School Success: The Politics and Culture of Educational Achievement." *Anthropology & Education Quarterly* 18 (1987): 335–356.

Farella, John R. *The Main Stalk: A Synthesis of Navajo Philosophy*. Tucson: University of Arizona Press, 1984.

Faris, James C. *The Nightway: A History and a History of Documentation of a Navajo Ceremonial*. Albuquerque: University of New Mexico Press, 1990.

Foley, Douglas E. *The Heartland Chronicles*. Philadelphia: University of Pennsylvania Press, 1995.

———. "On Writing Reflexive Realist Narratives." In *Being Reflexive in Critical Educational and Social Research*, edited by G. Shacklock and J. Smyth, 110–129. Bristol, PA: Falmer Press, 1998.

———. "The Silent Indian as a Cultural Production." In *The Cultural Production of the Educated Person*, edited by B. A. Levison, D. E. Foley, and D. C. Holland, 79–91. Albany: State University of New York Press, 1996.

Foucault, Michel. *Discipline & Punish: The Birth of the Prison*. New York: Vintage Books, 1995.

Francisco, Nia. "Brown Children." In *Blue Horses for Navajo Women*, 3–4. Greenfield Center, NY: Greenfield Review Press, 1988.

Frisbie, Charlotte Johnson. *Kinaaldá: A Study of the Navaho Girl's Puberty Ceremony*. Salt Lake City: University of Utah Press, 1993.

Glen, John M. *Highlander, No Ordinary School, 1932–1962*. Lexington: University Press of Kentucky, 1988.

Hale, Janet Campbell. "The Only Good Indian." In *Reinventing the Enemy's Language: Contemporary Native Women's Writings of North America*, edited by J. Harjo and G. Bird, 123–148. New York: W. W. Norton, 1997.

Harjo, Joy. "Perhaps the World Ends Here." In *Reinventing the Enemy's Language: Contemporary Native Women's Writings of North America*, edited by J. Harjo and G. Bird, 556–557. New York: W. W. Norton, 1997.

———. "Remember." In *She Had Some Horses*, 40. New York: Thunder's Mouth Press, 1997.

Holland, Dorothy, and Jean Lave. *History in Person: Enduring Struggles, Contentious Practice, Intimate Identities*. Santa Fe: School of American Research Press, 2001.

House, Deborah. *Language Shift among the Navajos*. Tucson: University of Arizona Press, 2002.

Hurst, Michael T. "Bluff City, Utah." *Blue Mountain Shadows* 1, no. 1 (1988): 15–30.

Iverson, Peter. *Diné: A History of the Navajos*. Albuquerque: University of New Mexico Press, 2002.

Jones, Kumen. "Preface to the Writings of Kumen Jones." Unpublished manuscript in possession of the author.

King, Beth. "The Utah Navajos Relocation in the 1950s." In *Life along the San Juan River, The Bluff Legacy Project, Canyon Echo*. 1996.

Kluckhohn, Clyde. *Navaho Witchcraft*. Boston: Beacon Press, 1963.

Kluckhohn, Clyde, and Dorothea Leighton. *The Navaho: Revised Edition*. Cambridge, MA: Harvard University Press, 1974.

Lamphere, Louise. *To Run after Them: Cultural and Social Bases of Cooperation in a Navajo Community*. Tucson: University of Arizona Press, 1977.

———. *Weaving Women's Lives: Three Generations in a Navajo Family*. Albuquerque: University of New Mexico Press, 2007.

Lee, Tiffany S. "If They Want Navajo to Be Learned, Then They Should Require It in All Schools: Navajo Teenagers' Experiences, Choices, and Demands Regarding Navajo Language." *Wicazo Sa Review* 22, no. 1 (2007): 7–33.

Lefler, Ellen. "Memories of the Ute Roundup." *Blue Mountain Shadows* 4 (1989): 28.

Liebler, H. Baxter. *Boil My Heart for Me*. Salt Lake City: University of Utah Press, 1994.

Lurie, Nancy Oestreich. "Relations between Indians and Anthropologists." In *Handbook of North American Indians*, vol. 4, *History of Indian-White*

Relations, edited by W. E. Washburn and W. C. Sturtevant, 548–556. Washington, D.C.: Smithsonian Institution Press, 1989.

Lyman, Albert R. *Indians and Outlaws: Settling of the San Juan Frontier*. Salt Lake City: Bookcraft, Inc., 1962.

———. *The Outlaw of Navajo Mountain*. Salt Lake City, UT: Bookcraft, 1962.

Malkki, Liisa. "National Geographic: The Rooting of Peoples and the Territorialization of National Identity among Scholars and Refugees." *Cultural Anthropology* 7, no. 1 (1992): 24–44.

Maryboy, Nancy, and David Begay. "The Navajos." In *A History of Utah's American Indians*, edited by F. Cuch, 265–314. Salt Lake City: Utah State Division of Indian Affairs; Utah State Division of History, 2000.

McCarty, Teresa. *A Place to Be Navajo: Rough Rock and the Struggle for Self-Determination in Indigenous Schooling*. Mahwah, NJ: Lawrence Erlbaum Associates, 2002.

McCarty, Teresa, T. Borgoiakova, P. Gilmore, K. Lomawaima, and M. Romero, eds. "Indigenous Epistemologies and Education: Self Determination, Anthropology, and Human Rights." *Anthropology & Education Quarterly* 36, no. 1 (2005): 1-7.

McPherson, Robert. "Canyons, Cows and Conflicts: A Native American History of Montezuma Canyon, 1874–1933." *Utah Historical Quarterly* 60, no. 3 (1992): 238–258.

———. *A History of San Juan County: In the Palm of Time*. Salt Lake City: Utah Historical Society, 1995.

———. *Navajo Land, Navajo Culture: The Utah Experience in the Twentieth Century*. Norman: University of Oklahoma Press, 2001.

———. *The Northern Navajo Frontier 1860–1900: Expansion through Adversity*. Albuquerque: University of New Mexico Press, 1988.

———. "Paiute Posey and the Last White Uprising." *Blue Mountain Shadows* 4 (1989): 7–14.

Mills, Charles. *The Racial Contract*. Ithaca, NY: Cornell University Press, 1997.

Morris, Irvin. *From the Glittering World: A Navajo Story*. Norman: University of Oklahoma Press, 1997.

Morris, Tonya. "Posey: A Leader of the Witapunuche Utes." *Blue Mountain Shadows* 4 (1989): 15–20.

Nagel, Joane. *American Ethnic Renewal: Red Power and the Resurgence of Identity and Culture*. New York: Oxford University Press, 1996.

Northsun, Nila. "99 things to Do before You Die." In *Reinventing the Enemy's Language: Contemporary Native Women's Writings of North America*, edited by J. Harjo and G. Bird, 395–397. New York: W. W. Norton, 1997.

Ogbu, John. "Variability in Minority School Performance: A Problem in Search of an Explanation." *Anthropology & Education Quarterly* 18 (1987): 312–334.

Owens, Louis. "As If an Indian Were Really an Indian." In *Native American Representations*, edited by G. M. Bataille, 11–24. Lincoln: University of Nebraska Press, 2001.

Peterson, Charles S. *Look to the Mountains*. Provo, UT: BYU Press, 1975.

Pratt, Richard Henry. *Battlefield and Classroom: Four Decades with the American Indian, 1867–1907*, edited by R. M. Utley. New Haven, CT: Yale University Press, 1964.

Ration, Tom. "Smith Lake, New Mexico." In *The Sacred: Ways of Knowledge, Sources of Life*, edited by P. V. Beck, A. L. Walters, and N. Francisco, 278–279. Tsaile, AZ: Diné College Press, 1996.

Reichard, Gladys A. *Navaho Religion: A Study of Symbolism*. Tucson: University of Arizona Press, 1983.

Reid, Betty. *Navajo Women: Sáanii*. Tucson: Rio Nuevo Publishers, 2007.

Roberts, Ryan, and Jenny Hurst. "Indian Education." *Blue Mountain Shadows* 9 (1991): 69–74.

Roessel, Ruth. *Women in Navajo Society*. Rough Rock, AZ: Navajo Resource Center, 1981.

Schwarz, Maureen Trudelle. *Molded in the Image of Changing Woman: Navajo Views on the Human Body and Personhood*. Tucson: University of Arizona Press, 1997.

Shumway, Gary. "Blanding: The Making of a Community." In *San Juan County Utah: People, Resources, and History*, edited by A. K. Powell, 131–151. Salt Lake City: Utah State Historical Society, 1983.

Shumway, Helen N. *The First Forty Years: History of San Juan High School*. San Juan County, UT: Blue Mountain Shadows, 1994.

Smith, Christopher. "Baffled by Burial Decision. Indians and Scientist Say Ruling Was Racist." *Salt Lake Tribune*, March 1, 1998.

———. "State Asks That Grave-Robbing Charges Be Reinstated." *Salt Lake Tribune*, March 21, 1998.

Smith, Donna. "The Integration of the San Juan County School District." *Blue Mountain Shadows* 21 (1999): 27–38.

Standing Bear, Luther. *Land of the Spotted Eagle*. Lincoln: Board of Regents of the University of Nebraska, 2006.

Swisher, Karen, and John Tippeconnic, eds. *Next Steps: Research and Practice to Advance Indian Education*. Charleston, WV: Eric Clearinghouse on Rural Education and Small Schools, 1999.

Tapahonso, Luci. "A Birthday Poem." In *Blue Horses Rush In*, 79–80. Tucson: University of Arizona Press, 1977.

———. *Blue Horses Rush In*. Tucson: University of Arizona Press, 1977.

———. "For Misty Starting School." In *A Breeze Swept Through: Poetry*, 20–21. Albuquerque: West End Press, 1987.

———. "Hard to Take." In *Seasonal Woman: Luci Tapahonso*, 17–18. Santa Fe, NM: Tooth of Time Books, 1982.

———. "Notes for the Children." In *Blue Horses Rush In*, 35–37. Tucson: University of Arizona Press, 1977.

Tate, Laverne Powell. "Elk Mountain." *Blue Mountain Shadows* 4 (1990): 6–19.

Tedlock, Barbara. *The Beautiful and the Dangerous: Encounters with the Zuni Indians.* New York: Penguin Books, 1992.

Tew, William T. Journal, March 30, 1881. Utah State Historical Society, photocopy.

Tohe, Laura. "The Names." In *No Parole Today*, 4–5. Albuquerque: West End Press, 1999.

———. "Our Tongues Slapped into Silence." In *No Parole Today*, 2–3. Albuquerque: West End Press, 1999.

Topper, M. D. "Mormon Placement: The Effects of Missionary Foster Families on Navajo Adolescents." *Ethos* 7, no. 2 (1979): 142–160.

"Treaty between the United States of American and the Navajo Tribe of Indians." Las Vegas: KC Publications, 1968.

Trueba, Henry T. "Culturally Based Explanation of Minority Students' Academic Achievement." *Anthropology & Education Quarterly* 19 (1988): 270–287.

Ulrich, Laurel, and Dell Fox. "L is for Indian: An Alphabet for Little Saints." Pamphlet produced in Salt Lake City.

U.S. Department of Health, Education and Welfare. Office for Civil Rights. "Task Force Findings Specifying Remedies Available for Eliminating Past Educational Practices Ruled Unlawful under *Lau vs. Nichols*." Washington, D.C.: Department of Health, Education and Welfare, 1975.

Vizenor, Gerald. *Manifest Manners: Postindian Warriors of Survivance.* Hanover, NH: Wesleyan University Press, 1994.

Vizenor, Gerald, and A. Robert Lee. *Postindian Conversations.* Lincoln: University of Nebraska Press, 1999.

Wax, Murray, Rosalie Wax, and Robert Dumont. *Formal Education in an American Indian Community.* Atlanta: Emory University, 1964.

Wilkins, David. *The Navajo Political Experience.* Landham, MD: Rowman & Littlefield, 2003.

Wilson, Waziyatawin Angela, and Michael Yellow Bird, eds. *For Indigenous Eyes Only: A Decolonization Handbook.* Santa Fe, NM: School of American Research, 2005.

Witherspoon, Gary. *Language and Art in the Navajo Universe.* Ann Arbor: University of Michigan Press, 1977.

Wyman, Leland C. "Navajo Ceremonial System." In *Handbook of North American Indians*, edited by A. Ortiz and W. C. Sturtevant, 10: 536–557. Washington, D.C.: Smithsonian Institution, 1983.

Yazzie, Ethelou. *Navajo History.* Many Farms, AZ: Navajo Community College Press, 1971.

Zolbrod, Paul. *Diné Bahane': The Navajo Creation Story.* Albuquerque: University of New Mexico Press, 1984.

Index

About the Author

Donna Deyhle is a professor in the Department of Education, Culture and Society and the coordinator of the American Indian Studies Program in the Ethnic Studies Program at the University of Utah. Her research and fieldwork has focused on educational issues in cross-cultural settings in Brazil, Peru, Australia, and various American Indian reservations in the United States. She has taught on-site teacher training programs on the Navajo reservation and at Laguna, Acoma, and Zuni Pueblos. Her professional interests in anthropology and education, critical theory, and social justice have led to publications on parent involvement in the *International Journal of Qualitative Research in Education*, on break-dancers in the *Anthropology & Education Quarterly*, on cross-cultural child development in *Theory Into Practice* (with M. LeCompte), on cultural integrity and racism in the *Harvard Educational Review*, on Navajo mothers and daughters in the *Anthropology & Education Quarterly* (with F. Margonis), and on break dancing and heavy metal in *Youth & Society*. She also has written reviews of the field of American Indian education in the *Review of Research in Education*, and the *Routledge International Companion to Multicultural Education* (both with K. Swisher), and on Indigenous education in the *Sage International Handbook of Curriculum and Instruction* (with T. Stevens, R. Trinidad, and K. Swisher). In recognition of the excellence of her research, in 2002 she received the George and Louise Spindler Award for a distinguished career in educational anthropology from the Council on Anthropology and Education of the American Anthropological Association. In 2008, she received the Distinguished Diversity Senior Scholar Award from the University of Utah.